Lecture Notes in Computer Science 7985

Commenced Publication in 1973
Founding and Former Series Editors:
Gerhard Goos, Juris Hartmanis, and Jan van Leeuwen

James Heather   Steve Schneider
Vanessa Teague (Eds.)

E-Voting
and Identity

4th International Conference, Vote-ID 2013
Guildford, UK, July 17-19, 2013
Proceedings

 Springer

Volume Editors

James Heather
University of Surrey
Guildford, Surrey, GU2 7XH, UK
E-mail: j.heather@surrey.ac.uk

Steve Schneider
University of Surrey
Guildford, Surrey, GU2 7XH, UK
E-mail: s.schneider@surrey.ac.uk

Vanessa Teague
The University of Melbourne
Parkville VIC 3010, Australia
E-mail: vjteague@unimelb.edu.au

ISSN 0302-9743   e-ISSN 1611-3349
ISBN 978-3-642-39184-2   e-ISBN 978-3-642-39185-9
DOI 10.1007/978-3-642-39185-9
Springer Heidelberg Dordrecht London New York

Library of Congress Control Number: 2013941244

CR Subject Classification (1998): E.3, D.4.6, K.6.5, C.2, J.1, K.4.4, K.5.2

LNCS Sublibrary: SL 4 – Security and Cryptology

Typesetting: Camera-ready by author, data conversion by Scientific Publishing Services, Chennai, India

Printed on acid-free paper

Springer is part of Springer Science+Business Media (www.springer.com)

Preface

This is the fourth edition of the International Conference on E-Voting and Identity (VoteID). Previous VoteID conferences were held in Tallinn, Estonia (2011), Luxembourg (2009) and Bochum, Germany (2007). This year's VoteID takes place in Guildford, UK, on 17–19 July 2013, hosted by the University of Surrey, preceded by a special session on "Voting Systems Demonstrations" exhibiting recent practical developments in voting systems.

Countries around the world are increasing their deployment of electronic voting, though in many places the trustworthiness of their systems remains controversial. Vote-ID has always maintained a strong focus on designing trustworthy voting systems, but the breadth of interpretations of trustworthiness seems to widen every year. This year's papers include a range of works on end-to-end verifiable election systems, verifiably correct complex tallying algorithms, human perceptions of verifiability, formal models of verifiability and, of course, attacks on systems formerly advertised as verifiable.

To be trustworthy is one thing, but to be trusted is quite another. The increasing practical application of electronic voting technologies implies a need for us to understand the wider implications of gaining and deserving public trust. This year's Vote-ID boasts some prestigious invited speakers on this theme: David Birch, a founding Director of Consult Hyperion, will be speaking on "Suppose Electronic Voting Works? What Then?"; Robert Krimmer, Senior Adviser on New Voting Technologies in the Election Department of the OSCE's Office for Democratic Institutions and Human Rights (OSCE/ODIHR), gives a talk entitled "The Election Observation of New Voting Technologies"; Philip Stark, Professor and Chair of Statistics, UC Berkeley, speaks on "E2E to Hand-to-Eye: Verifiability, Trust, Audits"; and Baroness Onora O'Neill of Bengarve CBE FBA Hon FRS F Med Sci, Chair of the Equality and Human Rights Commission, delivers our keynote address on the subject of "Trustworthiness before Trust".

The Programme Committee selected 12 papers for presentation at the conference out of a total of 26 submissions. Each submission was reviewed by at least four Programme Committee members.

We would like to thank everyone who helped in bringing this conference together: the authors for their submissions; the Programme Committee and the external reviewers for their conscientious and timely efforts in reviewing and discussing the submissions; Maggie Burton, who provided such excellent support for the local arrangements; and Consult Hyperion and IBM for their generous sponsorship that allowed us to extend invitations to the guest speakers, as well as funding a number of student stipends. Finally, we thank our home institutions, The University of Melbourne and University of Surrey, for their support.

July 2013

James Heather
Steve Schneider
Vanessa Teague

Organization

Program Committee

Josh Benaloh	Microsoft Research
Jeremy Clark	Carleton University
J Paul Gibson	Telecom & Management SudParis
Joseph Hall	Center for Democracy & Technology
James Heather	University of Surrey
Hugo Jonker	University of Luxembourg
Aggelos Kiayias	University of Connecticut
Reto Koenig	Berne University of Applied Sciences
Helger Lipmaa	University of Tartu
Olivier Pereira	Universite catholique de Louvain
Mark Ryan	University of Birmingham
Peter Ryan	University of Luxembourg
Steve Schneider	University of Surrey
Berry Schoenmakers	Eindhoven University of Technology
Vanessa Teague	The University of Melbourne
Melanie Volkamer	Technische Universität Darmstadt
Poorvi Vora	The George Washington University
David Wagner	University of California, Berkeley
Douglas Wikström	KTH Royal Institute of Technology
Zhe Xia	Wuhan University of Technology

Additional Reviewers

Grewal, Gurchetan S.
Joaquim, Rui
Llewellyn, Morgan
Mauw, Sjouke
Peacock, Thea
Phillips, Joshua

Table of Contents

Scaling Privacy Guarantees
in Code-Verification Elections

Aggelos Kiayias[1,*] and Anthi Orfanou[2]

[1] National and Kapodistrian University of Athens, Athens, Greece
aggelos@kiayias.com
[2] Columbia University, New York, NY
anthi@cs.columbia.edu

Abstract. Preventing the corruption of the voting platform is a major issue for any e-voting scheme. To address this, a number of recent protocols enable voters to validate the operation of their platform by utilizing a platform independent feedback: the voting system reaches out to the voter to convince her that the vote was cast as intended. This poses two major problems: first, the system should not learn the actual vote; second, the voter should be able to validate the system's response without performing a mathematically complex protocol (we call this property "human verifiability"). Current solutions with convincing privacy guarantees suffer from trust scalability problems: either a small coalition of servers can entirely break privacy or the platform has a secret key which prevents the privacy from being breached. In this work we demonstrate how it is possible to provide better trust distribution without platform side secrets by increasing the number of feedback messages back to the voter. The main challenge of our approach is to maintain human verifiability: to solve this we provide new techniques that are based on either simple mathematical calculations or a novel visual cryptography technique that we call *visual sharing of shape descriptions*, which may be of independent interest.

Keywords: Electronic voting, elections integrity, visual cryptography.

1 Introduction

The integrity of the voting platform is a critical feature of electronic voting systems. If an attacker controls the voting platform then it can not only breach voter privacy but also manipulate the election results. For this reason, as e-voting systems increasingly find their way to real-world deployments, the security properties of the voting platform have become a major consideration. This problem is particularly exacerbated in the case of Internet voting where the voter is supposed to use a general purpose system (PC) for ballot casting. In this context

---

* Supported by project FINER of Greek Secretariat of Research and Technology, ERC project CODAMODA and Marie Curie grant RECUP. Also partly supported by an EAC grant from the VoTeR center - University of Connecticut.

J. Heather, S. Schneider, and V. Teague (Eds.): VoteID 2013, LNCS 7985, pp. 1–24, 2013.

the problem has been generally identified as the *untrusted platform problem*. To solve the problem a general methodology has arisen that enables the human operator of the ballot casting PC to validate its operation (i.e., that it has cast the proper vote) by receiving a suitable feedback from the system. This approach, even if we assume the existence of such feedback channel for free[1], it has to additionally overcome two major challenges: First, the system should be able to provide such feedback without breaching the privacy of the voter and learning its vote. Second, the validation protocol should not be mathematically complex since then this would require the utilization of the PC again to complete it; in other words, the protocol should be "human-verifiable" i.e., easily executed by a human in the verifier side. We first explain how these problems have been addressed in the literature so far and then we present our results.

1.1   Previous Work

An ingenious idea to resolve the untrusted platform problem was proposed by Chaum [4]: in *code voting* the system provides to the voter a code that uniquely corresponds to his proper vote but the actual correspondence is hidden. The system used pre-encrypted ballots and return codes, requiring the voters to enter pseudo-random numbers in order to cast a vote. The scheme guarantees privacy and integrity against malicious computers however codes need to be generated via a multiparty protocol and distributed privately, something that substantially increases the complexity of the system. Later the idea of code voting was applied in voting schemes like those in [23,13].

Subsequent work in code verification protocols cf. [14,11] simplified the ballot casting procedure and made it compatible with standard encrypted ballot casting systems (so that previous tallying mechanisms can be readily applied, as those in [12,1,2,15,20,7]). More specifically, Heiberg et al. propose in [14] a code verification protocol that uses random security codes. These are reconstructed as the vote is transfered from the PC to the messenger through the vote collector, by a proxy oblivious transfer scheme. Gjøsteen in [10,11] uses pseudo-random codes, generated as the composition of three pseudo-random functions, owned by the PC, the vote collector and the messenger respectively. These papers focused on the vote collection and feedback system which is comprised of two servers, a vote collector and a messenger who collaborate to produce the validation code that is transmitted as feedback back to the user. The separation of these two servers is an essential feature and their collaboration breaks privacy in the protocols of [14,11]. To address this serious privacy issue (as well as a few other problems), Lipmaa presented an adaptation of Gjøsteen's protocol in [16], that prevents the coalition of the servers from breaching privacy by relying on a secret stored on the PC. In this case, the vote collector and messenger server coalition is still unable to breach privacy unless somehow they get access to the PC secret-key. While this addresses partially the privacy concern it increases the

---

[1] For example an SMS to a smartphone has been suggested as an implementation of the feedback mechanism.

key-management requirements of the protocol on the PC side. Given the above, it remains as an open question to provide better privacy guarantees without using a secret key on the PC side.

Part of our techniques to be presented below are related to visual cryptography. Naor and Shamir [19] introduced visual cryptography and proposed a visual secret sharing protocol that shares black and white images. In their system each pixel is mapped to a certain shape and can be subdivided to a number of black and white sub-pixels. The scheme considers a pixel as black if the number of black sub-pixels exceeds a certain threshold and analogously white if the black sub-pixels are below a threshold. The final pixels are revealed visually by overlaying a number of shares. While very interesting, the techniques of visual cryptography have found little applications in real world systems. Chaum exploited visual cryptography for visual receipts in supervised electronic voting (elections through voting booths) [5]. The scheme uses a 2-out-of-2 secret sharing scheme to share the written form of the vote in two complementary sheets that reveal the vote when combined, while none of the sheets leaks information on its own. The voters keep one sheet and verify their ballot by comparing it with a copy posted on the bulletin board. The use of visual cryptography was later found to be non-essential and the original system was simplified in a way that obviates the visual cryptography part, [22].

1.2 Our Results

In this work we tackle the problem of scaling the privacy guarantee in code verification voting systems without requiring any secret-keys on the PC side. Our approach to achieve this is by increasing the number of feedback messages back to the voter in order to enable the distribution of the messenger functionality. The main challenge of this approach is to maintain human verifiability: to solve this we provide new techniques that are based on either a simple mathematical calculation that the voter is supposed to execute or a novel visual cryptography technique that we call *visual sharing of shape descriptions* and is detailed below.

In general we follow the same initial setup as the voting systems of [14,10,16], i.e., the voter interacts with her PC to generate an encrypted vote. This vote however, is transmitted to *a set* of voting servers: in our scalable system we need not distinguish between types of servers as in previous protocols — all of our servers behave in identical fashion. The voting servers provide feedback to the user through an untappable channel (as the single messenger did in the previous protocols cited above). Each feedback by itself carries no information that can be tied to a specific voter choice. Nevertheless, the voter is able to validate her vote by appropriately synthesizing the feedback she receives from the servers. We consider the cases where the feedback may be the vote itself, a visual representation of the vote (explained below) or a voter dependent security code. In the latter case it is also required to have another out-of-band channel for the distribution of the security codes (as in [14,11,4]). The first two cases though, highlight a unique feature of our methodology: since there is a set of voting servers that each one of them is incapable of extracting something useful from the feedback they return to the voter, it is actually possible for the synthesized feedback to be the actual vote that was casted.

We give two constructions that address the problem of human verifiability (via the synthesis of the voting server feedback messages). In the first case we assume that the voter is capable of executing addition of decimal numbers, i.e., the voter should be capable of verifying that, e.g., the two-digit decimal numbers 32 and 92 sum up to a number that ends in 44. While for some people this may be an easy task, it can be argued by some that it is a tall order for the general population who may not be accustomed to perform mathematical calculations. For this reason we introduce an entirely different technique that is related to (but distinct from) visual cryptography and may be of independent interest.

A visual sharing of shape descriptions is a way to perform secret-sharing of a set of *shape descriptions*. For example a shape description can be the following: "a full circle." In this setting the voter may be given two or more images and we assume that she is capable of deciding (in her mind) whether the overlay of the images matches the shape description she is given. In the case of a full circle, for example, a question that the voter is assumed to be able to answer is the following: does the overlay of ◗ and ◖ amount to a full circle? In our second vote verification protocol the voter validates the PC operation by answering queries such as this one.

We present our protocols for the case that the voting server feedback synthesizes back to the actual vote, however, as mentioned, our protocols can be easily adapted to the code verification setting (as in [14,11]). In this setting a code generation phase takes place before the elections and the codes are sent to the voter through an out-of-band communication channel (called the pre-channel that for instance is paper mail sent ahead of the elections). Then, the voting servers will obtain a *share* of the code that corresponds to the submitted vote and will forward it, through another out-of-band channel (the post-channel), to the voter as feedback that will be synthesized as above using our techniques. An attacker may view the contents of at most one of these channels, in order to guarantee privacy.

2   Cryptographic Preliminaries and Tools

Public Key Cryptosystem. A public key cryptosystem is a triple of algorithms $\langle Gen, Enc, Dec \rangle$. The randomized Gen algorithm on input the security parameter 1^k outputs a secret/public key pair $(pk, sk) \leftarrow Gen(1^k)$. The Enc_{pk} randomized algorithm on input pk, a message m and randomness r outputs a ciphertext $c = Enc_{pk}(m, r)$. The deterministic Dec_{sk} algorithm on input sk and a ciphertext $c \in C$ outputs a message $m' = Dec_{sk}(c)$. For a correct encryption scheme it holds that if $(pk, sk) \leftarrow Gen(1^k)$ then $Dec_{sk}(Enc_{pk}(m, r)) = m$.

The ElGamal cryptosystem works over a finite cyclic group G_q of prime order q, generated by $\langle g \rangle$. Gen selects a secret key $sk \leftarrow \mathbb{Z}_q$ and sets $pk = g^{sk}$. A message $m \in G$ is encrypted as $\langle c_1, c_2 \rangle = Enc_{pk}(m, r) = \langle m \cdot pk^r, g^r \rangle$, with randomness $r \in \mathbb{Z}_q$. On input $\langle c_1, c_2 \rangle$ the decryption algorithm outputs

$m' = Dec_{sk}(\langle c_1, c_2 \rangle) = c_1/c_2^{sk}$. The cryptosystem is multiplicatively homomorphic as for all $m_1, m_2, r_1, r_2 \in \mathbb{Z}_q$ it holds that $Enc_{pk}(m_1, r_1) \cdot Enc_{pk}(m_2, r_2) = Enc_{pk}(m_1 \cdot m_2, r_1 + r_2)$. An additively homomorphic variant is derived if we encrypt g^m instead of m. The ElGamal cryptosystem is IND-CPA secure under the decisional Diffie-Hellman assumption.

Commitments. A commitment scheme is a triple of algorithms $\langle Gen, Com, Open \rangle$. The randomized Gen algorithm on input 1^k outputs a public key h. The randomized Com_h algorithm on input h, a message m and randomness r and outputs a commitment $c = Com_h(m, r)$. The $Open$ algorithm on input a commitment c and the de-commiting values m, r verifies that $c = Com_h(m, r)$. A commitment scheme satisfies the statistically hiding property if the distributions of commitments for two different messages are indistinguishable. It satisfies the computationally binding property if any polynomial-time adversary cannot open a commitment to two different values with non-negligible probability. The Pedersen commitment scheme [21] works over a finite cyclic group G_q of prime order q generated by $\langle g \rangle$. The message and randomness space is $\mathbb{Z}_q$ and the cipherspace G_q. $Gen(1^k)$ outputs a key $h = g^\alpha$ for $\alpha \leftarrow \mathbb{Z}_q$ and algorithm Com_h, on input $m, r \in \mathbb{Z}_q$ outputs $c = g^m h^r$. The scheme is statistically hiding and computationally binding under the decisional Diffie-Hellman assumption.

Signatures. A digital signature scheme is a triple of algorithms $\langle Gen, Sign, Ver \rangle$. The randomized Gen algorithm on input 1^k outputs a verification/signing key pair $(vk, sk) \leftarrow Gen(1^k)$. The randomized $Sign_{sk}$ algorithm on input the signing key sk, a message m and randomness r outputs a signature $\sigma = Sign_{sk}(m, r)$ and the Ver_{vk} algorithm, on input the verification key vk, a message m and a signature σ accepts the signature as valid or rejects it. Security for signatures is defined as existentially unforgeability against chosen message attack (EUF-CMA), stating that no polynomial forger can produce a valid signature for a message that he has not seen before, assuming black box access to a signing oracle. For our purposes we rely on any EUF-CMA signature scheme and we assume the existence of a public key infrastructure that can be used to digitally sign messages. All participants of the protocol, i.e. the voter's PCs and the online voting servers, are assumed to support these operations.

Proofs of Knowledge. A proof of knowledge is a communication protocol between two entities, a Prover and a Verifier. The prover possesses a valid witness w for a publicly known predicate R, such that $R(w) = 1$ and wants to convince the verifier without revealing the witness. A special case of proofs of knowledge are the 3-message Σ-protocols whose communication transcript is of the form $\langle com, chl, ans \rangle$. The prover makes the first step to send a commitment com to the verifier. The response of the verifier is a randomly chosen challenge chl. The prover terminates the protocol by sending an answer message ans and the verifier checks the validity of some conditions. Any Σ-protocol can be made non interactive in the random oracle model by using the Fiat-Shamir heuristic [8]. The techniques of [6] allow us to produce conjunctions and disjunctions of Σ-protocols that satisfy special soundness and honest-verifier zero-knowledge.

The well known Schnorr protocol for proving knowledge of a discrete logarithm forms the basis of all necessary proofs of knowledge we discuss. Bit commitment proofs of the form $pk(r \mid h^r = C \ \lor \ h^r = (C/g))$, for Pederesen bit commitments C on a public key h, are an immediate consequence of the disjunctions of Schnorr protocols, known as Schnorr "OR" proofs. The proof $pk(\alpha, r_1, r_2 \mid C_1 = g^\alpha h_1^{r_1} \land C_2 = g^\alpha h_2^{r_2})$ that two Pedersen commitments C_1, C_2 over the public keys h_1, h_2 hide the same value α, is also derived from Schnorr's protocol. By employing the techniques of [6] the previous proof can be generalized to "OR" proofs for the statement $pk(\alpha, \beta, r_1, r_2 \mid C_1 = g^\alpha h_1^{r_1} \land C_2 = g^\beta h_2^{r_2} \land (\alpha = \beta \ \lor \ \alpha = \beta + u \ \lor \ \ldots \ \lor \ \alpha = \beta + \lambda u))$, stating that the hidden values α, β of the two commitments satisfy the relation $\alpha = \beta + iu$, for some $i \in \{0, \ldots, \lambda\}$ and a publicly known value u.

Finally range proofs are proofs of knowledge showing that a committed value x in a commitment C lies in a specific range of values, such as $[0, m-1]$, for $m \geq 2$. For Pedersen commitments such a proof will be denoted as $pk(\alpha, r \mid C = g^\alpha h^r \ \land \ x \in [0, m-1]$). For the purposes of our protocol we employ the range proof from [17]. Alternatively one could use any efficient range proof in exponents, like the generalization of [17] presented in [3]. The proof modifies the classic bit-length range proof of [18] to arbitrary ranges. The proof of [17] writes number $\alpha \in [0, m-1]$ in the form $\alpha = \sum_{j=0}^{\lfloor \log_2(m-1) \rfloor} \mu_j H_j$, where $H_j = \lfloor (m - 1 + 2^j)/2^{j+1} \rfloor$ and $\mu_j \in \{0, 1\}$. Then it commits to all values μ_j and uses bit commitment proofs to show that $\mu_j \in \{0, 1\}$, requiring $k = \lfloor \log_2(m-1) \rfloor + 1$ single bit proofs. For small values of m the proof remains efficient for our purpose. Both the prover and the verifier precompute the coefficients H_j and the verifier can confirm that the committed values μ_j represent α by checking that $g^\alpha = \prod_{j=0}^{k-1} (g^{\mu_j})^{H_j}$.

The Communication Channels. We require the existence of secure communication channels for vote verification. We use the term "untappable channel" to refer to a private channel that prevents an adversary from intercepting sent messages, keeping the information sent through this channel perfectly secret to all other parties. We assume the existence of an one-way untappable channel from the voting servers to the voter to transfer the receipts. This channel can be viewed either as a unique untappable channel used by all servers, or alternatively as a set of communication channels (one from each server to the voter) requiring that one of them should be untappable. Two channels are referred as "a pair of out-of-band communication channels" when they are both secure, authenticated and independent of the PC. In our case we will need a channel from the elections authorities to the voters for receipt distribution and a channel from the voting servers to the voters for verification. For both "out-of-band" channels we prohibit the attacker from modifying their contents. However we may allow the attacker to read the contents of at most one of these channels. We also require the existence of a broadcast channel between the PC and the voting servers, where the PC posts public information required by them.

3   The Vote Verification Protocol

The Security Model. We define the notion of security of our scheme in terms of privacy and integrity. Throughout our discussion we refer to malicious entities. In our setting a malicious PC wants to violate integrity by modifying the vote. We recall that privacy is not relevant against such an attacker, since the PC knows the vote. A set of malicious (honest but curious) voting servers want to violate privacy by learning the vote, as by their construction they cannot alter encrypted submitted ballots. We ask that the following requirements are met:

Cast as intended: We consider the following game between two entities, an adversary A and an honest challenger C: We give A access to the public keys PK and the voter identities ID, and in the code verification setting to the verification codes CS possessed by the voters. A picks a voter V from the ID set, corrupts her PC and lets V cast a ballot for candidate x. Then C runs the whole voting protocol and outputs the encryption of a vote E, the secret receipt R and the public auxiliary information Pub of the protocol. Let Q be a predicate that on input the receipt R and the public information Pub outputs 1 iff R is consistent with Pub. In the code verification setting the codes CS are also part of Q's input, whose output is 1 iff all its input arguments are consistent. A wins the game if $Q(R, Pub, (CS)) = 1$ and $Dec_{sk}(E) \neq x$. A voting protocol with receipts satisfies the "cast as intended" property if it holds that $Pr[A(PK, Pub, ID, (CS))$ wins$] \leq \epsilon(k)$, where $\epsilon(k)$ is a negligible function in the security parameter k.

(t, n)-*Vote secrecy:* We consider the following game between an adversary A and an honest challenger C: We give A have access to the public keys set PK, to the voter identities ID and, in the code verification setting, to the codes CS possessed by the voters. A picks and corrupts $t < n$ out of n servers. A picks a voter identity from the ID set and two candidates x_0, x_1 of his choice and gives them to the challenger. Then C runs the vote casting by picking at random a bit $b \leftarrow \{0,1\}$ and encrypting message x_b as $E = Enc_{pk}(x_b)$. Then C runs the voting protocol and outputs the encrypted vote E, the secret receipt R and all other auxiliary public information and secret information Pub, Sec, sending E, Pub and the appropriate share of Sec_i to server S_i. A in possession of Pub and the private values $\{Sec_i\}_{i \in [j_1, \ldots, j_t]}$ of t compromised servers, outputs a bit b^*. A wins the game if $b^* = b$. A voting protocol satisfies "(t, n)-vote secrecy" if it holds that $Pr[A(PK, Pub, ID, (CS), E, \{Sec_i\}_{i \in [j_1, \ldots, j_t]})$ wins$] \leq 1/2 + \epsilon(k)$, where $\epsilon(k)$ is a negligible function.

As we mentioned before, our solution focuses only on the vote submission phase, like previously suggested protocols [14,16]. The final stage of tallying is considered a separate procedure and correct tallying can be guaranteed by employing a suitable protocol. To address coercion one may allow revoting. However, similarly to previous approaches [14,11,16], this clashes with the cast as intended property since there is no means to guarantee that the servers will send to the tallier the most recent vote submitted by a voter. We note that in case of a wrong receipt we accuse the PC of being malicious (since it is assumed to be the most vulnerable component). Note that if the voting servers' goal is to break privacy, sending wrong receipts will not be useful to them. Still if a server wants to disrupt the election it can create confusion by not issuing receipts, however a voter that verifies her vote will notice that an error has occurred.

3.1 Instantiation of the Vote Verification Protocol

We are now ready to describe the vote verification protocol. Let $n \geq 2$ be the desired number of voting servers and M be the set of m candidates that participate in the elections, represented as globally known elements in $\mathbb{Z}_m$. Moreover let G_q be a subgroup of $\mathbb{Z}_p$ of prime order q over which we implement ElGamal encryption and Pedersen commitments. Our message space is $\mathbb{Z}_u$, where u is an additional system parameter. Specifically u is chosen so as to facilitate the vote reconstruction and verification by the voter. We set $u = \min_\lambda 10^\lambda$ such that $m \leq 10^\lambda < q$. As we consider small scale elections with at most a few hundred options in total, typical values for u will be 100 or 1000. By this trick we avoid the modular additions that would be otherwise required by the vote verification step of the voter, which is simplified to addition of λ-digit decimal numbers. By introducing n voting servers ($2 \leq n < q$), the voter needs to add the corresponding n numbers.

Let us consider the ElGamal key pairs (pk_t, sk_t) of the tallier and the commitment scheme (g, h) that are generated in a key generation phase prior to the elections. During vote submission a voter casts her ballot through her PC voting for candidate $x \in \mathbb{Z}_m$. Then the PC splits the vote by picking $n - 1$ random shares $x_1, \ldots, x_{n-1} \in \mathbb{Z}_u$ and adjusting x_n such that $x = \sum_{i=1}^n x_i \bmod u$. The PC computes the commitments $(C_1, \ldots, C_n) = (g^{x_1} h^{r_1}, \ldots, g^{x_n} h^{r_n})$ to the shares and sends them, through the broadcast channel, to the voting servers $S_1, \ldots, S_n$ along with the encrypted vote $E_t = (E_x, E_t) = (g^x pk_t^r, g^r)$. The PC needs to prove in zero knowledge that the shares and the vote satisfy the relation $x = \sum_{i=1}^n x_i \bmod u$, and opens the commitment C_i to server S_i who verifies its validity. In addition the PC needs to prove that the encrypted candidate corresponds to a valid value in the range $[0, m-1]$. By this we prevent a malicious PC from submitting forged ballots of the form $y = x + ku$ that would yield a correct receipt modulo u.

The PC prepares a non-interactive witness indistinguishable proof of knowledge of the above statements denoted as $\pi = PK(x, r, \{x_i, r_i\}_{i=1}^n \mid E_x = g^x pk_t^r \wedge x \in [0, m-1] \wedge \{C_i = g^{x_i} h^{r_i}\}_{i=1}^n \wedge x = \sum_{i=1}^n x_i \bmod u)$, using standard variations of the Schnorr proof and adapting the techniques of [6]. We note that the proof requires that $n \cdot u < q$ to work properly. From the results of [6] it follows that the proof satisfies correctness, special soundness and honest verifier zero knowledge, however we provide a security proof in appendix D. In our instantiation we will use the non-interactive version of the proof by using the Fiat-Shamir heuristic [8]. Each online server S_i verifies the proof π, decrypts and obtains the share x_i and verifies compatibility with commitment C_i. Upon successful verification of all these steps, the server sends the value x_i through the untappable channel to the voter who verifies the vote by performing a regular addition with possible carry drop beyond the most significant digit ($x = \sum_{i=1}^n x_i \bmod 10^\lambda$). In this protocol we allow re-voting as a measure against vote coercion.

The Proof of Knowledge π: Public Input: $\langle p, q, g, u \rangle$ the system parameters, h, pk_t the commitment key and the tallier's public key, m the number of candidates and $k = \lfloor \log_2(m-1) \rfloor + 1$, $E_t = (E_x, E_r) = (g^x pk_t^r, g^r)$, $\{C_i = g^{x_i} h^{r_i}\}_{i=1}^n$. Prover's Input: $x, r, \{x_i, r_i\}_{i=1}^n$.

1. The Prover:
   (a) *Range proof:* For $j = 0, \ldots, k-1$ computes $\mu_j \in \{0,1\}$ s.t. $x = \sum_{j=0}^{k-1} \mu_j H_j$ where $H_j = \lfloor ((m-1) + 2^j)/2^{j+1} \rfloor$
   (b) *Range proof:* For $j = 0, \ldots, k-1$:
      i. Picks $z_j \leftarrow \mathbb{Z}_q$ s.t. $\sum_{j=0}^{k-1} z_j H_j = r$.
      ii. Commits to μ_j as $\mathcal{E}_j = g^{\mu_j} pk_t^{z_j}$.
      iii. If $\mu_j = 0$ it picks $w_j, c_{2j}, \rho_{2j} \leftarrow \mathbb{Z}_q$ and sets $y_{1j} = pk_t^{w_j}$, $y_{2j} = pk_t^{\rho_{2j}} (\mathcal{E}_j/g)^{-c_{2j}}$.
      iv. if $\mu_j = 1$ it picks $w_j, c_{1j}, \rho_{1j} \leftarrow \mathbb{Z}_q$ and sets $y_{1j} = pk_t^{\rho_{1j}} (\mathcal{E}_j)^{-c_{1j}}$, $y_{2j} = pk_t^{w_j}$.
   (c) *Valid shares:* If $\sum_{i=1}^n x_i = x + (i-1)u \bmod q$, with $i \in \{1, 2, \ldots, n\}$, it picks $w, \rho_a, \rho_b, \{c_j, s_j, \rho'_{1j}, \rho'_{2j}\}_{j \neq i} \leftarrow \mathbb{Z}_q$ and sets $a_i = g^w pk_t^{\rho_a}$, $b_i = g^w h^{\rho_b}$, $\{a_j = (E_x)^{-c_j} g^{s_j} pk_t^{\rho'_{1j}}, b_j = (\prod_{l=1}^n C_l/g^{(j-1)u})^{-c_j} g^{s_j} h^{\rho'_{2j}}\}_{i \neq j}$.
   (d) It sends $(\{a_i, b_i\}_{i=1}^n, \{\mathcal{E}_j, y_{1j}, y_{2j}\}_{j=0}^{k-1})$ to the Verifier.
2. The Verifier picks $c \leftarrow \mathbb{Z}_q$ and sends it to the Prover.
3. The Prover:
   (a) *Range proof:* For $j = 0, \ldots, k-1$:
      i. If $\mu_j = 0$ it sets $c_{1j} = c - c_{2j}$, $\rho_{1j} = w_j + c_{1j} z_j$.
      ii. if $\mu_j = 1$ it sets $c_{2j} = c - c_{1j}$, $\rho_{2j} = w_j + c_{2j} z_j$.
   (b) *Valid shares:* If $\sum_{i=1}^n x_i = x + (i-1)u \bmod q$, with $i \in \{1, 2, \ldots, n\}$, it sets $c_i = c - \sum_{i \neq j} c_j$, $s_i = w + xc_i$, $\rho'_{1i} = \rho_a + rc_i$, $\rho'_{22} = \rho_b + (\sum_{l=1}^n r_l) c_i$.
   (c) It sends $(\{c_i, s_i, \rho'_{1i}, \rho'_{2i}\}_{i=1}^n, \{c_{1j}, c_{2j}, \rho_{1j}, \rho_{2j}\}_{j=0}^{k-1})$ to the Verifier.
4. The Verifier accepts if all the following tests succeed, otherwise it rejects:
   (a) *Range proof:* For $j = 0, \ldots, k-1$: $c = c_{1j} + c_{2j}$ and $pk_t^{\rho_{1j}} = y_{1j}(\mathcal{E}_j)^{c_{1j}}$ and $pk_t^{\rho_{2j}} = y_{2j}(\mathcal{E}_j/g)^{c_{2j}}$.
   (b) *Range proof:* $E_x = \prod_{j=0}^{k-1} \mathcal{E}_j^{H_j}$.
   (c) *Valid shares:* $c = \sum_{i=1}^n c_i$ and for $i = 1, \ldots, n$: $g^{s_i} pk_t^{\rho'_{1i}} = a_i (E_x)^{c_i}$ and $g^{s_i} h^{\rho'_{2i}} = b_i (\prod_{l=1}^n C_l/g^{(i-1)u})^{c_i}$.

The Vote Verification Protocol: Let M be the set of m candidates, n the number of servers, (pk_{S_i}, sk_{S_i}), (pk_t, sk_t) be the public/secret key pairs of server S_i $(i = 1, \ldots, n)$ and the tallier respectively, (sk_V, vk_V) and (sg_{S_i}, vk_{S_i}) be the signing/verification key pairs of voter V and server S_i, h the commitment public key and $\langle p, q, g, u \rangle$ the system parameters.

- The voter V:
  1. Submits a vote for candidate $x \in \mathbb{Z}_m$.
  2. Waits for shares $x_1, \ldots, x_n$ from the servers and checks that $x = x_1 + \cdots + x_n \bmod u$.
- The PC $(sk_V, pk_t, \{pk_{S_i}\}_{i=1}^n)$ on input x by the voter:

1. Picks $x_1, \ldots, x_{n-1} \leftarrow \mathbb{Z}_u$ and sets $x_n = x - \sum_{j=1}^{n-1} x_j \bmod u$.
2. Picks $r \leftarrow \mathbb{Z}_q$ and encrypts x as $E_t = (E_x, E_r) = Enc_{pk_t}(g^x, r)$.
3. For all $i = 1, \ldots, n$ picks $\rho_i, r_i, r_i' \leftarrow \mathbb{Z}_q$ and encrypts x_i as $e_i = Enc_{pk_{S_i}}(x_i, \rho_i)$ and commits to it as $C_i = g^{x_i} h^{r_i}$. Then it encrypts the randomness r_i as $R_i = Enc_{pk_{S_i}}(r_i, r_i')$.
4. Prepares the non interactive proof $\pi = PK(x, r, \{x_i, r_i\}_{i=1}^n \mid E_x = g^x pk_t^r \wedge \{C_i = g^{x_i} h^{r_i}\}_{i=1}^n \wedge x = \sum_{i=1}^n x_i \bmod u \wedge x \in [0, m-1])$.
5. Signs the vote $\sigma = Sign_{sk_V}(E_t, \pi)$.
6. For all $i = 1, \ldots n$ sends to Server S_i $D_i = (e_i, R_i)$ and sends $B = (E_t, \{C_j\}_{j=1}^n, \pi, \sigma, V)$ through the broadcast channel to all servers.
- The Server S_i $(sg_{S_i}, sk_{S_i}, vk_V)$ on input D_i, B performs the following tests. If any step fails it declares a forgery and stops:
  1. Decrypts the de-committing values of D_i to obtain r_i, x_i, verifies the valid opening of $C_i = g^{x_i} h^{r_i}$ and that $x_i \in \mathbb{Z}_u$.
  2. Verifies the proof π and the signature σ.
  3. Signs the vote E_t, $\sigma' = Sign_{sg_{S_i}}(E_t)$, stores it and sends x_i to the voter V through the untappable channel.
- The Tallier: When the election is over the tallier gets the signed votes from a sever, verifies the server's signatures and runs a decryption protocol.

3.2   Security and Performance

We now discuss the security offered by the vote verification protocol. We guarantee that the protocol meets our security requirements in the corruption scenario where the voter's PC is corrupted or a subset of $t \leq n-1$ out of n voting servers are honest-but-curious, i.e. they follow the protocol but share their information with the attacker. We state that if a voter successfully verifies her vote and does not revote, then we guarantee that the vote was cast as intended and remains secret from the voting servers.

Cast as intended: In order for a corrupted PC to succeed in submitting a message $x' \in \mathbb{Z}_q$ instead of a valid candidate $x \in [0, m-1]$ selected by the voter, it must be the case that the receipts are equal, that is $x = x' \bmod u$. Thus x' must be of the form $x' = x + ku \bmod q$, for a $k \in \mathbb{Z}$. Since we assume the execution of the voting protocol by the honest challenger all voting servers check that they receive compatible values in the correct range. Then the range proof guarantees that $x' \in \mathbb{Z}_m \subset \mathbb{Z}_u$, and thus $k = 0$ giving us $x' = x \bmod q$.

(t, n)-*Vote secrecy:* Without loss of generality assume that the adversary controls the first $t < n$ servers and let $x_0, x_1 \in [0, m-1]$ be the candidates chosen by the adversary and given to the voting system. The challenger choses b from $\{0, 1\}$ and generates the n shares $x_{b1}, \ldots, x_{bn} \in \mathbb{Z}_u$, forming the receipt $x_b = \sum_{i=1}^n x_{bi} \bmod u$. The adversary obtains the the private shares $x_{b1}, \ldots, x_{bt}$ of the receipt and the publicly announced vales $C_i = g^{x_{bi}} h^{r_i}$ for all $i = 1, \ldots, n$ and $E = (g^{x_b} pk^r, g^r)$. Since we use a (n, n)-secret sharing scheme the adversary needs all n shares to reconstruct the receipt, while with fewer he obtains a random value $\sum_{i=1}^t x_{bi} \bmod u$ in $\mathbb{Z}_u$. From the statistically hiding property of Pedersen commitments and ElGamal encryption it is guaranteed that he cannot distinguish between x_0, x_1 from E or from the commitments C_i, for $i = 1, \ldots, n$.

We cannot guarantee security against coalitions of malicious computers and malicious voting servers, as in this scenario the malicious voting servers trivially learn the vote from the PC. The PC submits a fake ballot undetected as long as it collaborates with one malicious server who deviates from the protocol and sends a modified value to the voter so that she reconstructs a correct receipt.

Complexity. We calculate the complexity of the n-server protocol, $(2 \leq n < q)$ for m candidates, counting the number of the *online* exponentiations, signings and signature verifications. Values that can be pre-computed like H_j for the range proofs, the votes g^x and the values g^{iu} that appear in the proofs are not counted. The PC performs $6n + 2$ exponentiations for vote encryption and commitments to the shares, $4k$ for the range proof and $5(n - 1) + 3$ for the valid share proof, a total of $4(\lfloor \log_2(m - 1) \rfloor + 1) + 11n$ exponentiations. In addition it performs a single signing. Each server S_i performs 4 exponentiations for decryptions and commitment verifications, $5k$ for verifying the range and $5n$ for verifying the valid shares, a total of $5(\lfloor \log_2(m - 1) \rfloor + 1) + 5n + 4$ exponentiations. Additionally the sever performs one signing and one signature verification.

3.3   Instantiation of a Code Verification Protocol

With a simple adaptation our protocol can be transformed to use voter dependent security codes as receipts, relaxing the untappable channel requirement. Following the approach of [14,10,16], we assume a code generation phase before the elections and we use a pair of out-of-band channels, a pre-channel for code delivery to the voters and a post-channel for sending the receipts to the voters.

We sightly change the protocol by creating the security codes through an onetime pad scheme. For each voter V we pick a random value $b_V \in \mathbb{Z}_u$ and set $Code_V[x] = x + b_V \mod u$, for all candidates x. We also pick $n - 1$ random values $b_{V_1}, \ldots, b_{V_{n-1}} \in \mathbb{Z}_m$ and set appropriately b_{V_n} such that $\sum_{i=1}^{n} b_{V_i} = b_V$. We send through the pre-channel the pairs $(x, code_V[x])$ to the voter V. Also the pairs (V, b_{V_i}) need to be given to each server S_i. The voting protocol remains the same, except for the servers' last step, where they send $\alpha_i = x_i + b_{V_i} \mod u$ through the post-channel. Finally the voter reconstructs the security code as $c = \sum_{i=1}^{n} \alpha_i = \sum_{i=1}^{n} x_i + b_{V_i} = x + b_V$ and compares it to the value $Code_V[x]$.

We do not allow revoting as the security of the one-time pad scheme collapses otherwise. The protocol has the same security guarantees with the vote verification protocol and additionally an observer of the pre-channel gets no information about the voting process and an observer of the post-channel gets no information about the vote x from the code $c = x + b_V \mod u$, due to the perfect secrecy of one-time pad. To allow revoting we should use an untappable post-channel. Although in this case we do not relax the untappable channel assumption, voterdependent receipts can still be useful as a means against coercion.

4   A Visual Vote Verification Protocol

In this section we introduce visual vote verification. This method enables the generation of visual receipts that even though individually leak no information about the submitted vote, overlaying them enables the verification of it. Even though the notion is general, here we will consider the case of two voting servers and an untappable channel to forward the receipts, allowing revoting.

First we introduce a formal cryptographic primitive that we call n-Visual Sharing of Shape Descriptions (n-VSSD). The main idea is that each voter choice will correspond in a unique way to a certain shape. Shapes can be split in n different parts, without revealing information about the initial image; still a person can easily verify that the parts overlay back to the shape. Using a VSSD we show how visual vote verification can be facilitated. Due to lack of space the proofs of this section can be found in appendix B.

The n-VSSD. Let M be the set of $m \geq 2$ distinct messages which we want to represent visually and share in $n \geq 2$ different parts. Let D_x be the set of visual descriptions for message $x \in M$ (we note that we allow each message to have more than one visual representation, i.e., $|D_x| \geq 1$). Also let Λ be a commutative semigroup equipped with an operation $\vee$ that will be called the visual alphabet. The splitting function is a probabilistic function $P : M \to \Lambda^n$, that given a message $m \in M$ outputs a valid "splitting" of it, consisting of n shares in Λ. Then we ask for the following properties:

- Solvability: $\forall x \in M \; \forall \langle v_1, \ldots, v_n \rangle \in P(x)$ it holds that $\vee_{i=1}^{n} v_i \in D_x$.
- (t, n)-Resilience: Let w be an n-tuple of the form $\langle (A \cup \{\#\}), \ldots, (A \cup \{\#\}) \rangle$, where the symbol $\#$ represents a share of unknown value in Λ and A represents known shares in Λ, such that w has $t < n$ known shares A (i.e., different than $\#$). Then there is a constant $0 < c < 1$ such that for all w of the previous form it holds that $Prob_{v \leftarrow P(x)}[w \in v] = c$.

The solvability property corresponds to correctness, requiring the correct reconstruction of a visual description of the initial message from all its n shares. The (t, n)-resilience property corresponds to threshold security, stating that any observer in possession of t or less shares of an image cannot distinguish between the initial message they may belong to, as the ordered t shares can be part of any message with equal probability.

4.1   A 2-VSSD Instantiation

Let us first consider two shape descriptions: *full circle* and *half circle*. These two shape descriptions can be visually represented by a completely black circle and by a circle that is half white in its left or right part. We can correspond these two shapes to a set of messages $M = \{0, 1\}$ say, such that, 0 corresponds to full circle and 1 corresponds to half circle. Next we define the visual alphabet Λ to contain two half circles as defined above: half white in the left and half white in the right part. Observe now that $P(0)$ may contain any pair of the two complementary elements from Λ, while $P(1)$ may contain any pair of elements from Λ where the same half circle appears twice.

As bitstrings, we can denote the full circle by 11, while the half-circle by 10 or 01, thus having $D_0 = \{11\}$ and $D_1 = \{01, 10\}$. Our alphabet is $\Lambda = \{01, 10\}$ and the operation $\vee$ is the bitwise OR operation in the elements of Λ applied coordinate-wise. In this case the message corresponding to a shape $bb' \in \cup_{x \in M} D_x$ can be simply recovered as $x = b \oplus b'$ (where $\oplus$ stands for the x-or operation). The splitting function is then defined as follows: $P(0)$ is uniformly chosen from $\{(10, 01), (01, 10)\}$ while $P(1)$ is uniformly chosen from $\{(01, 01), (10, 10)\}$.

Proposition 1. *Let $M = \{0, 1\}$. The $(M, \{D_x\}_{x \in M}, \Lambda, P)$ scheme defined above is a 2-VSSD that satisfies $(1, 2)$-resilience.*

A Scheme for Arbitrary M. Let the set M be an arbitrary set of size $m \geq 2$ (corresponding, say, to m different election candidates). Without loss of generality consider $M = \mathbb{Z}_m$. Let $\langle M^*, \{D_x^*\}_{x \in M^*}, \Lambda^*, P^* \rangle$ be the 2-VSSD defined above and $k = \lfloor \log_2(m-1) \rfloor + 1$. Let $\Lambda = \{10, 01\}^k$ and let $\vee$ be the bitwise OR operation. We next need to determine the visual description set D_x and the splitting function $P(x)$ for each $x \in M$. Let $(b_{k-1} \ldots b_0) \in \{0, 1\}^k$ be the binary encoding for a message $x \in M$. We define the set D_x by processing each bit $b_j \in M^* = \{0, 1\}$ of x separately and independently from the others. Specifically a bitstring $(d_{k-1} \ldots d_0)$ is in D_x iff for all $j = 0, \ldots, k-1$ $d_j \in D_{b_j}^*$. Similarly the function $P(x)$ applies in each bit of x the splitting function P^* such that the tuple $(a_{k-1} \ldots a_0, a'_{k-1} \ldots a'_0)$ is in $P(x)$ iff for all $j = 0, \ldots k-1$ $(a_j, a'_j) \in P^*(b_j)$. We provide a detailed example in appendix A.

message bit	shape description	visual	split 1	split 2
0	full circle	●	(10,01): ◐ ◑	(01,10): ◑ ◐
1	half circle	◑ or ◐	(01,01): ◑ ◑	(10,10): ◐ ◐

Fig. 1. The 2-VSSD for $M^* = \{0, 1\}$ with visual alphabet Λ^*

Proposition 2. *For any $m \in \mathbb{N}$, the scheme $(M = \mathbb{Z}_m, \{D_x\}_{x \in M}, \Lambda, P)$ defined above is a 2-VSSD that satisfies $(1, 2)$-resilience.*

4.2   Instantiation of the Visual Vote Verification Protocol

Let us proceed to the visual vote verification protocol that uses the above 2-VSSD. As usual the voter votes for candidate x through her PC, which encrypts it for the tallier. It also generates the visual shares $P(x) = (v_1, v_2)$ that yield the visual description $v_0 = v_1 \vee v_2$, with $v_0 \in D_x$. The PC prepares a proof of compatibility of the visual description, the shares and the vote: It commits through Pedersen commitments $C_{0_j}, C_{1_j}, C_{2_j}$ to each bit $j = 0, \ldots, 2k-1$ of v_0, v_1, v_2 respectively, and proves the validity of bit commitments. Moreover it proves that the splitting is valid, i.e. that for each bit j $v_{0_j} = v_{1_j} \vee v_{2_j}$. To do so we observe that the latter is true if and only if the commitment $C_j = (C_{1_j})(C_{2_j})^2(C_{0_j})^3$ hides a value in $\{0, 4, 5, 6\}$. In addition the PC proves that $v_0 = (v_{0_{2k-1}} v_{0_{2k-2}} \cdots v_{0_1} v_{0_0})$ is a valid visual description of x, i.e. $v_0 \in D_x$. That is for each bit b_j, $j = 0, \ldots, k-1$ in the binary encoding of x, it holds that $b_j = v_{0_{2j+1}} \oplus v_{0_{2j}} = v_{0_{2j+1}} + v_{0_{2j}}$ mod 2. Since we have proved that all values v_{0_j} are bits and for all $j = 0, \ldots, k-1$ $(v_{0_{2j+1}} v_{0_{2j}}) \in \bigcup_{x \in M^*} D_x^*$, i.e. $(v_{0_{2j+1}} v_{0_{2j}}) \in \{01, 10, 11\}$, the latter relation is equivalent to proving that $b_j = 2 - v_{0_{2j+1}} - v_{0_{2j}}$. Thus we prove knowledge of the value x in the encryption E_x and then prove that the commitment $\prod_{j=0}^{k-1} (\frac{g^2}{C_{0_{2j+1}} \cdot C_{0_{2j}}})^{2^j}$ also hides the same value x. The full interactive proof of knowledge is denoted as $\pi' = PK(x, \rho, \{(v_{i_j}, r_{i_j})_{i=0,1,2}\}_{j=0}^{2k-1} \mid \{(C_{i_j} = g^{v_{i_j}} h^{r_{i_j}})_{i=0,1,2}\}_{j=0}^{2k-1} \wedge (\{(v_{i_j})_{i=0,1,2}\}_{j=0}^{2k-1} \in \{0,1\}) \wedge (v_{1_j} + 2v_{2_j} + 3v_{0_j} \in \{0, 4, 5, 6\})_{j=0}^{2k-1} \wedge E_x = g^x pk_t^\rho \wedge (x = \sum_{j=0}^{k-1} (2 - v_{0_{2j+1}} - v_{0_{2j}}) 2^j))$. Due to lack of space its full description is given in appendix C. For our protocol we will use the non-interactive version by the Fiat-Shamir heuristic. Its security follows from the results of [6], however we provide a proof in appendix D.

Each server S_i $(i = 1, 2)$ needs to verify the proof π' and the validity of the share v_i. The servers store the shares v_i for all $v_i \in \Lambda$, as well as their corresponding images that will be sent back to the voters. Let $\tilde{v}_i$ be the number whose binary encoding is the bitstring $v_i = (v_{i_{2k-1}} v_{i_{2k-2}} \cdots v_{i_1} v_{i_0}) \in \Lambda$, i.e. $\tilde{v}_i = \sum_{j=0}^{2k-1} v_{i_j} 2^j$. Each server S_i stores a database of all valid shares $v_i \in \Lambda$ and their images, indexed by the corresponding value $\tilde{v}_i$. By this construction we do not need to open all bit commitments $\{C_{i_j} = g^{v_{i_j}} h^{r_{i_j}}\}_{j=0}^{2k-1}$ of the bits of v_i to server S_i, in order to verify the validity of the share. Instead the PC can open to server S_i a single commitment $C_i' = \prod_{j=0}^{2k-1} (C_{i_j})^{2^j}$ as $g^{\tilde{v}_i} h^{\rho_{\tilde{v}_i}}$ with $\rho_{\tilde{v}_i} = \sum_{j=0}^{2k-1} r_{i_j} 2^j$, so that the server can verify that the bit commitments C_{i_j} correspond to a valid share v_i. We note that $\tilde{v}_i$ needs to be in $\mathbb{Z}_q$ so we should have $2^{2k} - 1 < q$. If all verifications are successful the server S_i sends the image indexed by $\tilde{v}_i$ to the voter through the untappable channel.

The Visual Vote Verification Protocol: Let M be the set of m candidates, $k = \lfloor \log_2(m-1) \rfloor + 1$, $(pk_{S_i}, sk_{S_i}), (pk_t, sk_t)$ be the public/secret key pairs of server S_i $(i = 1, 2)$ and the tallier respectively, (sk_V, vk_V) and (sg_{S_i}, vk_{S_i}) be the signing/verification key pairs of voter V and server S_i, h the commitment public key and $\langle p, q, g \rangle$ the system parameters.

- The voter V votes for candidate x through her PC and waits for the images from the voting servers. Upon receiving them she verifies that their overlaying is a correct shape description for candidate x.
- The PC $(sk_V, pk_t, pk_{S_1}, pk_{S_2})$ on input x by the voter:
  1. Generates a valid visual splitting $(v_1, v_2) \leftarrow P(x)$ for candidate x and its visual representation $v_0 = v_1 \vee v_2 \in D_x$.
  2. Picks $r, \rho \leftarrow \mathbb{Z}_q$ and encrypts the vote $E_t = (E_x, E_\rho) = Enc_{pk_t}(g^x, \rho)$.
  3. For each $j = 0, \ldots, 2k-1$ commits to the j-th bit of v_0, v_1, v_2 as $C_{i_j} = g^{v_{i_j}} h^{r_{i_j}}$ for $i = 0, 1, 2$ and $\{r_{i_j}\}_{i=0,1,2}^{j=0,\ldots,2k-1} \leftarrow \mathbb{Z}_q$.

4. Let $\tilde{v}_1, \tilde{v}_2 \in \mathbb{Z}_q$ be the values whose binary representation is $v_1, v_2 \in \{0,1\}^{2k}$. Then for $i = 1, 2$ the PC encrypts the opening randomness $\rho_{\tilde{v}_i} = \sum_{j=0}^{2k-1} r_{ij} 2^j$ as $R_{v_i} = Enc_{pks_i}(\rho_{\tilde{v}_i}, r_i')$, for $r_i' \leftarrow \mathbb{Z}_q$ and the values $\tilde{v}_i$ as $e_{v_i} = Enc_{pks_i}(\tilde{v}_i, r_i)$, for $r_i \leftarrow \mathbb{Z}_q$.
5. Prepares the non-interactive proof of knowledge $\pi' = PK(x, \rho, \{(v_{i_j}, r_{i_j})_{i=0,1,2}\}_{j=0}^{2k-1} \mid ((C_{i_j} = g^{v_{i_j}} h^{r_{i_j}})_{i=0,1,2})_{j=0}^{2k-1} \wedge (\{(v_{i_j})_{i=0,1,2}\}_{j=0}^{2k-1} \in \{0,1\}) \wedge (v_{1_j} + 2v_{2_j} + 3v_{0_j} \in \{0,4,5,6\})_{j=0}^{2k-1} \wedge (E_x = g^x pk_t^{\rho}) \wedge (x = \sum_{j=0}^{k-1} (2 - v_{0_{2j+1}} - v_{0_{2j}}) 2^j)$.
6. Signs the encrypted message and the proof.
7. Sends to server S_i, for $i = 1, 2$, $D_i = (e_{v_i}, R_{v_i})$ and posts $B = (E_t, \{(C_{i_j})_{i=0,1,2}\}_{j=0}^{2k-1}, \pi', sing_{sk_V}(E_t, \pi'), V)$ to the broadcast channel.

- The Server S_i $(sg_{S_i}, sk_{S_i}, vk_V, \langle \tilde{v}_i, v_i, image(v_i) \rangle_{v_i \in \Lambda})$ on input D_i, B performs the following tests. If any step fails it declares a forgery and stops:
  1. Verifies the voter's signature and proof π'.
  2. Decrypts e_{v_i}, R_{v_i} to obtain $\tilde{v}_i, \rho_{v_i}$, checks that $\tilde{v}_i$ is a valid entry in the database $\langle \tilde{v}_i, v_i, image(v_i) \rangle_{v_i \in \Lambda}$ and checks that $g^{\tilde{v}_i} h^{\rho_{v_i}} = \prod_{j=0}^{2k-1} (C_{i_j})^{2^j}$.
  3. Sends the corresponding image of $v_i \in \Lambda$ to the voter through the untappable channel. It signs and stores the vote $sign_{sg_{S_i}}(E_t)$.
- The Tallier: Obtains from a server the votes E_t and runs a suitable protocol.

Security. *Cast as intended:* Let x be the vote submitted by the voter and x' the forged vote such that $Dec_{sk_t}(E_t) = x'$. In order for x' to create a valid receipt v_0 for x it should hold that $v_0 \in D_x$, which implies that for all $j = 0, \ldots, k-1$ $(v_{0_{2j+1}} v_{0_{2j}}) \in D_{b_j}^*$ where b_j is the j-th bit of x, and thus $v_{0_{2j+1}} \oplus v_{0_{2j}} = b_j$. It follows that $\sum_{j=0}^{k-1} (v_{0_{2j+1}} \oplus v_{0_{2j}}) 2^j = \sum_{j=0}^{k-1} b_j 2^j = x$. Since proof π' guarantees that E_t and $\sum_{j=0}^{k-1} (v_{0_{2j+1}} \oplus v_{0_{2j}}) 2^j$ hide the same value, we have that $x = x'$.

(1,2)-Vote secrecy: Without loss of generaltiy let the attacker control server S_1 and let $x_0, x_1 \in \mathbb{Z}_m$ be the candidates chosen by the attacker. The challenger randomly selects and encrypts x_b $(b \in \{0,1\})$ and produces the shares $(v_1, v_2) \in P(x_b)$. The public commitments and encryptions do not reveal information to the attacker, who neither extracts information from v_1 since $Prob[(v_1, \#) \in P(x_0)] = Prob[(v_1, \#) \in P(x_1)]$ from the $(1,2)$-resilience property.

Complexity. The PC needs 10 exponentiations for encryptions and commitments, $12k$ exponentiations for bit commitments and $44k+3$ exponentiations for generating the proof π', a total of $56(\lfloor \log_2(m-1) \rfloor + 1) + 15$ online exponentiations and one signing. Each server S_i does 4 exponentiations for decryptions and commitment openings, $56k+5$ for verifying π' and k for checking the compatibility of the share and its bits, a total of $57(\lfloor \log_2(m-1) \rfloor + 1) + 9$ exponentiations, one signing and one signature verification.

Extensions. The 2-VSSD scheme we presented can be extended to n-VSSD in a number of possible ways. We leave it as future work to determine which ones might be more suitable for human verifiability. We also leave it as open question to develop the case where resiliency is achieved for $t > 1$ but we conjecture that it is possible to obtain a general n-VSSD ($n > 2$) with (t, n)-resilience for $t > 1$ using techniques that were developed for *colored* visual secret sharing [25].

References

1. Bayer, S., Groth, J.: Efficient zero-knowledge argument for correctness of a shuffle. In: Pointcheval, D., Johansson, T. (eds.) EUROCRYPT 2012. LNCS, vol. 7237, pp. 263–280. Springer, Heidelberg (2012)
2. Boneh, D., Golle, P.: Almost entirely correct mixing with applications to voting. In: Proceedings of the 9th ACM Conference on Computer and Communications Security, CCS 2002, pp. 68–77. ACM, New York (2002)
3. Chaabouni, R., Lipmaa, H., Shelat, A.: Additive combinatorics and discrete logarithm based range protocols. In: Steinfeld, R., Hawkes, P. (eds.) ACISP 2010. LNCS, vol. 6168, pp. 336–351. Springer, Heidelberg (2010)
4. Chaum, D.: Surevote. International patent WO 01/55940 A1 (2001)
5. Chaum, D.: Secret-ballot receipts: True voter-verifiable elections. IEEE Security & Privacy 2(1), 38–47 (2004)
6. Cramer, R., Damgård, I., Schoenmakers, B.: Proofs of partial knowledge and simplified design of witness hiding protocols. In: Desmedt, Y.G. (ed.) CRYPTO 1994. LNCS, vol. 839, pp. 174–187. Springer, Heidelberg (1994)
7. Cramer, R., Gennaro, R., Schoenmakers, B.: A secure and optimally efficient multi-authority election scheme. In: Fumy, W. (ed.) EUROCRYPT 1997. LNCS, vol. 1233, pp. 103–118. Springer, Heidelberg (1997)
8. Fiat, A., Shamir, A.: How to prove yourself: Practical solutions to identification and signature problems. In: Odlyzko, A.M. (ed.) CRYPTO 1986. LNCS, vol. 263, pp. 186–194. Springer, Heidelberg (1987)
9. Gjøsteen, K.: Analysis internet voting protocol. Technical Report (2010), http://www.regjeringen.no
10. Gjøsteen, K.: Analysis of an internet voting protocol. IACR Cryptology ePrint Archive 2010:380 (2010)
11. Gjøsteen, K.: The norwegian internet voting protocol. In: Kiayias, A., Lipmaa, H. (eds.) VoteID 2011. LNCS, vol. 7187, pp. 1–18. Springer, Heidelberg (2012)
12. Groth, J.: A verifiable secret shuffle of homomorphic encryptions. In: Desmedt, Y.G. (ed.) PKC 2003. LNCS, vol. 2567, pp. 145–160. Springer, Heidelberg (2003)
13. Heather, J., Ryan, P.Y.A., Teague, V.: Pretty good democracy for more expressive voting schemes. In: Gritzalis, D., Preneel, B., Theoharidou, M. (eds.) ESORICS 2010. LNCS, vol. 6345, pp. 405–423. Springer, Heidelberg (2010)
14. Heiberg, S., Lipmaa, H., van Laenen, F.: On E-vote integrity in the case of malicious voter computers. In: Gritzalis, D., Preneel, B., Theoharidou, M. (eds.) ESORICS 2010. LNCS, vol. 6345, pp. 373–388. Springer, Heidelberg (2010)
15. Jakobsson, M., Juels, A., Rivest, R.L.: Making mix nets robust for electronic voting by randomized partial checking. In: Proceedings of the 11th USENIX Security Symposium, pp. 339–353. USENIX Association, Berkeley (2002)
16. Lipmaa, H.: Two simple code-verification voting protocols. IACR Cryptology ePrint Archive, 2011:317 (2011)
17. Lipmaa, H., Asokan, N., Niemi, V.: Secure vickrey auctions without threshold trust. In: Blaze, M. (ed.) FC 2002. LNCS, vol. 2357, pp. 87–101. Springer, Heidelberg (2003)

18. Mao, W.: Guaranteed correct sharing of integer factorization with off-line share-holders. In: Imai, H., Zheng, Y. (eds.) PKC 1998. LNCS, vol. 1431, pp. 60–71. Springer, Heidelberg (1998)
19. Naor, M., Shamir, A.: Visual cryptography. In: De Santis, A. (ed.) EUROCRYPT 1994. LNCS, vol. 950, pp. 1–12. Springer, Heidelberg (1995)
20. Andrew Neff, C.: A verifiable secret shuffle and its application to e-voting. In: Proceedings of the 8th ACM Conference on Computer and Communications Security, CCS 2001, pp. 116–125. ACM, New York (2001)
21. Pedersen, T.P.: Non-interactive and information-theoretic secure verifiable secret sharing. In: Feigenbaum, J. (ed.) CRYPTO 1991. LNCS, vol. 576, pp. 129–140. Springer, Heidelberg (1992)
22. Ryan, P.Y.A.: A variant of the chaum voter-verifiable scheme. In: WITS, pp. 81–88 (2005)
23. Ryan, P.Y.A., Teague, V.: Pretty good democracy. In: Christianson, B., Malcolm, J.A., Matyáš, V., Roe, M. (eds.) Security Protocols 2009. LNCS, vol. 7028, pp. 111–130. Springer, Heidelberg (2013)
24. Schnorr, C.-P.: Efficient identification and signatures for smart cards. In: Brassard, G. (ed.) CRYPTO 1989. LNCS, vol. 435, pp. 239–252. Springer, Heidelberg (1990)
25. Verheul, E.R., Van Tilborg, H.C.A.: Constructions and properties of k out of n visual secret sharing schemes. Des. Codes Cryptography 11(2), 179–196 (1997)

Appendix A

We provide an example of the visual description of a scheme with 4 candidates along with the relevant splittings. The visual alphabet for this representation is $\Lambda = \{01, 10\}^2$.

Message	Shape	D_x	$P(x)$
00	Two full circles	●●	(◐◑, ◐◑)(◐◑, ◐◑)
			(◑◐, ◑◐)(◑◐, ◑◐)
01	Full circle followed by half circle	●◐	(◐◑, ◑◐)(◐◑, ◑◐)
		●◑	(◐◑, ◑◐)(◐◑, ◑◐)
10	Half circle followed by full circle	◐●	(◐◑, ◐◑)(◐◑, ◐◑)
		◑●	(◑◐, ◑◐)(◑◐, ◑◐)
11	Two half circles	◐◑, ◐◑	(◐◑, ◐◑)(◐◑, ◐◑)
		◑◐, ◑◐	(◑◐, ◑◐)(◑◐, ◑◐)

Fig. 2. Visual descriptions and splittings of 4 candidates

The depiction of the splittings along with the relevant shares exhibits the solvability property, while for a randomly selected share w in Λ, say $w = ◐◑$, it holds that $Prob[(◐◑, \#) \in P(00)] = Prob[(◐◑, \#) \in P(01)] = Prob[(◐◑, \#) \in P(10)] = Prob[(◐◑, \#) \in P(11)] = 1/4$, satisfying $(1,2)$-resilience. The same holds for the rest of the cases with $w = ◑◐$, $w = ◐◑$, $w = ◑◐$ and the symmetric case $(\#, w)$.

Appendix B

Proof of Proposition 1

Proof. For the message 0 the description set is $D_0 = \{11\}$ and possible splittings are $P(0) \in \{(10, 01), (01, 10)\}$, and analogously for the message 1 $D_1 = \{01, 10\}$ and $P(1) \in \{(01, 01), (10, 10)\}$.

Solvability: For message 0 we have $10 \vee 01 = 11 \in D_0$ and $01 \vee 10 = 11 \in D_0$. Similarly for message 1, we have $01 \vee 01 = 01 \in D_1$ and $10 \vee 10 = 10 \in D_1$.

(1,2)-Resilience: The 2-tuples with one known and one unknown element in Λ we need to consider are $(01, \#), (10, \#), (\#, 01), (\#, 10)$. The function P

outputs one of the possible valid splittings uniformly at random and thus we have $Prob[(01, \#) \in P(0)] = Prob[(01, \#) \in P(1)] = \frac{1}{2}$, $Prob[(10, \#) \in P(0)] = Prob[(10, \#) \in P(1)] = \frac{1}{2}$ and $Prob[(\#, 01) \in P(0)] = Prob[(\#, 01) \in P(1)] = \frac{1}{2}$, $Prob[(\#, 10) \in P(0)] = Prob[(\#, 10) \in P(1)] = \frac{1}{2}$.

Proof of Proposition 2

Proof. **Solvability:** Let $(a_{k-1} \ldots a_0, a'_{k-1} \ldots a'_0)$ be a splitting in $P(x)$. From the construction of P for all $j = 0, \ldots, k-1$ $(a_j, a'_j) \in P^*(b_j)$ where b_j is the j-th bit of x. Then from proposition 1 for all $j = 0, \ldots, k-1$ it holds that $d_j = a_j \vee a'_j$ is in $D^*_{b_j}$, which implies that $(d_{k-1} \ldots d_0) \in D_x$ as requested.

(1,2)-Resilience: Let $(a_{k-1} \ldots a_0, \#_k)$ denote the tuple with exactly one known element $(a_{k-1} \ldots a_0)$ in $\Lambda = \{01, 10\}^k$. Thus for all $j = 0, \ldots, k-1$ $a_j = 01$ or $a_j = 10$, i.e. $a_j \in \Lambda^*$. Since the splitting function $P(x)$ handles each bit b_j of x independently from the others, we have that for all $x \in M$ $Prob[(a_{k-1} \ldots a_0, \#_k) \in P(x)] = Prob[(a_{k-1}, \#) \in P^*(b_{k-1})] \times \cdots \times Prob[(a_0, \#) \in P^*(b_0)]$, where $b_j \in M^*$ is the j-th bit of x. Since from proposition 1 we have that for all $a_j \in \Lambda^*$ $Prob[(a_j, \#) \in P^*(0)] = Prob[(a_j, \#) \in P^*(1)] = \frac{1}{2}$ we conclude that for all $x \in M$ $Prob[(a_{k-1} \ldots, a_0, \#_k) \in P(x)] = (\frac{1}{2})^k$ as requested. The case of $(\#_k, a_{k-1} \ldots a_0)$ is symmetrical.

Appendix C

The proof π': Public Input: $\langle p, q, g \rangle$, $h, pk_t, m, k = \lfloor \log_2(m-1) \rfloor + 1$, $E_t = (E_x, E_\rho) = (g^x pk_t^\rho, g^\rho)$, $\{C_{1_j} = g^{v_{1_j}} h^{r_{1_j}}, C_{2_j} = g^{v_{2_j}} h^{r_{2_j}}, C_{0_j} = g^{v_{0_j}} h^{r_{0_j}}\}_{j=0}^{2k-1}$. Let $d_1 = 1, d_2 = g^4, d_3 = g^5, d_4 = g^6$.

Prover's Input: $x, \rho, \{v_{1_j}, r_{1_j}, v_{2_j}, r_{2_j}, v_{0_j}, r_{0_j}\}_{j=0}^{2k-1}$.

1. The Prover:
   (a) *Bit proof:* For $j = 0, \ldots, 2k-1$:
       i. For $i = 0, 1, 2$:
          – If $v_{i_j} = 0$ it picks $w_{ij}, c_{2ij}, \rho_{2ij} \leftarrow \mathbb{Z}_q$ and sets $y_{1ij} = h^{w_{ij}}$, $y_{2ij} = h^{\rho_{2ij}} (C_{i_j}/g)^{-c_{2ij}}$.
          – Else if $v_{1_j} = 1$ it picks $w_{ij}, c_{1ij}, \rho_{1ij} \leftarrow \mathbb{Z}_q$ and sets $y_{1ij} = h^{\rho_{1ij}} (C_{i_j})^{-c_{1ij}}$, $y_{2ij} = h^{w_{ij}}$
   (b) *OR proof:* For $j = 0, \ldots, 2k-1$:
       i. If $1v_{1_j} + 2v_{2_j} + 3v_{0_j} = 0$ (case $0 \vee 0 = 0$) set $t = 1$. If $1v_{1_j} + 2v_{2_j} + 3v_{0_j} = 4$ (case $1 \vee 0 = 1$) set $t = 2$. If $1v_{1_j} + 2v_{2_j} + 3v_{0_j} = 5$ (case $0 \vee 1 = 1$) set $t = 3$. If $1v_{1_j} + 2v_{2_j} + 3v_{0_j} = 6$ (case $1 \vee 1 = 1$) set $t = 4$.
       ii. It picks $w_{tj}, \{c_{\lambda j}, \rho_{\lambda j}\}_{\lambda=1,2,3,4}^{\lambda \neq t} \leftarrow \mathbb{Z}_q$ and sets $y_{tj} = h^{w_{tj}}$ and $\{y_{\lambda j} = h^{\rho_{\lambda j}} (\frac{(C_{1_j})(C_{2_j})^2 (C_{0_j})^3}{d_\lambda})^{-c_{\lambda j}}\}_{\lambda=1,2,3,4}^{\lambda \neq t}$.
   (c) It picks $w, \rho_1, \rho_2 \leftarrow \mathbb{Z}_q$ and sets $y_1 = g^w pk_t^{\rho_1}$, $y_2 = g^w h^{\rho_2}$.
   (d) It sends (y_1, y_2), $(y_{1j}, y_{2j}, y_{3j}, y_{4j})_{j=0}^{2k-1}$, $((y_{1ij}, y_{2ij})_{j=0}^{2k-1})_{i=0,1,2}$ to the Verifier.
2. The Verifier picks $\mathbf{c} \leftarrow \mathbb{Z}_q$ and sends it to the Prover.

3. The Prover:
   (a) *Bit proof:* For $j = 0, \ldots, 2k - 1$:
       - For $i = 0, 1, 2$:
         i. If $v_{i_j} = 0$ it sets $c_{1ij} = \mathbf{c} - c_{2ij}$, $\rho_{1ij} = w_{ij} + c_{1ij} r_{i_j}$.
         ii. Else if $v_{i_j} = 1$ it sets $c_{2ij} = \mathbf{c} - c_{1ij}$, $\rho_{2ij} = w_{ij} + c_{2ij} r_{i_j}$.
   (b) *OR proof:* For $j = 0, \ldots, 2k - 1$:
       - It sets $c_{tj} = \mathbf{c} - (\sum_{\lambda=1,2,3,4}^{\lambda \neq t} c_{\lambda j})$ and $\rho_{tj} = w_{tj} + c_{tj}(r_{1_j} + 2r_{2_j} + 3r_{0_j})$.
   (c) It sets $s = w + \mathbf{c}x$, $\rho_1' = \rho_1 + \mathbf{c}\rho$, $\rho_2' = \rho_2 - \mathbf{c}(\sum_{j=0}^{k-1}(r_{0_{2j+1}} + r_{0_{2j}})2^j)$.
   (d) It sends to the Verifier (s, ρ_1', ρ_2'), $((c_{\lambda j}, \rho_{\lambda_j})_{\lambda=1,2,3,4})_{j=0}^{2k-1}$ and $((c_{1ij}, c_{2ij}, \rho_{1ij}, \rho_{2ij})_{j=0}^{2k-1})_{i=0,1,2}$.
4. The Verifier accepts if all the following tests succeed, otherwise it rejects:
   (a) For $j = 0, \ldots, 2k - 1$:
       i. *Bit proof:* For $i = 0, 1, 2$: $\mathbf{c} = c_{1ij} + c_{2ij}$, $h^{\rho_{1ij}} = y_{1ij}(C_{i_j})^{c_{1ij}}$ and $h^{\rho_{2ij}} = y_{2ij}(C_{i_j}/g)^{c_{2ij}}$.
       ii. *OR proof:* $\mathbf{c} = \sum_{\lambda=1}^{4} c_{\lambda j}$ and for $\lambda = 1, 2, 3, 4$:
       $$h^{\rho_{\lambda j}} = y_{\lambda j}\left(\frac{(C_{1_j})(C_{2_j})^2(C_{0_j})^3}{d_\lambda}\right)^{c_{\lambda j}}.$$
   (b) $g^s pk_t^{\rho_1'} = y_1(E_x)^{\mathbf{c}}$ and $g^s h^{\rho_2'} = y_2(\prod_{j=0}^{k-1}(\frac{g^2}{C_{0_{2j+1}} \cdot C_{0_{2j}}})^{2^j})^{\mathbf{c}}$.

Appendix D

Security Proof for Proof of Knowledge π

Proof. **Completeness:** Executing the protocol with an honest prover and a honest verifier, we have that in step 4 condition (b) holds since $\prod_{j=0}^{k-1} \mathcal{E}_j^{H_j} =$
$\prod_{j=0}^{k-1}(g^{\mu_j} pk_t^{z_j})^{H_j} = g^{\sum_{j=0}^{k-1} \mu_j H_j} pk_t^{\sum_{j=0}^{k-1} z_j H_j} = g^x pk_t^r = E_x$.
Let i^* be the value such that $\sum_{i=1}^{n} x_i = x + (i^* - 1)u$. Then condition (c) holds since $\sum_{i=1}^{n} c_i = c$ and for all $i = 1, \ldots, n$ with $i \neq i^*$ we have that:

$$a_i(E_x)^{c_i} = ((E_x)^{-c_i} g^{s_i} pk_t^{\rho_{1i}'})(E_x)^{c_i} = g^{s_i} pk t^{\rho_{1i}'}$$

and

$$b_i(\prod_{l=1}^{n} C_l/g^{(i-1)u})^{c_i} = (\prod_{l=1}^{n} C_l/g^{(i-1)u})^{-c_i} g^{s_i} h^{\rho_{2i}'}(\prod_{l=1}^{n} C_l/g^{(i-1)u})^{c_i} = g^{s_i} h^{\rho_{2i}'}.$$

For i^* it holds that:

$$a_{i^*}(E_x)^{c_{i^*}} = (g^w pk_t^{\rho_a})(g^x pk_t^r)^{c_{i^*}} = g^{w+xc_{i^*}} pk_t^{\rho_a + rc_{i^*}} = g^{s_{i^*}} pk_t^{\rho_{1i^*}'}$$

and

$$b_{i^*}(\prod_{l=1}^{n} C_l/g^{(i^*-1)u})^{c_{i^*}} = g^w h^{\rho_b}(\prod_{l=1}^{n} g^{x_l} h^{r_l}/g^{(i^*-1)u})^{c_{i^*}} =$$

$$= g^w h^{\rho_b}(g^{\sum_{l=1}^{n} x_l - (i^*-1)u} h^{\sum_{l=1}^{n} r_l})^{c_{i^*}} = g^{w+(\sum_{l=1}^{n} x_l - (i^*-1)u)c_{i^*}} h^{\rho_b + (\sum_{l=1}^{n} r_l)c_{i^*}} =$$

$$= g^{w+xc_{i*}} h^{\rho_b + (\sum_{l=1}^{n} r_l)c_{i*}} = g^{s_{i*}} h^{\rho'_{2i*}}.$$

Finally condition (a) holds as for all $j = 0, \ldots, k-1$: $c = c_{1j} + c_{2j}$, and if $\mathcal{E}_j = g^0 pk_t^{z_j}$, we have that:

$$y_{1j}(\mathcal{E}_j)^{c_{1j}} = pk_t^{w_j}(pk_t^{z_j})^{c_{1j}} = pk_t^{w_j + c_{1j} z_j} = pkt^{\rho_{1j}}$$

and

$$y_{2j}(\mathcal{E}_j/g)^{c_{2j}} = pk_t^{\rho_{2j}}(\mathcal{E}_j/g)^{-c_{2j}}(\mathcal{E}_j/g)^{c_{2j}} = pk_t^{\rho_{2j}}.$$

Otherwise if $\mathcal{E}_j = g^1 pk_t^{z_j}$ then:

$$y_{1j}(\mathcal{E}_j)^{c_{1j}} = pk_t^{\rho_{1j}}(\mathcal{E}_j)^{-c_{1j}}(\mathcal{E}_j)^{c_{1j}} = pk_t^{\rho_{1j}}$$

and

$$y_{2j}(\mathcal{E}_j/g)^{c_{2j}} = pk_t^{w_j}(g^1 pk_t^{z_j}/g^1)^{c_{2j}} = pk_t^{w_j + z_j c_{2j}} = pk_t^{\rho_{2j}}.$$

Special Soundness: Let

$$\langle A, c, B \rangle =$$

$$= \langle (\{a_i, b_i\}_{i=1}^n, \{\mathcal{E}_j, y_{1j}, y_{2j}\}_{j=0}^{k-1}), c, (\{c_i, s_i, \rho'_{1i}, \rho'_{2i}\}_{i=1}^n, \{c_{1j}, c_{2j}, \rho_{1j}, \rho_{2j}\}_{j=0}^{k-1}) \rangle$$

and

$$\langle A, \tilde{c}, \tilde{B} \rangle =$$

$$= \langle (\{a_i, b_i\}_{i=1}^n, \{\mathcal{E}_j, y_{1j}, y_{2j}\}_{j=0}^{k-1}), \tilde{c}, (\{\tilde{c}_i, \tilde{s}_i, \tilde{\rho'_{1i}}, \tilde{\rho'_{2i}}\}_{i=1}^n, \{\tilde{c_{1j}}, \tilde{c_{2j}}, \tilde{\rho_{1j}}, \tilde{\rho_{2j}}\}_{j=0}^{k-1}) \rangle$$

be two accepting communication transcripts for the same first message A with $c \neq \tilde{c}$.

Since both transcripts are accepting we have that from condition (c) for $i = 1, \ldots, n$:

$$g^{s_i} pk_t^{\rho'_{1i}} = a_i(E_x)^{c_i} \quad \text{and} \quad g^{\tilde{s}_i} pk_t^{\tilde{\rho'_{1i}}} = a_i(E_x)^{\tilde{c}_i}$$

and

$$g^{s_i} h^{\rho'_{2i}} = b_i(\prod_{l=1}^{n} C_l/g^{(i-1)u})^{c_i} \quad \text{and} \quad g^{\tilde{s}_i} h^{\tilde{\rho'_{2i}}} = b_i(\prod_{l=1}^{n} C_l/g^{(i-1)u})^{\tilde{c}_i}.$$

Then since $c \neq \tilde{c}$ for some $i \in \{1, \ldots, n\}$ there are $c_i \neq \tilde{c}_i$ so that we have:

$$\frac{g^{s_i} pk_t^{\rho'_{1i}}}{g^{\tilde{s}_i} pk_t^{\tilde{\rho'_{1i}}}} = (E_x)^{c_i - \tilde{c}_i} \Leftrightarrow g^{\frac{s_i - \tilde{s}_i}{c_i - \tilde{c}_i}} pk_t^{\frac{\rho'_{1i} - \tilde{\rho'_{1j}}}{c_i - \tilde{c}_i}} = E_x$$

so we can extract a valid opening for $E_x = g^{w_i} pk_t^{v_{1i}}$ with $w_i = \frac{s_i - \tilde{s}_i}{c_i - \tilde{c}_i}$ and $v_{1i} = \frac{\rho'_{1i} - \tilde{\rho'_{1j}}}{c_i - \tilde{c}_i}$.

In addition since:

$$\frac{g^{s_i} pk_t^{\rho'_{2i}}}{g^{\tilde{s}_i} pk_t^{\tilde{\rho'_{2i}}}} = (\prod_{l=1}^{n} C_l/g^{(i-1)u})^{c_i - \tilde{c}_i} \Leftrightarrow g^{\frac{s_i - \tilde{s}_i}{c_i - \tilde{c}_i}} pk_t^{\frac{\rho'_{2i} - \tilde{\rho'_{2i}}}{c_i - \tilde{c}_i}} = \prod_{l=1}^{n} C_l/g^{(i-1)u}$$

we also extract a valid opening for $\prod_{l=1}^{n} C_l/g^{(i-1)u} = g^{w_i} pk_t^{v_{2i}}$ with w_i and $v_{2i} = \frac{\rho'_{2i} - \tilde{\rho}'_{2i}}{c_i - \tilde{c}_i}$.

From condition (a) we have that since $c \neq \tilde{c}$ for all $j = 0, \ldots, k-1$, either $c_{1j} \neq \tilde{c_{1j}}$ or $c_{2j} \neq \tilde{c_{2j}}$. We also have that:

$$pk_t^{\rho_{1j}} = y_{1j}(\mathcal{E}_j)^{c_{1j}} \quad \text{and} \quad pk_t^{\tilde{\rho_{1j}}} = y_{1j}(\mathcal{E}_j)^{\tilde{c_{1j}}}$$

and

$$pk_t^{\rho_{2j}} = y_{2j}(\mathcal{E}_j/g)^{c_{2j}} \quad \text{and} \quad pk_t^{\tilde{\rho_{2j}}} = y_{2j}(\mathcal{E}_j/g)^{\tilde{c_{2j}}}.$$

Then in the case that $c_{1j} \neq \tilde{c_{1j}}$ we have that:

$$\frac{pk_t^{\rho_{1j}}}{pk_t^{\tilde{\rho_{1j}}}} = \frac{(\mathcal{E}_j)^{c_{1j}}}{(\mathcal{E}_j)^{\tilde{c_{1j}}}} \Leftrightarrow pk_t^{\frac{\rho_{1j} - \tilde{\rho_{1j}}}{c_{1j} - \tilde{c_{1j}}}} = \mathcal{E}_j$$

so we can extract a valid opening for $\mathcal{E}_j = pk_t^{z_{1j}}$ with $z_{1j} = \frac{\rho_{1j} - \tilde{\rho_{1j}}}{c_{1j} - \tilde{c_{1j}}}$. Similarly in the case that $c_{2j} \neq \tilde{c_{2j}}$ from $\frac{pk_t^{\rho_{2j}}}{pk_t^{\tilde{\rho_{2j}}}} = \frac{(\mathcal{E}_j/g)^{c_{2j}}}{(\mathcal{E}_j/g)^{\tilde{c_{2j}}}}$ we extract a valid opening for $\mathcal{E}_j/g = pk_t^{z_{2j}}$ with $z_{2j} = \frac{\rho_{2j} - \tilde{\rho_{2j}}}{c_{2j} - \tilde{c_{2j}}}$.

HV Zero Knowledge: We can create a simulator for the prover given the public input $G, q, g, pk_t, h, E_x, \{C_i\}_{i=1}^{n}$ as follows: We randomly pick $c \leftarrow \mathbb{Z}_q$ and for $i = 1, \ldots n$ we pick $c_{1i}, s_i, \rho'_{1i}, \rho'_{2i} \leftarrow \mathbb{Z}_q$ and set $c_{2i} = c - c_{1i} \bmod q$. For $j = 0, \ldots, k-1$ we pick $c_{1j}, \rho_{1j}, \rho_{2j} \leftarrow \mathbb{Z}_q$ and set $c_{2j} = c - c_{1j} \bmod q$. We fix the second and the third message of the communication protocol to be $\langle c, (\{c_i, s_i, \rho'_{1i}, \rho'_{2i}\}_{i=1}^{n}, \{c_{1j}, c_{2j}, \rho_{1j}, \rho_{2j}\}_{j=0}^{k-1})\rangle$. Then we set the first message A to be $A = (\{(E_x)^{-c_i} g^{s_i} pk_t^{\rho'_{1i}}, (\prod_{l=1}^{n} C_l/g^{(i-1)u})^{-c_i} g^{s_i} h^{\rho'_{2i}}\}_{i=1}^{n}$, $\{\mathcal{E}_j, pk_t^{\rho_{1j}}(\mathcal{E}_j)^{-c_{1j}}, pk_t^{\rho_{2j}}(\mathcal{E}_j/g)^{-c_{2j}}\}_{j=0}^{k-1})$.

Security Proof for Proof of Knowledge π'

Proof. **Completeness:** Executing the protocol with an honest prover and a honest verifier, we have that in step 4 condition (b) holds since

$$y_1(E_x)^{\mathbf{c}} = g^w pk_t^{\rho_1}(g^x pk_t^\rho)^{\mathbf{c}} = g^{w+cx} pk_t^{\rho_1 + c\rho} = g^s pk_t^{\rho'_1}$$

and

$$y_2(\prod_{j=0}^{k-1}(\frac{g^2}{C_{0_{2j+1}} \cdot C_{0_{2j}}})^{2^j})^{\mathbf{c}} =$$

$$= g^w h^{\rho_2}(g^{(\sum_{j=0}^{k-1}(2-v_{0_{2j+1}} - v_{0_{2j}})2^j)} h^{(-\sum_{j=0}^{k-1}(r_{0_{2j+1}} + r_{0_{2j}})2^j)})^{\mathbf{c}} = g^{w+cx} h^{\rho'_2} = g^s h^{\rho'_2}.$$

Condition (ai) holds as for all $j = 0, \ldots, 2k-1$ and for all $i = 0, 1, 2$: $\mathbf{c} = c_{1ij} + c_{2ij}$, and if $C_{i_j} = g^0 h^{r_{ij}}$, we have that:

$$y_{1ij}(C_{i_j})^{c_{1ij}} = h^{w_{ij}}(h^{r_{ij}})^{c_{1ij}} = h^{\rho_{1ij}}$$

and

$$y_{2ij}(C_{i_j}/g)^{c_{2ij}} = (h^{\rho_{2ij}}(C_{i_j}/g)^{-c_{2ij}})(C_{i_j}/g)^{c_{2ij}} = h^{\rho_{2ij}}.$$

Otherwise if $C_{i_j} = g^1 h^{r_{ij}}$ we have that:

$$y_{1ij}(C_{i_j})^{c_{1ij}} = (h^{\rho_{1ij}}(C_{i_j})^{-c_{1ij}})(C_{i_j})^{c_{1ij}} = h^{\rho_{1ij}}$$

and

$$y_{2ij}(C_{i_j}/g)^{c_{2ij}} = h^{w_{ij}}(gh^{r_{ij}}/g)^{c_{2ij}} = h^{w_{ij}+c_{2ij}r_{ij}} = h^{\rho_{2ij}}.$$

Regarding condition (aii), for $j = 0, \ldots, 2k-1$, we present the case for general $t \in \{1, 2, 3, 4\}$ with $d_t = g^\alpha$, i.e. $(v_{1_j}) + 2(v_{2_j}) + 3(v_{0_j}) = \alpha$, with $\alpha \in \{0, 4, 5, 6\}$. The condition holds as $\mathbf{c} = c_{1j} + c_{2j} + c_{3j} + c_{4j}$ and for t : $y_{tj}\left(\dfrac{(C_{1_j})(C_{2_j})^2(C_{3_j})^3}{d_t}\right)^{c_{tj}} =$

$$= h^{w_{tj}}\left(\frac{g^{(1v_{1_j}+2v_{2_j}+3v_{0_j})}h^{(1r_{1_j}+2r_{2_j}+3r_{0_j})}}{g^\alpha}\right)^{c_{tj}} =$$

$$= h^{w_{tj}}\left(\frac{g^\alpha h^{(1r_{1_j}+2r_{2_j}+3r_{0_j})}}{g^\alpha}\right)^{c_{tj}} = h^{w_{tj}+c_{1j}(1r_{1_j}+2r_{2_j}+3r_{0_j})} = h^{\rho_{1j}}.$$

For $\lambda \neq t$ the proof is simulated and thus $y_{\lambda j}\left(\dfrac{(C_{1_j})(C_{2_j})^2(C_{3_j})^3}{d_\lambda}\right)^{c_{\lambda j}} =$

$$= \left(h^{\rho_{\lambda j}}\left(\frac{(C_{1_j})(C_{2_j})^2(C_{3_j})^3}{d_\lambda}\right)^{-c_{\lambda j}}\right)\left(\frac{(C_{1_j})(C_{2_j})^2(C_{3_j})^3}{d_\lambda}\right)^{c_{\lambda j}} = h^{\rho_{\lambda j}}.$$

Special Soundness:

Let $\langle A, c, B\rangle$, $\langle A, \tilde{c}, \tilde{B}\rangle$ be two accepting communication transcripts for the same first message A with $c \neq \tilde{c}$ and

$$A = ((y_1, y_2), (y_{1j}, y_{2j}, y_{3j}, y_{4j})_{j=0}^{2k-1}, ((y_{1ij}, y_{2ij})_{j=0}^{2k-1})_{i=0,1,2})$$

and

$$B = ((s, \rho_1', \rho_2'), ((c_{\lambda j}, \rho_{\lambda j})_{\lambda=1,2,3,4})_{j=0}^{2k-1}, ((c_{1ij}, c_{2ij}, \rho_{1ij}, \rho_{2ij})_{j=0}^{2k-1})_{i=0,1,2})$$

and

$$\tilde{B} = ((\tilde{s}, \tilde{\rho_1'}, \tilde{\rho_2'}), ((\tilde{c_{\lambda j}}, \tilde{\rho_{\lambda j}})_{\lambda=1,2,3,4})_{j=0}^{2k-1}, ((\tilde{c_{1ij}}, \tilde{c_{2ij}}, \tilde{\rho_{1ij}}, \tilde{\rho_{2ij}})_{j=0}^{2k-1})_{i=0,1,2}).$$

Then for condition (ai) of step 4, since $c \neq \tilde{c}$, for $j = 0, \ldots, 2k-1$ and $i = 0, 1, 2$ either $c_{1ij} \neq \tilde{c_{1ij}}$ or $c_{2ij} \neq \tilde{c_{2ij}}$. In the first case we have $h^{\rho_{1ij}} = y_{1ij}(C_{i_j})^{c_{1ij}}$ and $h^{\tilde{\rho_{1ij}}} = y_{1ij}(C_{i_j})^{\tilde{c_{1ij}}}$ whose division gives us

$$h^{\rho_{1ij}-\tilde{\rho_{1ij}}} = (C_{i_j})^{c_{1ij}-\tilde{c_{1ij}}} \Leftrightarrow h^{\frac{\rho_{1ij}-\tilde{\rho_{1ij}}}{c_{1ij}-\tilde{c_{1ij}}}} = C_{i_j}$$

i.e. we extract $\zeta = \frac{\rho_{1ij}-\tilde{\rho_{1ij}}}{c_{1ij}-\tilde{c_{1ij}}}$ as a valid opening for C_{i_j}. In the second case we have that $h^{\rho_{2ij}} = y_{2ij}(C_{i_j}/g)^{c_{2ij}}$ and $h^{\tilde{\rho_{2ij}}} = y_{2ij}(C_{i_j}/g)^{\tilde{c_{2ij}}}$ and similarly $h^{\frac{\rho_{2ij}-\tilde{\rho_{2ij}}}{c_{2ij}-\tilde{c_{2ij}}}} = (C_{i_j}/g)$, i.e.we extract $\zeta' = \frac{\rho_{2ij}-\tilde{\rho_{2ij}}}{c_{2ij}-\tilde{c_{2ij}}}$ as a valid opening for (C_{i_j}/g).

From condition (aii) for $j = 0, \ldots, 2k - 1$ and $\lambda = 1, 2, 3, 4$ we have that $h^{\rho_{\lambda j}} = y_{\lambda j}(\frac{(C_{1_j})(C_{2_j})^2(C_{0_j})^3}{d_\lambda})^{c_{\lambda j}}$ and $h^{\rho_{\tilde{\lambda} j}} = y_{\lambda j}(\frac{(C_{1_j})(C_{2_j})^2(C_{0_j})^3}{d_\lambda})^{c_{\tilde{\lambda} j}}$ whose division yields $h^{\rho_{\lambda j} - \rho_{\tilde{\lambda} j}} = (\frac{(C_{1_j})(C_{2_j})^2(C_{0_j})^3}{d_\lambda})^{c_{\lambda j} - c_{\tilde{\lambda} j}}$. Since $c \neq \tilde{c}$ for each $j = 0, \ldots, 2k - 1$ there is a $\lambda \in \{1, 2, 3, 4\}$ such that $c_{\lambda j} \neq c_{\tilde{\lambda} j}$. Thus $h^{\frac{\rho_{\lambda j} - \rho_{\tilde{\lambda} j}}{c_{\lambda j} - c_{\tilde{\lambda} j}}} = (\frac{(C_{1_j})(C_{2_j})^2(C_{0_j})^3}{d_\lambda})$, concluding that we can extract $\eta = \frac{\rho_{\lambda j} - \rho_{\tilde{\lambda} j}}{c_{\lambda j} - c_{\tilde{\lambda} j}}$ as a valid opening for $C'_j = \frac{(C_{1_j})(C_{2_j})^2(C_{0_j})^3}{d_\lambda}$.

Finally from condition (b) we have that $g^s pk_t^{\rho'_1} = y_1(E_x)^c$ and $g^{\tilde{s}} pk_t^{\rho'_1} = y_1(E_x)^{\tilde{c}}$ from which we have that $g^{\frac{s - \tilde{s}}{c - \tilde{c}}} h^{\frac{\rho'_1 - \rho'_1}{c - \tilde{c}}} = E_x$, i.e. we extract $\alpha = \frac{s - \tilde{s}}{c - \tilde{c}}$, $\beta = \frac{\rho'_1 - \rho'_1}{c - \tilde{c}}$ as a valid opening for $E_x = g^\alpha h^\beta$.

Similarly from

$$g^s h^{\rho'_2} = y_2 \left(\prod_{j=0}^{k-1}\left(\frac{g^2}{C_{0_{2j+1}} \cdot C_{0_{2j}}}\right)^{(2^j)}\right)^c \text{ and } g^{\tilde{s}} h^{\rho'_2} = y_2 \left(\prod_{j=0}^{k-1}\left(\frac{g^2}{C_{0_{2j+1}} \cdot C_{0_{2j}}}\right)^{(2^j)}\right)^{\tilde{c}}$$

we extract $\alpha = \frac{s - \tilde{s}}{c - \tilde{c}}$ and $\beta' = \frac{\rho'_2 - \rho'_2}{c - \tilde{c}}$ as a valid opening for

$$C'' = \left(\prod_{j=0}^{k-1}\left(\frac{g^2}{C_{0_{2j+1}} \cdot C_{0_{2j}}}\right)^{2^j}\right).$$

HV Zero Knowledge: There is a simulator that can simulate the communication transcript. On input $G, q, g, pk_t, h, E_x, \{(C_{i_j})_{j=0,\ldots,2k-1}\}_{i=0,1,2}$ it picks randomly a value $c \in \mathbb{Z}_q$. It also picks uniformly at random $s, \rho'_1, \rho'_2 \in \mathbb{Z}_q$. For $\lambda = 1, 2, 3, 4$ and for $j = 0, \ldots, 2k - 1$ it picks $c_{\lambda j}, \rho_{\lambda j} \in \mathbb{Z}_q$ such that $\sum_{\lambda=1}^{4} c_{\lambda j} = c$. For $i = 0, 1, 2$ and $j = 0, \ldots, 2k-1$ it picks $c_{1ij}, c_{2ij}, \rho_{1ij}, \rho_{2ij} \in \mathbb{Z}_q$ such that $c_{1ij} + c_{2ij} = c$. We define the second and the third message of the communication transcript to be respectively c and

$$B = ((s, \rho'_1, \rho'_2), ((c_{\lambda j}, \rho_{\lambda j})_{\lambda=1,2,3,4})_{j=0}^{2k-1}, ((c_{1ij}, c_{2ij}, \rho_{1ij}, \rho_{2ij})_{j=0}^{2k-1})_{i=0,1,2}).$$

We now set the first message of the transcript to be A:

- $(y_1, y_2) = (g^s pk_t^{\rho'_1}(E_x)^{-c}, g^s h^{\rho'_2}(\prod_{j=0}^{k-1}(\frac{g^2}{C_{0_{2j+1}} \cdot C_{0_{2j}}})^{(2^j)})^{-c})$
- for $j = 0, \ldots, 2k - 1$, for $\lambda = 1, 2, 3, 4$: $y_{\lambda j} = h^{\rho_{\lambda j}}(\frac{(C_{1_j})(C_{2_j})^2(C_{0_j})^3}{d_\lambda})^{-c_{\lambda j}}$
- For $i = 0, 1, 2$, for $j = 0, \ldots, 2k - 1$:

$$(y_{1ij}, y_{2ij}) = (h^{\rho_{1ij}}(C_{i_j})^{-c_{1ij}}, h^{\rho_{2ij}}(C_{i_j}/g)^{-c_{2ij}}).$$

The final simulated transcript is $\langle A, c, B \rangle$.

On the Specification and Verification
of Voting Schemes

Bernhard Beckert[1], Rajeev Goré[2], and Carsten Schürmann[3]

[1] Karlsruhe Institute of Technology
beckert@kit.edu
[2] The Australian National University
Rajeev.Gore@anu.edu.au
[3] IT University of Copenhagen
carsten@itu.dk

Abstract. The ability to count ballots by computers allows us to design new voting schemes that are arguably fairer than existing schemes designed for hand-counting. We argue that formal methods can and should be used to ensure that such schemes behave as intended and are conform to the desired democratic properties. Specifically, we define two semantic criteria for single transferable vote (STV) schemes, formulated in first-order logic, and show how bounded model-checking can be used to test whether these criteria are met. As a case study, we then analyse an existing voting scheme for electing the board of trustees for a major international conference and discuss its deficiencies.

1   Introduction

The goal of any social choice function is to compute an "optimal" choice from a given set of preferences. Voting schemes in elections are a prime example of such choice functions as they compute a seat distribution from a set of preferences recorded on ballots. By voting scheme we mean a concrete description of a method for counting the ballots and computing which candidates are elected – as opposed to an actual computer implementation of such a scheme or a scheme describing the process of casting votes via computer. The difficulty in designing preferential voting schemes is that the optimisation criteria are not only multi-dimensional, but multi-dimensional on more than one level. On one level, we want to satisfy each voter, so each voter is a dimension. On a higher level, there are desirable global criteria such as "majority rule" and "minority protection" that are at least partly inconsistent with each other. It is well-known that "optimising" such theoretical voting schemes along one dimension may cause them to become "sub-optimal" along another.

This observation is not new and voting specialists have proposed a series of mathematical criteria [3] that can be used to compare various voting schemes with one another. A classic example is the notion of a Condorcet winner, defined as the candidate who wins against *each* other candidate in a one-on-one contest. Such a winner exists provided that there is no cycle in the one-to-one contest

J. Heather, S. Schneider, and V. Teague (Eds.): VoteID 2013, LNCS 7985, pp. 25–40, 2013.
© Springer-Verlag Berlin Heidelberg 2013

relation. A voting scheme is said to satisfy the Condorcet criterion if the Condorcet winner is guaranteed to be elected when such a winner exists. Another is the *monotonicity criterion* which requires that a candidate who wins a contest will also win if the ballots were changed uniformly to rank that candidate higher.

In practice, theoretical voting schemes are often simplified in many ways when used in real-world elections, typically to reduce their complexity to allow counting by hand. Such practical schemes may not satisfy general properties such as the Condorcet criterion simply because it is intractable to compute the Condorcet winner by hand, but they may satisfy some weaker version of "optimality" that is specific to that particular scheme. It may even happen that one among the optimal winners is chosen at random [2] (as allowed by the Australian Capital Territory's Hare-Clark Method) or that someone other than the optimal winner is elected.

Voting schemes also evolve over time – for national elections in the large, and local elections, union elections, share holder elections, and board of trustee elections in the small. Incremental changes to the electoral system, the tallying process and the related algorithms challenge the common understanding about what the voting scheme actually does. For example, since 1969 some local elections in New Zealand adopted Meeks' method [7], which is a voting scheme for preferential voting that uses fractional weightings in its computations and is too complex to count by hand. This also required an adjustment of understanding about who will now be elected. In general, it is often not clear whether changes to the electoral system improve or worsen the overall quality of a voting scheme with regard to the various dimensions of optimisation. Changes to the electoral system in Germany, for example, have created paradoxical situations where more votes for a party translate into fewer seats and fewer votes into more seats, and have prompted Germany's Supreme Court to intervene repeatedly (see, e.g., [6]).

Many jurisdictions are now using computers to count ballots according to traditional voting schemes. Using computers to count ballots opens up the possibility to use voting schemes which really are optimised along multiple dimensions, while retaining global *desiderata* such as the Condorcet criterion. The inherent complexity of counting ballots according to such schemes means that it may no longer be possible to "verify" the result by hand-counting, even when the number of ballots is small. It is therefore important to imbue these schemes with the trust accorded to existing schemes. Note that our focus is on trust in the voting scheme, not trust in the computer-based process for casting votes.

One way to engender trust in such complex yet "fairer" voting schemes is to specify the *desiderata* when the scheme is being designed, and then formally check that the scheme meets these criteria before proposing changes to the legislation to enact the scheme. Such formal analyses could contribute significant unbiased information into the political discussions that typically involve such legislative changes and also assure voters that the changes will not create paradoxical situations as described above.

Formal analysis, however, is only practicable when we possess formal specifications of the voting scheme. We argue that it is important to give declarative specifications of the properties of a voting scheme for two reasons: (1) For understanding their properties and how they change during the evolution process, so that improving a scheme in one aspect does not by accident introduce flaws w.r.t. other aspects. (2) For checking the correctness of the scheme from both an algorithmic and implementation perspective. We also argue that general criteria are not sufficient and criteria are needed that are tailor-made for specific (classes of) voting schemes.

The properties in question are difficult to state, to formalise, to understand. to analyse, and to describe declaratively (as opposed to algorithmically) because: the final voting scheme may have to compromise between the conflicting demands of multiple individual desirable properties; the voting scheme may evolve and we may have to revisit these desiderata; even when the properties can be made mathematically precise, the resulting mathematical statement cannot serve as a specification if the electoral law defines a voting scheme that does not (always) compute the optimal solution.

Contributions. Here, we show how seemingly innocuous revisions to a voting scheme can have serious implications on the desired properties of the system. As a running example, we use the preferential voting schemes single transferable vote (STV) that is used in large national elections world-wide, but also for smaller professional elections.

In Section 2, we define two tailor-made criteria to establish the desired properties of the voting scheme. Both criteria are formulated using first-order logic and are amenable for bounded model checking, which is the tool of choice for our formal analysis (Section 3). Subsequently, we discuss (Section 4) a particularly interesting variant of the Single Transferrable Vote Algorithm (CADE-STV) for the board of trustees of the International Conference on Automated Deduction (CADE). We explain its oddities and differences to standard STV, and give a historical account of the conception and the stepwise refinement of the algorithm. This paper extends our system description of a bounded model checking system for analysing voting schemes and its application to CADE-STV [1].

Related Work. Voting schemes have been investigated by social choice theorists for many decades. These tend to be mathematical analyses which prove various (relative) properties of different voting schemes: see [11]. Such work tends to concentrate on what we have referred to as theoretical schemes and is often couched in terms of a formal theorem and its proof in natural language.

There is also a significant body of research on various properties of vote-casting schemes, particular security properties [13].

There does not appear to be much existing work on the formal analysis of voting schemes using methods and tools from the computer aided verification and automated deduction communities in our sense, although there is some existing work on the formal analysis of actual implementations of such schemes [9,8,5].

2   Semantic Criteria for Analysing Voting Schemes

We focus on preferential voting schemes. Each vote consists of a partial linear order on candidates. Suppose that C candidates, numbered $1, 2, \ldots, C$, are competing for $S > 0$ vacant seats in an election. Furthermore, assume that $V \geq 1$

votes have been cast and are collected in a ballot box. It is commonly agreed that for $k \leq C$, a vote $[c_1, c_2, \ldots, c_k]$ ranks a subset of the candidates in decreasing order of preference so that each $c_i \in \{1, 2, \ldots, C\}$ and $c_i \neq c_j$ for $i \neq j$.

2.1   Basic Criteria

Many criteria that voting schemes preferably should satisfy have been proposed (for an overview see [3]). Below, we describe a few important examples. Note that, even though these basic criteria seem obvious and indispensable for voting schemes on first sight, they are in fact not always satisfied by each reasonable voting scheme. Most real-word voting schemes violate at least some basic criteria for some possible ballot box input.

An "obvious" and widely used criterion is the *majority criterion*, which states that, if a candidate c is ranked first by a majority of voters, then c must be elected. This is indeed satisfied by all reasonable preferential voting schemes that use votes ranking candidates. However, the majority criterion can be violated by preferential voting schemes where voters can attach a numerical preference to candidates instead of just ranking them (Borda count scheme).

Another "obvious" criterion is the *monotonicity criterion* [14]. Assume that there are two ballot boxes B and B' where B' results from B by raising the preference for a candidate c in one or more of the votes and leaving the votes otherwise unchanged (i.e., a vote of the form $[c_1, \ldots, c_{i-1}, c, c_{i+1}, \ldots, c_k]$ is replaced by $[c_1, \ldots, c_{j-1}, c, c_j, \ldots, c_{i-1}, c_{i+1}, \ldots, c_k]$ $(j < i)$. The monotonicity criterion states that, if c is elected using the ballot box B, then c must also be elected using B'. Surprisingly, some real-world voting schemes – including STV – do not satisfy monotonicity [14].

A further simple criterion is the *fill-all-seats criterion*, which states that all available seats are filled provided that there are sufficient candidates, i.e., $C \geq S$. In practice, this criterion is often used in a restricted form, e.g., candidates can be elected only if they reach a certain minimal quota.

2.2   Criteria Characterising the Election Result

The majority criterion fully describes the election result for the simple case of a single seat and a candidate with a majority of first preferences. But we desire criteria characterising the "right" result in increasingly complex situations.

An example is the *Condorcet criterion*. A candidate c is a Condorcet winner if c wins a one-to-one comparison against all other candidates, i.e., for all $c' \neq c$ there are more voters preferring c over c' than there are voters preferring c' over c. The *Condorcet criterion* states that a Condorcet winner c must be elected if there is one. And, as long as there are open seats and there are Condorcet winners among the remaining candidates, these must also be elected.

Note that Condorcet winners do not exist for all ballot boxes, so the Condorcet criterion does not specify the election result for all situations (but only for those where a clear winner exists). Moreover, it is well known that STV (which we use as a case study) does not satisfy the Condorcet criterion.

2.3   Tailor-Made Criteria for Preferential Voting Schemes

As stated previously, many more voting scheme criteria have been developed and are described in the literature. So, as a first approach to specifying and analysing a particular voting scheme, one could select some of these to characterise the scheme's properties. For a detailed analysis, however, that is not sufficient. General criteria cannot distinguish between variants of the same voting scheme (or the number of available general criteria would have to be very high). Moreover, there is a trade-off between two goals when defining voting scheme criteria:

Coverage. For as many different ballot boxes as possible, the criterion should apply and restrict the number of possible election results.

Restrictiveness. The number of possible election results for each ballot box should be restricted as much as possible.

For example, the majority and Condorcet criteria are very restrictive (they specify exactly one winner), but they do not have good coverage (they only apply if there is a clear winner). The fill-all-seats criterion, on the the other hand, has full coverage (it restricts the possible outcome for all ballot boxes), but it is not very restrictive.

Ideally, one would like to have an axiomatically defined criterion that allows exactly one result for every possible ballot box, i.e., has full coverage and is fully restrictive. But for many voting schemes used in practice, such criteria do not exist. In these cases, we rely on tailor-made criteria that strike a compromise between coverage and restrictiveness. For example, for our analysis of preferential voting, we have devised two tailor-made criteria that capture the essence of *preferential* voting (Criterion 2) with *proportional representation* (Criterion 1) and are applicable to our case study STV:

(1) There must be enough votes for each elected candidate.
(2) If the preferences of *all* voters w.r.t. two particular candidates are consistent, then that collective preference is not contradicted by the election result.

The first criterion only considers number of votes and ignores preferences, while the second criterion only considers preferences and ignores number of votes. This separation of the two dimensions (number of votes and preferences) is the key to finding strong criteria that can be described declaratively.

The two criteria compromise in different ways on the two goals of generality and restrictiveness: Criterion 1 has full coverage. It applies to all ballot-boxes without being too restrictive (as the order of preferences is not considered). Criterion 2 has lower coverage. It only applies if the voters' preferences are not contradictory. In that case, however, it is rather restrictive as only a small number of election results are permissible.

Criterion 2 is a weaker version of the the Condorcet criterion that, in contrast to Condorcet, is satisfied by STV. It assumes a preference to be collective if *all* voters agree (or at least not disagree), while the Condorcet criterion assumes a preference to be collective if it is supported by a *majority* of voters.

Criterion 1: Enough Votes for each Elected Candidate. This criterion captures that the votes can be partitioned with an assignment of exactly one class in the partition to each elected candidate such that, if Q is the quota, then:

1. There are exactly Q votes in each class that supports an elected candidate.
2. For each vote in a class that supports a candidate, that candidate occurs somewhere among the preferences of the supporting vote.

In the second condition above, the actual order of preferences is not taken into consideration. Thus, this is a weak property that can be satisfied by a wide variety of STV variants. But it is strict in that each vote counts only once.

Example 1. Assume there are four candidates A, B, C, D for two vacant seats, the votes to be counted are $[A, B, D], [A, B, D], [A, B, D], [D, C], [C, D]$, and the quota is $Q = 2$. The election result $[A, D]$ satisfies Criterion 1 using the partition $\{[A, B, D], [A, B, D]\}, \ \{[C, D], [D, C]\}, \ \{[A, B, D]\}$. The election result $[B, D]$ violates the majority criterion (as A despite its majority of first preferences is not elected). Nevertheless it satisfies Criterion 1 choosing the same partition as above (because the ordering of A and B is not considered), which shows that the criterion compromises on restrictiveness. But, the result $[A, B]$, which contradicts proportional representation, is not supported by this or any other partition (which shows that this criterion is indeed related to the requirement of proportional representation).

Formalisation. To formalise the criteria, we use first-order logic over the theories of natural numbers and arrays with the following notation in addition to the notation defined previously:

b: is the ballot box, where $b[i, j] \in \{1, \ldots, C\}$ is the number of the candidate that is ranked by vote i in the jth place. Thus i's preference is $[b[i, 1], b[i, 2], \ldots]$. If vote i ranks only $k \leq C$ candidates, then $b[i, j] = 0$ for $k < j \leq C$.

r: is the result, where $r[i]$ is the ith candidate that is elected ($1 \leq i \leq S$). If less than S candidates are elected, then $r[i] = 0$ for the empty seats.

Our criterion is formalised by a formula ϕ in which all the above (free) variables occur. We also use an existentially quantified variable a of type array that represents the partition and the assignment of classes in the partition to elected candidates as follows:

$a[i] = k$ if the ith vote supports the kth elected candidate $r[k]$. If the ith vote does not support any elected candidate, then $a[i] = 0$.

Then, the formula $\phi = \exists a(\phi_1 \wedge \ldots \wedge \phi_4)$ is the existentially quantified conjunction:

$$\forall i \big(1 \leq i \leq \mathsf{V} \to 0 \leq a[i] \leq \mathsf{S}\big) \tag{ϕ_1}$$

$$\forall i \big(1 \leq i \leq \mathsf{V} \to (a[i] \neq 0 \to r[a[i]] \neq 0)\big) \tag{ϕ_2}$$

$$\forall i \big((1 \leq i \leq \mathsf{V} \wedge a[i] \neq 0) \to \exists j(1 \leq j \leq \mathsf{C} \wedge b[i,j] = r[a[i]])\big) \tag{ϕ_3}$$

$$\begin{aligned}
\forall k \big((1 \leq k \leq \mathsf{S} \wedge r[k] \neq 0) \to \\
\exists count(count[0] = 0 \wedge \\
\forall i(1 \leq i \leq \mathsf{V} \to (a[i] = k \to count[i] = count[i-1] + 1) \wedge \\
(a[i] \neq k \to count[i] = count[i-1])) \wedge \\
count[\mathsf{V}] = \mathsf{Q}))
\end{aligned} \tag{ϕ_4}$$

Formulae ϕ_1 and ϕ_2 express well-formedness of the partition. Formula ϕ_3 expresses that only votes can support a candidate in which that candidate is somewhere ranked. Formula ϕ_4 expresses that each class supporting a particular elected candidate has exactly Q elements. To formalise this, we use an array $count$ such that $count[i]$ is the number of supporters among votes $1, \ldots, i$ that support the kth elected candidate.

Note, that this criterion assumes all seats to be filled and has to be relaxed if a voting scheme does not satisfy the fill-all-seats criterion or there are not enough candidates that can reach the quota.

2.4 Criterion 2: Election Result Consistent with Preferences

The idea of our second criterion is that, if there are two candidates a, b such that in the union of all votes' preferences there is an argument for ranking a over b but no argument for ranking b over a (i.e., a and b are not part of a cycle of preferences), then b must not be ranked higher than a in the election result.

Formalisation. That there is an argument for ranking a over b means that there are candidates $a = c[0], \ldots, c[k] = b$ and there are votes $v[1], \ldots, v[k]$ such that $v[i]$ prefers $c[i-1]$ over $c[i]$ $(1 \leq i \leq k)$.

That vote $v[i]$ prefers candidate c_1 over candidate c_2 can be formalised by:

$$\phi(v, i, c_1, c_2) = \exists j(1 \leq j \leq \mathsf{C} \wedge b[v[i], j] = c_1 \wedge \\ \forall j'(1 \leq j' < j \to b[v[i], j'] \neq c_2))$$

The first line of the above formula says that voter $v[i]$ gives the preference j to candidate c_1. The second line says that v does not give a higher preference $j' < j$ to c_2, i.e., gives c_2 lower preference or no preference at all.

Now, we can formalise that there is an argument for ranking a over b by:

$$\Phi(a, b) = \exists v \exists c \exists k (a = c[0] \wedge b = c[k] \wedge \\ \forall i(1 \leq i \leq k \to (1 \leq v[i] \leq \mathsf{V} \wedge 1 \leq c[i] \leq \mathsf{C} \wedge \\ \phi(v, i, c[i-1], c[i])))))$$

In a similar way as with ϕ, we can formalise the fact that the voting result gives a higher ranking to candidate c_1 than to candidate c_2 as follows:

$$\psi(c_1, c_2) = \exists j (1 \leq j \leq \mathsf{C} \wedge r[j] = c_1 \wedge \\ \forall j'(1 \leq j' < j \rightarrow r[j'] \neq c_2))$$

Then, using the formulas Φ and ψ the criterion can be formalised as follows:

$$\forall a \forall b \big((1 \leq a \leq \mathsf{C} \wedge 1 \leq b \leq \mathsf{C} \wedge a \neq b \wedge \Phi(a, b) \wedge \neg \Phi(b, a)) \rightarrow \neg \psi(b, a)\big)$$

2.5 Determinism

Another important criterion for voting schemes is *determinism*. Voting schemes can contain various non-determinisms that occur when candidates have the same number of votes or preferences. While that may not be a problem on an abstract level, for concrete elections it is important to clearly specify how these are to be resolved. Otherwise, choices by the election officials (or their computers) when counting the ballots could influence the election result, which is clearly undesirable.

3 Bounded Model Checking for Analysing Voting Schemes

In this section we discuss a technique for verifying that a voting scheme satisfies any of the aforementioned semantic criteria. This technique is called *bounded model checking*. It is well understood, and its application to voting schemes has been discussed in an earlier paper [1]. A bounded model checker examines an (arbitrarily small or large) finite state space of ballot boxes and tries to check if the provided semantic criteria hold for each box. If a model check run does not find a bad state, we have established that the criteria are satisfied, which by itself is not a proof but indicates the absence of programming bugs and conceptual problems. If the model checker finds a bad state, it is possible to extract a counter example for future inspection.

Besides a logical formulation of the criteria, the bounded model checking requires a formal description of the voting scheme, i.e. an implementation of the voting scheme in programming languages whose semantics is clearly defined. Fragments of programming languages with a clear mathematical foundation are preferred to capture the essence of the voting algorithm. In our earlier work we have shown that linear logic is adequate to express voting schemes, and that proof search within linear logic is tantamount to bounded model checking.

4 Case Study: Variants of the Single Transferable Vote Scheme

Single transferable vote (STV) is a preferential voting scheme [15] for multi-member constituencies aiming to achieve proportional representation according to the voters' preferences.

4.1   The Standard Version of STV

There are many versions of STV, but most are an extension or variant of the standard version that is shown in Figure 1.

For input and output of the algorithm, we use the same notation and encoding as in Section 2. There are V voters electing S of C candidates, and:

b: is the input ballot box, where $b[i, j]$ is the number of the candidate that is ranked by vote i in the jth place. If the vote does not rank all candidates, then $b[i, j] = 0$ for the empty places.

r: is the output election result, where $r[i]$ is the ith candidate that is elected $(1 \leq i \leq S)$. If less than S candidates are elected, then $r[i] = 0$ for the empty seats.

We assume the input for the algorithm to satisfy the following conditions (which are pre-conditions for running the standard STV algorithm): (1) $C \geq S$, (2) $V \geq 1$. and (3) votes are linear orders of a subset of the candidates, i.e., for all $1 \leq i \leq V$ and all $1 \leq j, j' \leq C$:

- $0 \leq b[i, j] \leq C$,
- if $b[i, j] \neq 0$ and $j \neq j'$ then $b[i, j] \neq b[i, j']$,
- if $b[i, j] = 0$ then $b[i, j'] = 0$ for all $j' \geq j$.

The initialisation part of the STV algorithm in particular computes a quota necessary to obtain a seat (line 5). Different definitions of quotas are used in practice, and the most common is the Droop quota $Q = \lfloor V/(S + 1) \rfloor + 1$.

To determine the election result, STV uses an iterative process, which repeats the following two steps until either a winner is found for every seat or the number of remaining candidates equals the number of open seats (lines 10–33).

1. If no candidate reaches the quota of first-preference votes, a candidate with a minimal number of first-preference votes is eliminated and that candidate is deleted from all ballots (lines 17–19).

2. Otherwise one of the candidates with Q or more first-preference votes is chosen (line 23) and declared elected (line 24). Of the first-preference votes for that candidate, Q are chosen and erased (lines 26–29). These are the votes that are considered to have been "used up". If the candidate has more than Q votes, the surplus votes remain in the ballot box. Finally, the elected candidate is deleted from all ballots still in the box.

The procedure for deleting a candidate c (lines 40–47 works by searching for the candidate in each vote and, if c is found to have preference j, then the candidate with preference $j + 1$ moves to preference j, the candidate with preference $j + 2$ moves to preference $j + 1$, and so on.

When the main loop of the standard STV algorithm as shown in Figure 1 terminates, either (a) all seats are filled, or (b) the number cc of remaining candidates is equal to the number of open seats. In case (b), a further step is needed to distribute some or all of the remaining candidates to the equal

```
───── Standard Version of STV ───────────────────────────────────────

 1  // Initialisation
 2  r   := [0, ..., 0];          // no one elected yet
 3  e   := 1;                    // e is the next seat to be filled
 4  cc := C;                     // cc is the number of (continuing) candidates
 5  Q   := ⌊V/(S + 1)⌋ + 1;      // Droop quota

 7  // Main loop: While not all seats filled and
 8  //                   there are more continuing candidates than open seats
 9  // In each iteration one candidate is elected or one candidate eliminated
10  while (e ≤ S) ∧ (cc > S − e + 1) do
11      // QuotaReached is the set of candidates for which the number of
12      // first-preference votes reaches or exceeds the quota Q
13      QuotaReached := {c | 1 ≤ c ≤ C ∧ #{v | 1 ≤ v ≤ V ∧ b[v, 1] = c} ≥ Q};
14      if QuotaReached = ∅ then
15          // no one has reached the quota,
16          // eliminate a weakest candidate by deletion from the ballot box
17          Weakest := {c | 1 ≤ c ≤ C ∧ #{v | 1 ≤ v ≤ V ∧ b[v, 1] = c} is minimal};
18          choose c ∈ Weakest;
19          delete(c);
20      else
21          // one or more candidates have reached the quota,
22          // elect one of them
23          choose c ∈ QuotaReached;
24          r[e] := c;  // put c in the next free seat
25          e := e + 1; // increase the number e of the next seat to be filled
26          do Q times                        // Q of the votes that
27              choose i ∈ {i | 1 ≤ i ≤ V ∧ b[i, 1] = c};  // give c top preference
28              for j = 1 to C do b[i, j] := 0; od        // get erased
29          od
30          delete(c);  // delete c from the ballot box
31      fi
32      cc := cc − 1;   // in any case we have one less continuing candidate
33  od

35  // Fill the empty seats
36  if e < S then
37      fill the remaining seats r[e, ..., S] with the remaining cc candidates

39  // procedure for deleting candidate c from votes in b
40  procedure delete(c) begin
41      for i = 1 to V do for j = 1 to C do
42          if b[i, j] = c then
43              for k = j to C − 1 do b[i, k] := b[i, k + 1] od;
44              b[i, C] := 0;
45          fi
46      od od
47  end
─────────────────────────────────────────────── Standard Version of STV ─────
```

Fig. 1. The standard STV algorithm

number of remaining seats. The default is to fill all the remaining seats with the remaining candidates (line 37). Alternatively, one may continue the main STV loop to see if the further candidates get elected (which may leave seats open).

Example 2. We consider the same situation as in Example 1, i.e., there are four candidates A, B, C, D for two vacant seats, and the votes to be counted are $[A, B, D], [A, B, D], [A, B, D], [D, C], [C, D]$. The Droop quota in this case is $Q = \lfloor 5/(2 + 1) \rfloor + 1 = 2$.

In the first iteration of the main loop, candidate A meets the quota and is hence elected. Two of the votes $[A, B, D]$ are erased, the third is a surplus vote. It is transformed into $[B, D]$ by deleting A from the ballots.

In the second iteration no candidate reaches the quota, thus the weakest of the remaining candidates B, C, D is eliminated – which one depends on the kind of tie-breaker used as all three have exactly one first-preference vote at that point. (1) If the tie-break eliminates B, the aforementioned transformed vote $[B, D]$ will be transformed again and will become a vote for D, so that D will be elected in the next iteration. (2) If the tie-break eliminates C, the vote $[C, D]$ will be transformed into a vote for D, and thus D will be elected. (3) If the tie-break eliminates D, then C will be elected, analogously, in the next iteration. In summary, the algorithm reports either $[A, D]$ or $[A, C]$ as the election result but not, for example, $[A, B]$ or $[B, D]$. If the number of second-preference votes is used as a tie-breaker, then B is eliminated first (case 1 above).

The standard STV algorithm has three choice points that are sources of non-determinism. These are resolved in different ways by different variants of STV:

1. Who is eliminated if several candidates have the same minimal number of first preferences (line 18)?
2. Who is elected if several candidates have reached the quota (line 23)?
3. How are the votes chosen that are deleted when an elected candidate has more than quote votes (line 27)?

Choice points (1) and (2) are typically handled – to some extent at least – by defining various kinds of tie-break rules. They can also be handled by declaring all weakest candidates eliminated resp. declaring all strongest candidates elected. That, however, is not always possible (there may not be enough open seats). And it can affect the election result in unexpected ways.

Choice point (3) can be eliminated using the notion of fractional votes. Instead of erasing a fraction of the votes that needs to be chosen, the same fraction of each vote is erased and the remaining fraction remains in the ballot box. This is done in many versions of STV used in real-world elections.

The above considerations illustrate that the STV algorithm as presented in this section is not only one but an entire family of vote counting algorithms. There are a number of parameters to play with: the quota, the choice of tie-breakers, placement of candidates once there are as many free seats as remaining candidates.

There are further options that – we argue in Section 4.2 – lead to election systems that can no longer be considered part of the STV family.

4.2   The CADE-STV Election Scheme

The bylaws of the Conference on Automated Deduction (CADE) specify an algorithm for counting the ballots cast for the election of members to its Board of Trustees [4]. The intention of the bylaws is to design a voting algorithm that takes the voters' preferences into account. The algorithm has been implemented in Java and used by several CADE Presidents and Secretaries in elections for the CADE Board of Trustees. It has later on also been used by TABLEAUX Steering Committee Presidents, including one of the authors, for the election of members to the TABLEAUX Steering Committee.

Pseudo code for the CADE-STV scheme is included in the CADE bylaws [4], which makes it an interesting target for formal analysis. CADE-STV differs from the standard version of STV as shown in Figure 1 in several ways:

Quota. Instead of the Droop quota, CADE-STV uses a quota of 50% of the votes – independently of the number of seats to be filled. That is, line 5 in Fig. 1 is changed to "$Q := \lfloor V/2 \rfloor + 1$".

Empty seats. CADE-STV does not fill seats that remain open at the end of the main loop, i.e., lines 36–37 are removed.

Restart. Each time a candidates c reaches the quota Q of first-preference votes and gets elected, the election for the next seat restarts with the original ballot box – with the only exception that the elected candidate c is deleted. Thus, (a) the Q votes used to elect c are not erased but are only changed by deleting c, and (b) weak candidates that have been eliminated are "resurrected" and take part in the election again. That is, (a) the code for erasing votes (lines 26–29) is removed and (b) replaced by code for resurrecting the eliminated candidates.

4.3   Effects of the Differences between CADE-STV and Standard STV

Effects of Restart. To illustrate the effect of the restart mechanism in CADE-STV on the election result, we consider an example:

Example 3. Let us run CADE-STV on Example 1. First, we compute the majority quota $Q = 3$. In the first iteration, A has three first preferences, which means that A is the majority winner and is seated. Since CADE-STV uses restart, A's votes are not deleted but are redistributed at the end of the first iteration. Now the ballot box contains $[B, D], [B, D], [B, D], [D, C], [C, D]$. Following the algorithm, we observe that now B is the majority candidate with 3 first preference votes and is seated. The election is over, and the election result is $[A, B]$ (which is different from the possible results $[A, D]$ or $[A, C]$ of standard STV).

Running our bounded model checker for analysing STV schemes that we have described in [1] on CADE-STV confirms that the election results computed by CADE-STV do not always satisfy Criterion 1, which is closely related to proportional representation (see Sect. 2.3). Indeed, our bounded model checker finds smaller counter examples than the one shown in Example 3, but these are not as illustrative.

The effect of the differences between standard STV and CADE-STV is further clarified by the following theorem and its corollary: in certain cases, there is no proportional representation in the election results computed by CADE-STV. See also Example 4 below.

Theorem 1. *If a majority of voters vote in exactly the same way $[c_1, \ldots, c_k]$, then CADE-STV will elect the candidates preferred by that majority in order of the majority's preference.*

Proof. Since a majority of voters choose c_1 as their first preference, no other candidate can meet the "majority quota". Thus c_1 is elected in the first round. When redistributing the ballots, each of the majority of ballots with c_1 as first preference have c_2 as second preference. All become first preferences for c_2. Thus candidate c_2 is guaranteed to have a majority of first preferences and is elected in round two, and so on until all vacancies are filled.   □

Corollary 1. *If the electorate consists of two diametrically opposed camps that vote for their candidates only, in some fixed order, then the camp with a majority will always get their candidates elected and the camp with a minority will never get their candidate elected.*

Standard STV does not use the restart mechanism and so it will elect the first ranked candidate of the majority, but will then reuse only the surplus votes and not all votes as done by CADE-STV. Thus the second preference from the majority is not necessarily the second person elected. Consequently, majorities do not rule outright in standard STV.

Effects of High Quota and No Filling of Empty Seats. No matter how many candidates there are and how many seats need to be filled, a candidate can only be seated by CADE-STV if he or she accumulates more than 50% of the votes. Any candidate with less than 50% of the vote is defeated. Thus, CADE-STV obviously violates the fill-all-seats criterion. But because of the high quota it also prevents proportional representation as candidates supported by a large minority can neither be elected via reaching the quota nor via filling seats left empty at the end of the main loop.

In fact, if the high quota of 50% and no filling of empty seats were the only changes w.r.t. standard STV, only a single candidate could be elected because more than 50% of the votes would be used up by electing that candidate. CADE-STV requires the restart mechanism to elect further candidates.

Example 4. Assume that there are 100 seats and two parties nominating candidates $A_1, \ldots, A_{100}$ and $B_1, \ldots, B_{100}$, respectively. Further assume that there are 51% of A-voters and 49% of B-voters. All A-voters vote $[A_1, \ldots, A_{100}]$ and all B-voters vote $[B_1, \ldots, B_{100}]$. Standard STV elects $A_1, \ldots, A_{51}, B_1, \ldots, B_{49}$, i.e., the result is a perfect proportional representation.

With a quota of 50% and no filling of empty seats, only A_1 gets elected and then nothing further happens, which is clearly undesirable. But CADE-STV uses, in addition, the restart mechanism. Therefore, like standard STV, it fills all seats. The result is different, however, because the votes used to elect $A_1, \ldots, A_{51}$ do not get erased. CADE-STV produces the election result $[A_1, \ldots, A_{100}]$.

The above example again shows that the majority can rule with CADE-STV and there is no proportional representation in that case (Corollary 1).

4.4   Observations on the History of CADE-STV

We discuss the history of the CADE-STV scheme because it illustrates the problem of evolving an election scheme without using formally specified semantic criteria and a formal definition of the input to the scheme. It is publicly known that there were lots of discussions among the CADE Trustees over a long period of evolving CADE-STV. But we do not know what the non-public deliberations actually where. The following is based on our interpretation of the publicly available material.

The Violation of Proportional Representation. The CADE-STV voting scheme is the result of a long discussion among the board of trustees that took place in the years 1994–1996. David A. Plaisted published various concerns about the existing voting scheme which can be found on his homepage [12].

One of Plaisted's concerns was that a minority supporting candidates standing for re-election could re-elect these candidates against the wishes of the majority as that majority is not sufficiently coordinated in its behaviour to elect alternative candidates [12]:

> *Of course, one of the main purposes of a democratic scheme is to permit the membership to vote a change in the leadership if there is a need for this. However, the new bylaws make this more difficult in several ways. The problem is that those who are unsatisfied with the scheme will tend to split their votes among many candidates (unless they are so disgusted as to put the trustee candidates at the very bottom of the list), but those who are satisfied will tend to vote for the trustee nominees. This means that the trustee nominees tend to be elected even if only a minority is happy with the scheme.*

We believe that because of Plaisted's concerns the board introduced the high 50% quota and did not include a mechanism for filling seats that remain empty. On first sight, this seems good because it solves the problem illustrated in Plaisted's scenario. But, as explained above, this deviation from the standard STV setup not only violates the fill-all-seats criterion but also the goal of proportional representation (see Example 4). Thus, the CADE-STV scheme protects the majority at the expense of the minority.

Also, as explained above, if the high quota and the remaining empty seats were the only changes, only a single candidate could be elected. So, in effect, one was forced to change the algorithm further. The result was that the restart mechanism was added to the algorithm, that reuses the original ballot box for each seat and does not erase votes (because then more candidates can be elected, see Example 4).

There would have been a different solution than using a restart that would have solved Plaisted's problem without restricting proportional representation as much: One could have used Standard STV with an additional rule that – before the main algorithm is started – anybody who does not appear (with arbitrary preference) on at least 50% of the votes is immediately eliminated.

Example 5. Using the same input ballots as in Example 4, the algorithm would then elect $[A_1, ..., A_{51}]$, which still suppresses the B minority, but at least gives the A party only those seats that are proportional to the A votes.

Well-Formedness and Interpretation of Input. Apparently, during some CADE elections, there was some confusion about the meaning of not listing a candidate at all on a ballot and how that should be translated into input for the CADE-STV voting scheme.

The instruction was given to the voters that not listing a candidate is the same as giving that candidate the lowest possible preference. But that is not the correct interpretation. It is easy to see that for both standard STV and CADE-STV, there is a difference between giving a candidate the lowest possible preference and not listing the candidate at all. For example, if there are candidates A, B, C, then $[A, B]$ is different from $[A, B, C]$. When candidates A and B get eliminated, $[A, B, C]$ turns into a vote for C and may help to elect C, which $[A, B]$ does not. One could transform a ballot of the form $[A, B]$ into an input vote $[A, B, C]$ (and, thus, make them equal by definition). But that only works if a single candidate is missing from the ballot. If more are missing, they would have to be put in the same spot on the ballot, which is not possible. Indeed, CADE-STV does not work correctly if input votes contain candidates with equal preference, i.e., if the pre-condition that a vote is a partial linear order is violated. As that pre-condition was never clearly specified, fixing the problem in CADE-STV was a lengthy process that took several years.

This shows that not formalising the pre-conditions which the input must satisfy is problematic. Besides the possibility of errors or unintended behaviour of the algorithm, it is important that the voters understand how their ballot is transformed into input for the algorithm.

5   Conclusion

We have discussed semantic criteria for desired properties of voting schemes. And our case study demonstrates the importance of such criteria both for formal analysis of voting schemes and their evolution and the development process. Semantic criteria need to be explicitly stated. A discussion of voting schemes using anecdotal descriptions of individual voting scenarios is not a good basis for making electoral laws.

In future work, we plan to implement more efficient analysis tools based on SMT solvers for checking that criteria are satisfied. This will allow to investigate larger classes of voting schemes and to use more complex criteria. We also plan to extend our analysis to criteria that measure the quality of election results based on difference measures [10] in addition to yes/no criteria.

References

1. Beckert, B., Goré, R., Schürmann, C.: Analysing vote counting algorithms via logic. And its application to the CADE election system. In: Bonacina, M.P. (ed.) CADE 2013. LNCS, vol. 7898, pp. 135–144. Springer, Heidelberg (2013)
2. Brams, S., Sanver, R.: Voter sovereignty and election outcomes (2003), http://www.nyu.edu/gsas/dept/politics/faculty/brams/sovereignty.pdf (accessed March 21, 2013) (retrieved)
3. Brandt, F., Conitzer, V., Endriss, U.: Computational social choice. In: Weiss, G. (ed.) Multiagent Systems. MIT Press (2012) (forthcoming), http://www.illc.uva.nl/~ulle/pubs/files/BrandtEtAlMAS2012.pdf
4. CADE Inc.: CADE Bylaws (effective November 1, 1996; amended July/August 2000), http://www.cadeinc.org/Bylaws.html (accessed January 20, 2013) (retrieved)
5. Cochran, D.: Formal Specification and Analysis of Danish and Irish Ballot Counting Algorithms. Ph.D. thesis, ITU (2012)
6. Court, F.C.: Provisions of the federal electoral act from which the effect of negative voting weight emerges unconstitutional. Press release no. 68/2008 (2008)
7. Hill, I.D., Wichmann, B.A., Woodall, D.R.: Single transferable vote by Meek's method. Computer Journal 30(3) (1987)
8. Kiniry, J.R., Cochran, D., Tierney, P.E.: Verification-centric realization of electronic vote counting. Tech. rep., School of Computer Science and Informatics, University College Dublin (2007)
9. McGaley, M., Gibson, J.P.: Electronic voting: A safety critical system. Tech. Rep. NUIM-CS-TR2003-02, Department of Computer Science, National University of Ireland, Maynooth (March 2003)
10. Meskanen, T., Nurmi, H.: Closeness counts in social choice. In: Braham, M., Steffen, F. (eds.) Power, Freedom, and Voting. Springer (2008)
11. Pacuit, E.: Voting methods. In: Zalta, E.N. (ed.) The Stanford Encyclopedia of Philosophy (Winter 2012)
12. Plaisted, D.A.: A consideration of the new cade bylaws, http://www.cs.unc.edu/Research/mi/consideration.html (accessed March 22, 2013) (retrieved)
13. Sun, Y., Zhang, C., Pang, J., Alcalde, B., Mauw, S.: A trust-augmented voting scheme for collaborative privacy management. Journal of Computer Security 20(4), 437–459 (2012)
14. Wikipedia: Monotonicity criterion, http://en.wikipedia.org/wiki/Monotonicity_criterion (accessed March 21, 2013) (retrieved)
15. Wikipedia: Single transferable vote, http://en.wikipedia.org/wiki/Single_transferable_vote (accessed January 20, 2013) (retrieved)

Formal Model-Based Validation
for Tally Systems

Dermot Cochran[1] and Joseph R. Kiniry[2]

[1] Siemens A/S, Ballerup, Denmark
dermot.cochran@siemens.com
[2] Technical University of Denmark, Lyngby, Denmark
jkin@imm.dtu.dk

Abstract. Existing commercial and open source e-voting systems have horrifically poor testing frameworks. Most tally systems, for example, are tested by re-running all past elections and seeing if the new system gives the same answer as an older, perhaps erroneous, system did. This amounts to a few dozen system tests and, typically, few-to-no unit tests. These systems are used today in a dozen countries to determine the outcome of national elections. This state-of-affairs cannot continue because it calls into question the legitimacy of elections in major European and North American democracies.

In this work, the ballot counting process for one of the most complex electoral schemes used in the world, Proportional Representation by Single Transferable Vote (PR-STV), is mechanically formally modeled. The purpose of such a formalization is to generate, using an algorithm of our design, a complete set of non-isomorphic test cases *per electoral scheme*, once and for all. Using such a system test suite, any digital election technology (proprietary or open source) can be rigorously evaluated for correctness. Doing so will vastly improve the confidence experts have—and can only improve the level of trust citizens have—in these digital elections systems.

1 Introduction

The electoral process consists of various different stages, from voter registration, through vote casting and tallying, to the final declaration of results. Some, but not all, aspects of the election process are apparently suitable for automation. For example, voter registration records can be stored in computer databases, and ballot counting can be done by machine. However, many attempts to introduce electronic counting of ballots have failed, or at least received much criticism, due to software and hardware errors, *including potential counting errors*, many of which are avoided through the appropriate use of formal methods and careful testing. The security aspects of elections, including voter privacy and election integrity, are an important concern, but are beyond the scope of this paper.

One of the potential advantages from automation is the *accuracy of vote counting*, so it is important to be able to prove that software can actually count ballots more accurately than the manual, labor-intensive process of counting

J. Heather, S. Schneider, and V. Teague (Eds.): VoteID 2013, LNCS 7985, pp. 41–60, 2013.
© Springer-Verlag Berlin Heidelberg 2013

paper ballots by hand, especially for complex voting schemes. Measured error rates for manual tallying of even simple electoral schemes range from around 0.5% to 1.5%. Mechanical tallying of (well-formed, unadulterated) digital ballots must have an error rate of 0%.

In this paper we focus mainly on the Irish voting scheme, as a case study, as it is one of the most complex electoral schemes in the world. By virtue of the design of this scheme and the manner in which we formalize it, we also mechanize two other popular voting schemes. We use the Alloy model finder [9] to describe the elections in terms of scenarios, consisting of equivalence classes of possible outcomes for each candidate in the election, where each outcome represents one branch through the algorithm. We show how test data is generated from a first-order logic representation of the counting algorithm using the Alloy model finder. This algorithm guarantees that we find the smallest number of ballots needed to test each scenario.

1.1   The Irish Voting Scheme

The Republic of Ireland uses Proportional Representation by Single Transferable Vote (PR-STV) for its national, local and European elections. Ireland uses Instant Runoff Voting (IRV) for its presidential elections and for by-elections to fill casual vacancies in Dáil Éireann. PR-STV is a multi-seat ranked choice voting system in which each voter ranks the candidates from first to last preference. IRV is PR-STV with just one remaining seat.

Manual recounts are often called for closely contested seats, as the results often vary slightly, indicating small errors in the manual process of counting votes. Paper-based voting with counting by hand is popular in Ireland, and recent attempts at automation were frustrated by subtle logic errors in the ballot counting software [2]. The potential for logic errors exist, in part, due to the complexities and idiosyncrasies with regard to tie breaking, especially involving the rounding up or down of vote transfers.

There has been some desire in Ireland to simplify matters. Referenda to introduce plurality (first past the post, where the candidate with the most votes is the winner, as is used in the U.S.A. and the U.K.) voting were rejected twice by the Irish electorate, once in 1959 and again in 1968 [20]. Since then, there have been no further legislative proposals to change the voting scheme used in Ireland.

The following are selected quotes from the Irish Commission on Electronic Voting (CEV) report on the previous electronic voting system used in Ireland (emphasis added) [3]:

- Design weaknesses, including *an error in the implementation of the count rules that could compromise the accuracy of an election*, have been identified and these have reduced the Commission's confidence in this software.
- The achievement of the full potential of the chosen system in terms of secrecy and accuracy depends upon a number of software and

hardware modifications, both major and minor, and more significantly, is dependent on the *reliability of its software being adequately
proven.*
- Taking account of the ease and relative cost of making some of these
modifications, the potential advantages of the chosen system, once
modified in accordance with the Commission's recommendations, can
make it a *viable alternative to the existing paper system in terms of
secrecy and accuracy.*

Thus, Ireland wishes to keep its current complicated voting scheme, is critical of
the existing attempts to implement that scheme in e-voting, but keeps the door
slightly ajar for the introduction of e-voting in the future.

1.2   Proportional Representation by Single Transferable Vote

Proportional Representation by Single Transferable Vote (PR-STV) achieves
proportional representation in multi-winner elections, and reduces to IRV for
single-winner elections.

The following flowchart outlines the algorithm used for counting preferences
ballots by PR-STV. A quota of preferences is chosen so that at most $N - 1$
candidates can reach the quota, where N is the number of seats to be filled. A
threshold number or percentage of votes is introduced to discourage unserious
candidates—to be on a ballot a candidate must put down a non-trivial deposit
(say, €1,000) and, if the number of vote for them does not reach the threshold,
they lose their deposit. The threshold is always less than the quota. The surplus
for a candidate is the number of votes in excess of the quota.

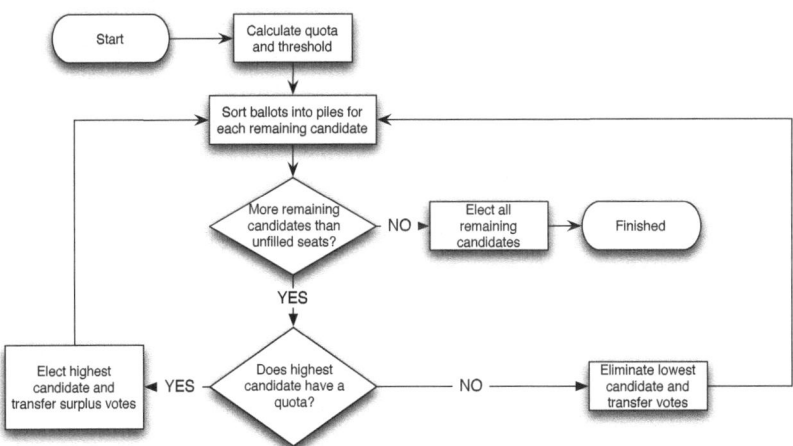

1.3   Vótáil

Vótáil is an open source Java implementation of Irish Proportional Representation by Single Transferable Vote (PR-STV). Its functional requirements, derived

from Irish electoral law, were formally specified using the Business Object Notation (BON) and refined to a model-based Java Modeling Language (JML) specification. While Normal and Extended Static Checking (ESC) were used to help verify and validate the correctness of the software, the system was not rigorously validated using system testing when it was first developed. Consequently, this new research enables us to rigorously validate this (lightly, formally) verified tally system, further increasing ones confidence in the system's correctness.

1.4   Related Work

Related work in this area is thin in peer-reviewed publication venues, as few groups in the world work on applying software engineering to electronic election systems. Some industrial and governmental work exists, but much that we are aware of is either under NDA or is word-of-mouth summaries of development practices at commercial firms.

Academic Work. Meagher wrote a Z and B specification (both are traditional formal methods with tool support [23]) for election to the board of Waterford Institute of Technology, which uses a variant of the Irish PR-STV system [17]. Kjölbro used a similar methodology for specification and implementation of the Danish Voting System [12]. Neither system has been rigorously validated through unit or system testing.

We are also aware of some unpublished work relating to a formalization of PR-STV in λ-Prolog by Lee Naish. It is our understanding that this system was verified but not validated.

Researchers at the Radboud University Nijmegen attempted to test two closed-source binaries implementing Scotland's tally system to ensure its compliance with the WIG-rule [18]. To do so they did a clean-room implementation of the Scottish STV system in the purely functional programming language CLEAN and then compared nearly 6,000 hand-written and automatically generated test runs between all three implementations [13,14]. It is perhaps surprising that they found a number of errors in the commercial implementations, given the ad hoc nature of their testing.

Researchers at the University College Dublin performed a similar exercise on behalf of the aforemented CEV to test the closed source "PowerVote" tally system. Their clean-room implementation was run in parallel to the closed source binary on a network of workstations for over one month on millions of randomly generated elections. Using this completely ad hoc technique they too found correctness errors in the closed source tally system.

Also of interest is a protocol for the tallying of encrypted STV ballots [22] and other work verifying properties of voting protocols (e.g., several papers by Delaune and colleagues), but none of this work focuses on rigorously developed or validated tally systems.

All of these systems, even those that are semi-rigorously validated (like those from Nijmegen), and *especially* all of those that are formally verified benefit from this new work. The latter is true since formally verified system often have errors due to un- or under-stated simplifications in the reasoning framework or verification tools that introduce soundness and completeness problems. Likewise, commercial systems that we and others have examined (research, open source, closed source, or leaked) tally systems all benefit from our work as well.

1.5   Outline of Paper

The next section of the paper describes voting schemes in more detail. The third section describes the system-under-test using a mathematical theory of ballots and ballot boxes. The fourth section outlines the process of deriving test data needed for each election configuration. The final section contains our conclusions and plans for future work.

2   Formalisation

We must represent the input data space in a precise mathematical way to formally reason about its properties with respect to the algorithm. In the following, all components of our model are described verbally, but of course the entire election model has been mechanically formalized. We do not have the space to review this entire first-order model, as it is nearly 1,000 lines of Alloy. The interested reader can download the specifications from http://www.javaforge.com/repository/5298.

The simplicity of our model and the underlying approach should not color the novelty of the approach nor the impact of the work. In fact, we believe that a simple model and algorithm are a strength of the work, as one need not be a logician or an expert in interactive theorem proving to understand and apply the results to new electoral schemes or to validate existing tally systems.

2.1   Mathematical Models

In this example, the core concepts of elections must all be modeled: *ballots, ballot boxes, candidates,* and *election results.*

Candidates. Citizens running for an election are identified by (distinct) names. The set of all candidates is denoted $\mathcal{C}$.

Ballot. An ordinal or preference ballot b is a strict total order on a set of candidates $\mathcal{C}$. The length of a ballot, $|b|$, is the number of preferences expressed. The minimum number of preferences is one, except in systems like that used in Australia where all preferences must be used. In a plurality voting scheme the maximum number of preferences is one. Otherwise, the maximum length of a ballot is the number of candidates in the election.

Ballot Box. An *unordered ballot box* is a bag (multiset) of ballots; an *ordered ballot box* is a vector of ballots, $[b_1 b_2 \ldots]$. Both are *ballot boxes*, denoted $\mathcal{B}$. As a bag can be modeled by a vector where order does not matter, we only use the latter formalization in the following. An ordered ballot box is used to model voting schemes in which surplus ballots are chosen randomly.

As a ballot is a vector, a *ballot box* is encoded as a matrix, where each column represents a single ballot. In such a representation, the top row of the matrix identifies the first preference candidate for each ballot. Each following row contains either a dash ('-'), meaning no preference, or the identifier of the next preference candidate.

2.2   Methodology

Here we describe the methodology we used to write the formal specification of PR-STV using the formalized candidate, ballot, and ballot box datatypes.

To write such a formal model one must be precise and meticulous. Our method is to go through the law, line by line, and identify every definition, algorithmic step, and claim therein. Definitions are mapped to datatype definitions (above). Informal algorithms are mapped to abstract state machines using these datatypes. And claims are mapped to theorems. All artifacts in the formal specification are carefully annotated with comments providing traceability to and from the law text.

Alloy permits one to specify formal models using a concise, typed first-order language. Theorems are written as assertions and are checked by the Alloy model finder by exploring the explicit state space of the model in a breadth-first fashion. The author of the specification stipulates the size of the primitive datatypes involved (e.g., the number of bits in an integer) so as to restrict the state space of exploration. For this case study, around 1,000 lines of Alloy specifications were written.

Consequently, by the time the specification is complete, the Alloy system has both guaranteed that the model is well-typed and gives strong evidence that it is sound because all theorems are checked using the model finder. Note that this automated consistency checking is *not* the same as providing a full interactive proof of a soundness theorem in a higher-order logical framework. Such formalization is an interesting and useful exercise, but we did not do it for this case study. Instead, checking the dozens of theorem stipulated in law text is more akin to the kind of validation that we are advocating in this work. It gives us high confidence, but not a proof, that the mechanical formalization is sound and complete.

3   Election Outcomes

A naive approach to validating/testing electoral systems (if they are tested at all) is to randomly generate enormous numbers of random ballot boxes and then to compare the results of executing two or more different implementations of the same voting scheme. If different results are found, then the ballots are counted manually to determine which result is correct [2].

This methodology is inadequate because, even if one generates billions of ballots in non-trivial election schemes, the fraction of the state space explored is vanishingly small. To make this fact clear, we analyze below the number of distinct ballot boxes in various schemes. Further examples are found in the Appendices.

3.1   Last Two Continuing Candidates

When there are just two continuing candidates and one remaining seat, the algorithm reduces to single winner plurality (first-past-the-post). In this case there are six possible election results (*candidate outcome events*) for each candidate.

Event	Description
W	The candidate is the poll-topper with the most votes.
W̲	The candidate is joint highest and only wins by tie-breaker.
L	The candidate loses, but receives enough votes to reach the threshold.
L̲	The candidate is joint highest and only loses by tie-breaker.
S	The candidate loses and does not reach the threshold.
S̲	The candidate is joint highest and loses by tie-breaker, but does not reach the threshold.

In plurality there is only one winner, so the winner is either in event W or W̲. If there is one loser, the 3 possible outcomes are:

Sub-Scenario	1st Event	2nd Event
1	W	L
2	W	S
3	W̲	L̲

Consequently, to test this particular election scenario, that of two continuing/remaining candidates and one remaining seat, there are three possible outcomes that must be exercised: one in which one candidate clearly wins and the other clearly loses, but showed well for himself (W L), another in which the loosing candidate was so unpopular as to not get his deposit back (W S), and the final outcome is when the two candidates tied and the outcome of the election was determined by a tie-breaking mechanism (W̲ L̲).

Clearly, even when analyzing as simple an election scenario such as this one, hand-identifying each outcome is complex, and hand-writing a test for each outcome is foolhardly.

Now, lets turn our attention to a slightly more complex scenario to start to see how the number of events impacts the number of scenarios.

3.2 Filling of Last Seat

When there is one remaining seat, but at least three continuing candidates, then the algorithm reduces to Instant Runoff Voting (IRV). For each continuing candidate the following event outcomes are possible.

Event	Description
ℍ	The candidate is the poll-topper with a majority of the first preferences and is elected.
ℚ	The candidate is elected during an intermediate round by receiving transfers.
𝕎	The candidate receives enough transfers to have a majority of the votes and is elected in the last round.
𝕎̲	The candidate is elected by tie-breaker in last round.
𝕃	The candidate is defeated as the lowest candidate in any round but reached the threshold.
𝕃̲	The candidate is defeated by tie-breaker in any round, but reached the threshold.
𝕊	The candidate is excluded as the lowest candidate in any round and did not reach the threshold.

Based upon these events, lets consider one simple scenario, focusing on two candidates, the winner and the highest loser (runner-up). In this scenario the following combinations of events are possible (the outcome ℚ is not possible because there are only two candidates and thus there will be no intermediate round).

1st Event	2nd Event	Description
𝕎	𝕃	The winner gets a majority and the loser reaches the threshold.
𝕎	𝕊	The winner gets a majority and loser does not reach the threshold.
𝕎̲	𝕃̲	The winner is elected by tie-breaker and the loser reaches the threshold.

Consequently, even though there are seven possible events, only three scenarios are possible. Thus, an increase in the number of possible events does not necessarily mean an increase in the number of scenarios.

3.3 PR-STV

PR-STV significantly complicates the picture of event types. For any winning candidate one of eight events can happen.

Event	Description
ℕ	The candidate is elected in the first round with a surplus containing at least one non-transferable vote
𝕋	The candidate is elected in the first round with at least one surplus vote
ℍ	The candidate is elected in the first round without surplus votes
𝕏	The candidate is elected after receiving vote transfers and then has a surplus with at least one non-transferable vote
𝔸	The candidate is elected during an intermediate round by receiving transfers and has a surplus to distribute
ℚ	The candidate is elected during an intermediate round by receiving transfers, but without a surplus
𝕎	The candidate is elected as the highest continuing candidate on last round.
𝕎̲	The candidate is elected by tie-breaker on the last round.

And for any losing candidate one of eight events can happen.

Event	Description
𝕃	The candidate is defeated as the lower continuing candidate on the last round.
𝕃̲	The candidate is defeated by tie-breaker on last round.
𝔼	The candidate is excluded as the lowest candidate in an earlier round but reached the threshold, all ballots are transferable
𝔻	The candidate is excluded in an earlier round and is below the threshold, all ballots are transferable
𝕊	The candidate is defeated in the last round and is below the threshold.
𝕊̲	The candidate is excluded by tie-breaker and is below the threshold.
𝔽	The candidate is excluded as the lowest candidate in an earlier round but reached the threshold, with at least one non-transferable ballot
𝕌	The candidate is excluded in an earlier round and is below the threshold with at least one non-transferable ballot

Deriving all possible outcomes for a simple election (say, five candidates running for three seats) is now a seriously non-trivial exercise. Thus, we need some means by which to automatically generate all possible legal outcomes of an election, and from that outcome, derive test data (i.e., a concrete ballot box) to exercise this particular corner of the election algorithm. This is the purpose of our formalization and algorithm, as presented in the sequel.

4   Procedure for Automated Test Generation

The question arises, how do we find witnesses for each outcome? That is, how do we find the smallest set of test ballots required for each outcome, while also showing that the system can scale to accept larger numbers of test ballots. Such stress testing can be achieved by running one test with the maximum number of ballots, but otherwise we would prefer to find the smallest sample ballot box for each outcome. When stress or performance tests are required then the same approach could be used to find both the smallest and largest set of input data for each outcome.

Ballot counting system tests are identified and generated in a complete and formal way, complementing existing hand-written unit tests [11]. To accomplish this task, one needs to be able to generate the ballots in each distinct kind of ballot box identified using the results of the earlier sections of this paper. Effectively, the question is one of, "Given the election outcome R, what is a legal set of ballots B that guarantees R holds?"

What follows is a fairly straightforward exercise of applying model finding to the problem of test case generation. While this idea, at its core, is not novel [19], the use of Alloy for such generation, particularly for critical systems such as election tally systems, is completely novel. The automatic generation of system tests in this space is far beyond what any research group or e-voting corporation has accomplished to-date.

4.1   Generation of Ballot Boxes

We outline a simple example to show how it is possible to derive test data from the equivalence class of ballot boxes.

Based upon the mechanized model of PR-STV, we used the SAT4J solver with Alloy running concurrently in a thread pool to perform this test generation. We suspect that a native solver would be faster, but might not be thread safe; see http://stackoverflow.com/tags/alloy for an explanation of why JNI solvers might not be thread safe.

Recall that each election outcome $\mathcal{O}$ is described by a single *election scenario*, $\mathcal{S}$, as described by a vector of *candidate outcome events*. We must derive from an outcome $\mathcal{O}$ a vector of ballots $\mathcal{B}$ that guarantees, when counted using the ballot counting algorithm of the election, exactly $\mathcal{O}$, assuming that ties are broken in a deterministic way. We write $\mathcal{B} \vdash_\mathcal{S} \mathcal{O}$ to mean counting $\mathcal{B}$ results in outcome $\mathcal{O}$ under scenario $\mathcal{S}$. Such a combination of ballots, outcome, and scenario is called an *election outcome configuration*.

In general, there are a large number of vectors of ballots that guarantee an election outcome. For practical reasons in validation, we wish to find the *smallest* vector that guarantees the outcome; i.e., given $\mathcal{O}$ and $\mathcal{S}$, find $\mathcal{B}$ such that $\forall b.b \vdash_\mathcal{S} \mathcal{O}.|\mathcal{B}| \leq |b|$.

For a given outcome $\mathcal{O}$, the conditions that a vector of ballots $\mathcal{B}$ must meet to fulfill scenario $\mathcal{S}$ is described using a first-order logical formula whose validity indicates $\mathcal{B} \vdash_\mathcal{S} \mathcal{O}$ holds. We denote this description Φ. Thus, $\mathcal{B} \vdash_\mathcal{S} \mathcal{O} \Leftrightarrow \Phi(\mathcal{B})$, or alternatively, $\Phi(\mathcal{B})\mathcal{B} \vdash_\mathcal{S} \mathcal{O}$.

Encoding in Alloy Modeling Language. Formally this is achieved using bounded checks in the Alloy Analyser [10].

Informally, to find the minimal sized $\mathcal{B}$, we iteratively describe election configurations $\mathcal{B} \vdash_S \mathcal{O}$ with monotonically increasing numbers of ballots, starting with a ballot box of size one. These descriptions consist of a set of definitions that describe the outcome and a single theorem that states that $\mathcal{O}$ is *not* possible. If the number of ballots is too small to produce the desired outcome, then the formulation of $\mathcal{B} \vdash_S \mathcal{O}$ will be inconsistent, and Alloy will return a satisfiable solution.

Alternatively, if the ballot box size is just large enough, Alloy will insist that the predicate is *invalid* and provide a counterexample proof context, whose values indicate the necessary values of all of the ballots in $\mathcal{B}$.

Example: Instant Runoff Voting. Consider 3 candidate IRV. Two possible outcome classes are QLE and WLE–no candidate has a majority so one is eliminated and then in the next round, one candidate has a majority. These are two distinct cases: firstly a ballot box of 3 ballots for A, 2 ballots for B, 1 ballot for C, and secondly a ballot box of 2 ballots for A, 2 ballots for B, and 1 ballot with (1st=C 2nd=A).

In both cases, no one has a majority, C is eliminated, and then A wins with a 3 to 2 majority. In both cases the threshold would be one vote. In both cases C is an Early Loser ($\mathbb{E}$) and B is a Loser ($\mathbb{L}$).

An Election Configuration Example. Consider a plurality election with two candidates ($|\mathcal{C}| = 2$). As discussed in the earlier examples, there are three scenarios associated with this election configuration: [WL], [WS], and [WL].

In the following, let T be a tiebreaker function that chooses a winner from a set of candidates.

As earlier, let $\mathcal{B}$ denote a ballot box and b a ballot. Let $b[n]$ be the nth preference of ballot b. Finally, as earlier, let τ be the threshold of votes for a given electoral system.

Formalization. Each candidate outcome is described by an definition that expresses the relationship between the number of votes that candidate receives and the outcome. Since most first-order theorem provers do not provide native support for the generalized summation quantifier, we use a generic encoding described by Leino and Monahan [15].

Axiomatization. We first need definitions that stipulate the well-formedness of ballots.

$$\forall b \in \mathcal{B} \,.\, b[1] \in |\mathcal{C}|$$

$$(\sum_{\mathcal{B}} b[1] = A) + (\sum_{\mathcal{B}} b[1] = B) = |\mathcal{B}|$$

Definition wf_b describes the well-formedness of ballots, while definition $\text{wf}_{\mathcal{B}}$ describes the well-formedness of the ballot box. If an electoral system permits empty preferences then this latter definition is modified to accommodate such.

Formalizing Scenarios. Next, we need to formalize the scenarios of this particular two candidate plurality election as follows, where the label of each formula indicates the semantics of event of the same name e.g., formula $\mathbb{W}$ describes the meaning of event $\mathbb{W}$.

As we commonly quantify over all ballots in $\mathcal{B}$, we write the quantifications over $\mathcal{B}$ rather than the more wordy $b \in \mathcal{B}$. Finally, we encode the set of ballots as the first index in the map b i.e., the second ballot's third preference is $b[2][3]$. Note that these summations are generalized quantifiers: $\sum(b[1] = A)$ means "count the number of ballots whose first preference is candidate A."

$$\sum_{\mathcal{B}} (b[1] = A) > \sum_{\mathcal{B}} (b[1] = B) \tag{$\mathbb{W}$}$$

$$\sum_{\mathcal{B}} (b[1] = A) = \sum_{\mathcal{B}} (b[1] = B) \wedge (T = A) \tag{$\underline{\mathbb{W}}$}$$

$$\tau \leq \sum_{\mathcal{B}} (b[1] = B) \tag{$\mathbb{L}$}$$

$$\sum_{\mathcal{B}} (b[1] = B) < \tau \tag{$\mathbb{S}$}$$

Note that the rightmost clause of formula $\underline{\mathbb{W}}$ states that the coin-flip function picked candidate one as the winner. Also remember that these are axioms of our theory of PR-STV elections, and thus redundant clauses repeating earlier axioms are unnecessary (e.g., repeating $\mathbb{W}$'s inequality in $\mathbb{L}$'s definition).

The Outcome Theorem. Now, we wish to try to prove a theorem that stipulates that, for a given scenario, an expected outcome is *not* possible for a given number of ballots.

After asserting to the theorem prover the above definitions (accomplished with the BG_PUSH command in the Alloy SAT4J solver and either the definition attribute or a push command in SMT-LIB [4,21]), we ask the prover to check the validity of the following theorem (by simply stating the theorem in Alloy or using the check-sat command in SMT-LIB), that captures the meaning of scenario [$\mathbb{W}\mathbb{L}$]:

$$|\mathcal{B}| = 1 \Rightarrow \neg(\mathbb{W} \wedge \mathbb{L})$$

If the prover responds with "valid," then we know that we need more than one ballot, and we make a new attempt:

$$|\mathcal{B}| = 2 \Rightarrow \neg(\mathbb{W} \wedge \mathbb{L})$$

Consequently, if that attempt also fails, we attempt to prove the theorem with three ballots:

$$|\mathcal{B}| = 3 \Rightarrow \neg(\mathbb{W} \wedge \mathbb{L})$$

at which time the prover returns an "invalid" response with a counterexample. The counterexample for this particular theorem will be of the form

$$b[1][1] = A \land b[2][1] = A \land b[3][1] = B$$

thereby providing a minimal ballot box that guarantees election outcome [WL]. Note that to check minimality we can attempt to prove the theorem $(W \land L) \Rightarrow 3 \leq |\mathcal{B}|$, though such a theorem is quite difficult for automated solvers to prove give the implicit quantification over ballot boxes and is, in general, can only be proven with an interactive theorem prover.

4.2 Open Source Implementation

The source code for all software and all mechanized theory is available under the terms of the MIT open source license and can be found the open source repository mentioned earlier.

5 Evaluation and Threats to Validity

To test our approach, we have used our methodology to test Vótáil, the afore-mentioned rigorously engineered tally system for Irish PR-STV. Vótáil was developed using a rigorous methodology with the application of several formal methods tools for design and implementation formal verification.

To test Vótáil (and other Irish PR-STV tally systems) we executed our election generator on a large sixteen core system for nearly one month. The specific algorithm we used gradually added candidates and seats to the election definition, essentially exploring all elections scenarios in a breadth-first fashion. The resulting log file tracing every election generation is over 700MB in size and we generated 137,000 elections. We terminated our test generation after generating elections with seven candidates vying for three seats as generating more complex election scenarios becomes increasingly computationally expensive.

To evaluate the quality of our system tests we executed all tests on Vótáil using Emma to perform coverage analysis [5]. Recall that Vótáil was developed using a rigorous development method including several static checkers and had already been lightly verified using ESC/Java2. Consequently, it would be some-what surprising to find errors in the implementation.

With our original model Emma reported that executing this test suite resulted a fraction below 100% statement coverage and 100% condition coverage. In order to achieve full statement coverage, the original Alloy model was expanded to include extra outcomes; in particular, we needed to model the possibility that a winning candidate might have no surplus votes.

Using this test suite we discovered two errors in its implementation, namely a null pointer exception and possible non-termination of a loop. On closer examination we discovered that both of these errors were not caught during the original formal verification of Vótáil due to under-specification (a missing loop invariant).

Of course, this level of coverage (100% statement and condition coverage) does *not* prove that the system is error-free. One could easily take the fixed set of system tests and code around its model coverage with sufficient effort. But what it does do is (a) provide strong evidence, *especially when combined with a rigorous development method and formal verification*, that the system is correct, and (b) raise the state-of-the-art for election tally system testing enormously.

6   Conclusions

The fact that we found errors in a tally system that was engineered using EAL level 7 methods and tools strongly supports our hypothesis that this kind of automated, domain-specific validation is critical for digital electronic voting systems worldwide.

Moving forward, we believe that it would be of great value to democracies around the world to formalize the other large handful of popular election schemes worldwide using the same software framework. By doing so we can generate a complete set of system tests for every tally scheme in widespread use. The lack of a standardized format for election data from the IEEE or similar is unfortunate, so perhaps we can make recommendations in this regard.

Of course, having all of these system tests generated is a useful outcome for everyone building election systems, academic and industrial alike, but is not a panacea. As advocated by others using applied formal methods, verification and validation of mission- and safety-critical systems is mandatory. Techniques go hand-in-hand toward ensuring that our critical software systems, like those of election software, are correct. This work simply provides a strong touchstone for the runtime validation side of things, while much work remains to be done with regards to verification and certification.

References

1. Bowler, S., Grofman, B.: Elections in Australia, Ireland, and Malta under the Single Transferable Vote: Reflections on an embedded institution. University of Michigan Press (2000)
2. Coyle, L., Cunnigham, P., Doyle, D.: Appendix 2D - second report of commission on electronic voting in Ireland: Secrecy, accuracy and testing of the chosen electronic voting system: Reliability and accuracy of data inputs and outputs (December 2004)
3. Department of Environment and Local Government, Commission on Electronic Voting in Ireland. Count requirements and commentary on count rules (June 23, 2000)
4. Detlefs, D., Nelson, G., Saxe, J.B.: Simplify: a theorem prover for program checking. Journal of the Association of Computing Machinery 52(3), 365–473 (2005)
5. https://github.com/jacoco
6. Farrell, D.M., McAllister, I.: The Australian electoral system: origins, variations, and consequences. New South Wales University Press, Ltd. (2006)
7. Gallagher, M.: Comparing proportional representation electoral systems: Quotas, thresholds, paradoxes and majorities. British Journal of Political Science 22(4), 469–496 (1992)

8. Gilmour, J.: Detailed description of the STV count in accordance with the rules in the Scottish local government elections order 2007. Representation 43(3), 217–229 (2007)
9. Jackson, D.: Alloy: A lightweight object modelling notation. ACM Transactions on Software Engineering and Methodology 11(2), 290 (2002)
10. Jackson, D.: Software Abstractions: logic, language and analysis. MIT Press, MA (2012)
11. Kiniry, J.R., Cochran, D., Tierney, P.E.: Verification-centric realization of electronic vote counting. In: Proceedings of the USENIX/Accurate Electronic Voting Technology on USENIX/Accurate Electronic Voting Technology Workshop. USENIX Association Berkeley, CA (2007)
12. Kjölbro, O.: Verifying the Danish Voting System. Master's thesis, IT University of Copenhagen (May 2011)
13. Koopman, P., Hubbers, E., Pieters, W., Poll, E., de Vries, R.: Testing the eSTV program for the Scottish local government elections. Technical report, Radboud University Nijmegen (2007)
14. Koopman, P., Plasmeijer, R.: Testing with functional reference implementations. In: Page, R., Horváth, Z., Zsók, V. (eds.) TFP 2010. LNCS, vol. 6546, pp. 134–149. Springer, Heidelberg (2011)
15. Leino, K.R.M., Monahan, R.: Reasoning about comprehensions with first-order SMT solvers. In: Proceedings of the 24th Annual ACM Symposium on Applied Computing, SAC 2009 (2009)
16. McGaley, M., Gibson, J.P.: Electronic voting: A safety critical system. Final Year Project Report, NUI Maynooth Department of Computer Science (2003)
17. Meagher, M.: Towards the development of an electronic count system using formal methods, MPhil thesis, University of Southampton (2001)
18. The Scottish Ministers, Scottish local government elections order 2007, rule 45–52 (December 2006)
19. Rayadurgam, S., Heimdahl, M.P.E.: Coverage based test-case generation using model checkers. In: Proceedings of the IEEE International Conference on the Engineering of Computer Based Systems (ECBS 2001), pp. 83–91. IEEE (2001)
20. Sinnott, R.: Irish voters decide: Voting behaviour in elections and referendums since 1918. Manchester Univ. Pr. (1995)
21. SMT-LIB: The satisfiability modulo theories library, http://combination.cs.uiowa.edu/smtlib/
22. Teague, V., Ramchen, K., Naish, L.: Coercion-resistant tallying for STV voting. In: Proceedings of the USENIX/Accurate Electronic Voting Technology Workshop (2008)
23. Wing, J.M.: A specifier's introduction to formal methods. Computer 23(9), 8–22 (1990)

A   Appendix: Voting Schemes

To analyze this challenge, a number of definitions are necessary to establish a clear nomenclature for the later formalisms of this paper. We focus first on voting schemes for context. Section 2, provided the formal definitions of all of the components informally mentioned here.

A *voting scheme* is an algorithm for counting ballots. A *preference voting scheme* requires the voter to rank two or more candidates ($\mathcal{C}$) in order of preference from first to last. A *plurality voting scheme* requires the voter to pick one candidate, and thus is equivalent to the preference scheme when the ranking list has unitary size.

The *election result* $(\mathcal{W}, \mathcal{L})$ consists of (1) the identification of the winner or winners of the election and (2) the identification of those candidates who achieved a certain *threshold* (denoted τ) of votes, e.g., 5 percent, needed either to qualify for public funding in future elections or to recoup a deposit paid. This threshold facet of our election model is not universal, but is a critical component in many electoral systems. Note that winners and losers are disjoint.

We denote a ballot box $\mathcal{B}$ as a set of ballots b. Mathematically, a voting scheme $\mathcal{E}$ is a function that takes a ballot box (a set of ballots) as its input, and produces an election result as its output. More formally, $\mathcal{E} : \mathcal{B} \to (\mathcal{W}, \mathcal{L})$ where $\mathcal{W} \subseteq \mathcal{C}$, $\mathcal{L} \subset \mathcal{C}$, and $\mathcal{W} \cap \mathcal{L} = \emptyset$.

Single Winner Plurality Voting. Plurality voting is one of the simplest possible voting schemes. The candidate with the most votes is the winner. When there is only one remaining seat and just two continuing candidates, then PR-STV reduces to single-winner Plurality.

Instant Runoff Voting (IRV). IRV allows the voter to rank one or more candidates in order of relative preference, from first to last.

IRV usually has a single winner, but the candidate with the most votes must also have a majority of all votes, otherwise the candidate with least votes is excluded and each ballot for that candidate is transferred to the next candidate in order of preference. This evaluation-and-transfer continues until one of the candidates achieves an overall majority.

When there is just one remaining seat, or a special election to fill a vacancy in one seat, then PR-STV reduces to IRV.

Order of Elimination. The candidate with the least number of votes credited to him or her in the curent round is selected for elimination. If there is an equality of votes, then previous rounds are considered. If two or more candidates have equal lowest votes in all rounds, then random selection is used.

Variants of PR-STV. To highlight the complexities of election schemes, consider the following variants of PR-STV. As schemes vary, so must testing/validation strategies. For example, Australia, Ireland, Malta, Scotland, and Massachusetts use different variants of PR-STV for their elections [1].

- **Australia** - Australia uses IRV to elect its House of Representatives and an open list system for its Senate, where voters can choose either to vote for individual candidates using all available preferences or to vote "above-the-line" for a party [6]. Australians (in many elections) vote either above the line or below the line, but ATL votes are still counted using PR-STV, after being transformed into a full preference ranking. (Effectively, an ATL vote proxies the vote to the chosen party.)

- **Ireland** - Ireland uses PR-STV for local, national and European elections. Transfers are rounded to the nearest whole ballot, so the order in which ballots are transferred makes a difference to the result [16]. Not all preferences need to be used, so voters may choose to use only one preference, as in Plurality voting, if desired.
- **Malta** - Malta uses PR-STV for local, national and European elections. For national elections Malta also adds additional members so that the party with the most first preference votes is guaranteed a majority of seats.
- **Scotland, UK** - Scotland uses PR-STV for local elections. Rather than randomly select which ballots to include in the surplus, fractions of each ballot are transferred, that gives a more accurate result but takes much longer to count if counted by hand [8].
- **Massachusetts, USA** - Cambridge in Massachusetts uses PR-STV for city elections. Candidates with less than fifty votes are eliminated in the first round and surplus ballots are chosen randomly.

The fact that a single complex voting scheme like PR-STV has this many variants in use highlights the challenges in reasoning about and validating a given software implementation. This fact makes our work that much more valuable, as each algorithm only need be analyzed *once* to derive a complete validation that may be used again and again over arbitrary implementations of a ballot counting algorithm.

Irish PR-STV. To give context, we now discuss the mechanics of Irish PR-STV in more detail.

Preference Ballots. The voter writes the number "1" beside his or her favorite candidate. There can only be one first preference.

The voter then considers which candidate would be his or her next preference if his or her favorite candidate is either excluded from the election or is elected with a surplus of votes.

The second preference is marked with "2" or some equivalent notation. The can be only one second preference; there cannot be a joint second preference. Likewise for third and subsequent preferences. Not all preferences need to be used.

Multi-seat constituencies. Each constituency is represented by either three, four or five seats.

The Droop Quota. The quota is calculated so that not all winners can reach the quota. The droop quota is $1 + \frac{V}{1+S}$, where V is the total number of valid votes cast and S is the number of vacancies (or seats) to be filled [7]. The quota is chosen so that any candidate reaching the quota is automatically elected, and so that the number of candidates that might reach the quota less than the number of seats.

For example, in a five-seat constituency a candidate needs just over one-sixth of the total vote to be assured of election.

Surplus. The surplus for each candidate, is the number of ballots in excess of the quota (if any). The surplus ballots are then available for redistribution to other continuing candidates.

The selection of which ballots belong to the surplus is a complex issue, depending on the round of counting. In the first round of counting, any surplus is divided into sub-piles for each second preference, so that the distribution of the ballots in the surplus is proportional to the second-preferences. In later rounds the surplus is taken from the last parcel of ballots received from other candidates. This surplus is then sorted into sub-piles according to the next available preference.

For example, if the quota is 9,000 votes and candidate A receives 10,000 first preference votes. The surplus is 1,000 votes. Suppose 5,000 ballots had candidate B as next preference, 3,000 had candidate C and 2,000 had candidate D. Then the surplus consists of 500 ballots taken from the 5000 for candidate B, 300 from the 3000 for candidate C and 200 from the 2000 for candidate D. Ideally each subset would also be sorted according to third and subsequent preference, but this does not happen under the current procedure for counting by hand, nor was it mandated in the previous guidelines for electronic voting in Ireland.

Exclusion of weakest candidates. When there are more candidates than available seats, and all surplus votes have been distributed, the continuing candidate with least votes is excluded. If two or more candidates have equal lowest votes (at all stages of the count) then one is chosen randomly for exclusion.

All ballots from the pile of the excluded candidate are then transferred to the next preference for a continuing candidate, or to the pile of non-transferable votes.

This continues until another candidate is elected with a surplus or until the number of continuing candidates equals the number of remaining seats.

Filling of Last Seat and Bye-elections. When there is only one seat remaining to be filled, i.e., the number of candidates having so far reached the quota is one less than the number of seats, or in a bye-election for a single vacancy, then the algorithm becomes the same as Instant Runoff Voting; no more surplus distributions are possible, and candidates with least votes are excluded until only two remain.

Last Two Continuing Candidates. When there are two continuing candidates and one remaining seat, then the algorithm becomes the same as single-seat first-past-the-post plurality; the candidate with more votes than the other is deemed elected to the remaining seat, without needing to reach the quota. If there is a tie then one candidate is chosen randomly.

B   Appendix: Detailed Examples

This appendix contains some more detailed examples for estimation the number of possible ballots, number of possible outcomes, and the number of distinct permutations of ballot papers.

B.1   Number of Distinct Ballots

The number of distinct permutations of non-empty preferences is $\sum_{l=1}^{C}(C)_l$, where $C = |\mathcal{C}|$ and partial ballots are allowed, so that the number of preferences used range in length from one to the number of candidates. For a ballot of length l, $(C)_l$ is the number of distinct preferences that can be expressed.

Examples and Encoding Ballots. This distinct ballot count is best understood, particularly for those unexcited by combinatorics, by examining cases for small C and enumerating all possible ballots.

Two Candidates. There are four different ways to vote for two candidates (named Alice and Bob): two ballots of length 1, and two ballots of length 2, that is $(2)_1 + (2)_2$:

Ballot	Alice	Bob	Encoding of Ballot	
1	1st	-	A	$-$
2	-	1st	B	$-$
3	1st	2nd	A	B
4	2nd	1st	B	A

$\boxed{A \mid -}$ has a different meaning than $\boxed{A \mid B}$. If we had an election with two ballots $\boxed{B \mid -}$ and $\boxed{A \mid B}$, then Bob would be the winner.

Note the symmetry of these four ballots. There are effectively only two different ballots if the candidates cannot be differentiated.

Number of Distinct Outcomes. If B is the number of distinct non-empty ballots that can be cast, and $V = |\mathcal{B}|$ is the number of votes cast, then the number of possible combinations of ballots is B^V if the order of ballots is important, and $\dfrac{B^V}{V!}$ if not.

A typical electoral configuration in Ireland is a five seat constituency with a typical voting population of 100,000 and 24 candidates. Consequently, the number of possible ballot boxes is $(\sum_{l=1}^{24}(24)_l)^{100,000}$, an astronomical number of tests that would be impossible to run.

To avoid this explosion, we partition the set of all possible ballot boxes into equivalence classes with respect to the counting algorithm chosen. We consider the equivalence class of election results for all three counting schemes.

Each election outcome is described by an *election scenario* that is a vector of *candidate outcome events*. Both of these terms are defined in the following.

The key idea is that election scenarios represent an equivalence class of election outcomes, thereby letting us collapse the testing state space due to symmetries in candidates. We will return to this point in detail below in the early examples.

Three Candidates. There are 15 legal ways to vote for three candidates called Alice, Bob, and Charlie:

Ballot	Alice	Bob	Charlie	Encoding		
1	1st	-	-	A	$-$	$-$
2	-	1st	-	B	$-$	$-$
3	-	-	1st	C	$-$	$-$
4	1st	2nd	-	A	B	$-$
5	1st	-	2nd	A	C	$-$
6	2nd	1st	-	B	A	$-$
7	-	1st	2nd	B	C	$-$
8	2nd	-	1st	C	A	$-$
9	-	2nd	1st	C	B	$-$
10	1st	2nd	3rd	A	B	C
11	1st	3rd	2nd	A	C	B
12	2nd	1st	3rd	B	A	C
13	3rd	1st	2nd	B	C	A
14	2nd	3rd	1st	C	A	B
15	3rd	2nd	1st	C	B	A

There are 3 ballots of length 1, 6 ballots of length 2 and 6 ballots of length 3, that totals $(3)_1 + (3)_2 + (3)_3 = 15$. Again, note the symmetry of these ballots, as there are only three different kinds of ballots in these fifteen ballots.

More than Three Candidates. Each additional candidate number n means one extra ballot of length 1, plus another C ballots in which the extra candidate is the last preference, plus every other way in which the candidate could be inserted into the existing set of ballots, in one of n positions along that ballot.

For example, when there are four candidates, the number of single preference ballots increases to 4, the number of length 2 ballots is $4 \times (4 - 1)$, the number of length 3 ballots is $4 \times (4 - 1) \times (4 - 2)$ and the number of full length ballots is $4!$, for a total of 64 ballots, of which there are only three equivalence classes.

Vote Casting in Any Preferred Constituency: A New Voting Channel

Jurlind Budurushi[1], Maria Henning[2], and Melanie Volkamer[1]

[1] CASED / TU Darmstadt, Germany
[2] provet, Universität Kassel, Germany
{jurlind.budurushi,melanie.volkamer}@cased.de,
{maria.henning}@uni-kassel.de
http://www.secuso.cased.de
http://www.uni-kassel.de/fb07/institute/iwr/

Abstract. In our society a rising number of people change their residence regularly. Insofar, mobility seems to be necessary even on Election Day, which is the reason why an increasing number of eligible voters use the opportunity of postal voting. Thereby, the abidance by the election principles, especially the freedom and secrecy of elections, is automatically transferred into the private sector. This would not be necessary if eligible voters had the possibility to cast their vote in any preferred constituency within the electoral area. Therefore, we investigate in this work if and how vote casting in any constituency can be constitutionally compliant, while maintaining the current electoral system. We also consider the integration of the new German electronic ID card for voter identification and authentication.

1 Introduction

The use of various services over the Internet is part of many peoples' everyday life. Through this, it is no longer required that the individual is present at a particular time or place to conduct its business. The need for this kind of mobility exists independent of special events, thus also on Election Day. For this reason, some countries provide postal voting in order to enable as many people as possible to participate in the election. Postal voting was established in Germany in 1956 with the third Federal Electoral Act [7]. Through this, voters who were not able to visit a polling station because of health reasons or any other issues were enabled to cast their vote at home. While in 1957 only 4,9 % used this option, for the elections to the 17th German Bundestag in 2009, about 21,4 % took the opportunity of postal voting (ref. to Table 1 in [2]). The increase of postal voters may be justified due to both: the rising mobility of the citizens, and the relaxation of application requirements for postal voting. But the shift of a democratic legitimized election to the private sector raises the question whether postal voting in its present form is still constitutionally compliant and in particular if it complies with the public nature of elections [25]. However, postal voting is an indispensable opportunity for voters, who cannot be present in the

J. Heather, S. Schneider, and V. Teague (Eds.): VoteID 2013, LNCS 7985, pp. 61–75, 2013.

polling station of their constituency because of health reasons or for those that cannot be in the election area on Election Day. In contrast, voters who are able to visit a constituency within the electoral area should be offered the additional opportunity to cast their vote in any preferred constituency. Through this new voting channel, voters would be as mobile and flexible as when using the opportunity of postal voting, but they would cast their vote in an environment that is controlled by the electoral committee. In addition the compliance with the election principles would be guaranteed.

In the following, we consider vote casting in any preferred constituency in the context of the elections for the German Bundestag on Election Day. Thereby, we investigate different possibilities of this new voting channel. Furthermore, we identify the advantages and disadvantages and compare all possibilities against each other from a legal and technical perspective. We do not aspire to change or suggest changes concerning the German electoral system, which means the composition of the German Bundestag and vote casting by selecting a candidate and the list of a party. While maintaining the current electoral system but voting from any constituency, two issues should be considered carefully: one is how to authenticate voters that vote in foreign constituencies and provide them with the respective ballot, and the other one is how to return the ballot to the local constituency in order to tally the votes.

This work considers legal implications of allowing voters to cast their vote from any constituency in Germany and respective technical solutions in order to realise this ambition. The findings of this work might also apply in countries that have similar legal requirements to Germany, especially member countries of the European Union (EU). However, legal requirements might be slightly different even within the EU. Therefore, a similar analysis, which could consider or could be based on this work, must be conducted for each country, individually.

2   General Possibility of Vote Casting in any Preferred Constituency

According to § 1.2 in conjunction with § 2.2 Federal Electoral Act the territory of Germany is divided into 299 electoral districts. Every electoral district is subdivided into constituencies. Thus, constituencies are the lowest spatial division of the electoral area from an organisational point of view (ref. to § 2, m.n. 5 in [29]). They are important in the context of casting the votes because they define the place where to do so. According to § 14.2 Federal Electoral Act, voters can cast their vote only in that constituency, in whose electoral register they are recorded in. According to § 14.3 a) Federal Electoral Act, the casting of votes in any preferred constituency within the electoral district requires the ownership of a ballot record which is only given in case of applying for it within a prescribed period.[1]

---

[1] A ballot record entitles the voter to do postal voting or to cast her vote in any constituency within the electoral district. For further information please see section 3.1.

The casting of votes in any preferred constituency of the electoral area is not compatible with the current regulations of electoral law. However, this is owned to the election process and not to the constitutional regulations. For instance, Article 38.1 sentence 1 of the Basic Law does not require that eligible voters cast their votes only in the constituency they are registered in. In case the checking of the eligibility to vote is guaranteed and it can be ensured that every eligible voter casts his or her vote only once and personally (see section 3), voters shall be able to cast their vote in any preferred constituency, not only in the one they are registered in. As the election system shall be maintained, it must be ensured that the cast vote is tallied in the constituency the respective voter is related to (see section 4).

3   Checking of Eligibility

The following remarks apply in case voters cast their vote in the constituency they are assigned to or in any preferred constituency.

3.1   Ballot Record

Voting by people from foreign constituencies could be made dependent on the submission of a ballot record. Insofar, it could be referred to the current regulations, whereas the grant of a ballot record is possible only on request, § 17.2 Federal Electoral Act, and voting by submission of a ballot record requires the presentation of an official identity document, § 59 Federal Electoral Code. Thus, in contrast to § 14.3 a) of the Federal Electoral Act, the possession of a ballot record would qualify for vote casting in any preferred constituency within the electoral area (and not only within the electoral district). This approach has the advantage that no new infrastructure is required in order to check the eligibility of voters in a foreign constituency. In that regard, the existing electoral registers can be used for checking the eligibility of voters in a foreign constituency, similar to postal voting. Those voters who have applied for a ballot record could cast their vote in any preferred constituency. Those who have not applied for a ballot record could cast their vote only in the constituency they are registered in.

However, this approach also has a number of disadvantages (which exist in the current implementation as well, but would affect a larger number of voters in our approach): The voter loses her right to vote in case she loses the ballot record. Furthermore, a coercer could conduct a forced-abstention attack by requiring the voter to hand out the ballot record. Both threats also exist in the current election system. Voters, who have received a ballot record and lost it subsequently, cannot refer to the issuance of it. The replacement of a lost ballot record is generally not considered in order to prevent a double vote (ref. to § 17, m.n. 15 in [29]). According to § 28.10 sentence 2 of the Federal Electoral Code, a new ballot record can be issued only with a credible assurance of a lack of access until 12 o'clock the day prior to the election. A further disadvantage of this approach is that only voters who have applied for a paper record within the prescribed period are able to cast their vote in an optional constituency. This could be solved by sending paper records to all eligible voters. However, this would strengthen all the disadvantages outlined above.

3.2   Centralised / Decentralised Electoral Register

If voting in any preferred constituency was provided the electoral committee could - according to the current regulations - only check the eligibility of voters registered in the respective electoral register. Thus, for checking the eligibility to vote of voters from foreign constituencies, the electoral committee would have to check the electoral register of the constituency the voter is registered in - easier to implement - a centralised electoral register[2], if this is legally permitted and feasible.

A centralised electoral register could easily be produced in the presence of a centralised Federal Register of Residents. However, a centralised Federal Register of Residents is neither provided in the current Framework Registration Act [8] nor in the Registration System Act for further development of the registration system, which passed the Germany Bundestag on 6/28/2012 but stands in a conciliation committee at the moment [11]. A draft which was written by a consultant and published on 12/6/2007 [24] focused the application of a centralised Federal Register of Residents. However, this concept was rejected by various data privacy experts. The criticism was not against such a register in general, but explicitly against the number and type of data, which were listed and considered in § 3 of the draft to be stored in the register. This includes an unjustifiable intervention in the law of informational self-determination, which results from Article 2.1 in conjunction with Article 1.1 Basic Law. Therefore, the establishment of a centralised electoral register cannot be fundamentally rejected. According to the principle of dedicated use in the Data Protection Law, voters' personal data may be used only for the specified purpose, namely to check the eligibility to vote. Beyond that, the centralised electoral register may store only that data which is required to check the eligibility to vote: first- and surname, birthday and current residential address.[3]

3.3   Voter Identification and Authentication, and Access to the Electoral Register

Classical Voter Identification and Authentication (I/A). Verification of the eligibility to vote requires a prior identification and authentication of the citizen. Currently eligible voters are notified in writing about their registration in the electoral register. This election notification also serves as a proof of identity (ref. to § 14, m.n. 9 in [29]). According to § 56.3 of the Federal Electoral

---

[2] The information on the centralised electoral register (server) can be replicated among several servers in order to avoid a single point of failure.

[3] The electoral registers get compiled on the basis of the population registers stored in the registry offices. Insofar, the surname, the first name, the date of birth and the residential address of eligible voters are transferred from one register to another one.

Code, voters shall submit the election notification on demand of the electoral committee. In case they do not submit the election notification, they must identify themselves. The submission of the election notification and the identification document is not necessary in any case, but at the behest of the electoral committee. It is not required in case of personal acquaintance between the voter and the electoral committee. However, the Federal Electoral Code does not permit the inference, whether a particular identity document shall be submitted. In that regard, each official document needs to be sufficient in order to provide a proof of identity. Therefore, the document should include a photo, as otherwise the verification of the identity is not guaranteed.

Electronic Electoral Register (EER). The right to vote can be checked against the voters personal data, which are stored on the de-/centralised electoral register. The transmission of personal data from the registration office to public authorities is already intended in § 18 Framework Registration Act and § 34 Registration System Act in case the personal data is necessary to fulfill their jurisdiction or necessary by the jurisdiction of the receiver to fulfill its corresponding tasks. In addition, according to § 14.1 sentence 2 Federal Electoral Code, the electoral register can be maintained through an automatic process as well.

The transmission of voters' personal data, namely first- and surname and current residential address, is necessary in order to check if the citizen is eligible to vote and whether he or she already cast a vote. The personal data could be transferred over a secured communication channel, for instance over telephone or Internet, which is already intended according to § 39.3 Registration System Act. The use of a telephone is impractical and therefore not further considered in this work. The access to the electoral register over the Internet would be secured by the application of standard cryptographic protocols for secure communication, like SSL/TLS [31]. The main disadvantages of an electronic electoral register, which is accessible over the Internet, are DoS/DDoS attacks. However, there are a number of techniques in order to mitigate such attacks, e.g. as presented in [30] and [21].

Regarding the transmission of personal data it is questionable, whether the electoral committee, as the receiver of the mentioned data, can be classified as a public authority in the context of the outlined regulations. On one hand, the municipal authorities carry out the statutory work assigned by the Federal Electoral Act on behalf of the federal government (ref. to No. 43 in [29]). On the other hand the electoral committee acts as an election body for the municipal authority. Insofar the personal data of voters could be transferred to the electoral committee directly. Thus, the access of the electoral committee to electoral registers of other constituencies is not generally forbidden.

EER and Classical Voter I/A. By checking the eligibility to vote over the Internet and maintaining the classical identification and authentication of voters, the electoral committee would have to enter the necessary data of the voter manually. The personal data of the voter could be taken by the presented document, captured electronically and sent as a request to check the eligibility to vote for the respective voter.

With this form of checking the eligibility to vote, a corresponding Public Key Infrastructure (PKI) [19] needs to be provided in order to ensure secure transmission of the personal data. This introduces additional costs. Another disadvantage of this approach is that the personal data transferred is confidential and secure only until the provided cryptographic encryption scheme is secure. Thus, an attacker who intercepts the encrypted personal data, which is transferred over the network, is able to determine who has participated in the election and who has not. Furthermore, this could violate the secrecy of the vote, depending on whether the ballot is electronically transferred and how it is transferred.

EER and (German) Electronic Identity Card for Voter I/A. Electronic identity cards (e-ID cards) have been already used in electronic voting for legally binding elections. Hereby, the most prominent examples are Estonia [12] and Austria [1]. Furthermore, the use of e-ID cards in electronic voting has been proposed in many scientific works, for instance [3], [4], [9], [20] and [26], and has been also analysed in [6]. In particular, the authors in [3] and [4] propose the use of the German electronic identity card "Der neue Personalausweis" (German e-ID card) in electronic voting.

Thus, the eligibility to vote could also be checked with the German e-ID card. The German e-ID card enables, due to its data fields, shown in Figure 1, and particularly due to its eID-Functionality, the so-called Restricted-ID, a unique service-related online authentication [16].

OperationsRequestorType	
DocumentType	AttributeRequestType
IssuingState	AttributeRequestType
DateOfExpiry	AttributeRequestType
GivenNames	AttributeRequestType
FamilyNames	AttributeRequestType
ArtisticName	AttributeRequestType
AcademicTitle	AttributeRequestType
DateOfBirth	AttributeRequestType
PlaceOfBirth	AttributeRequestType
Nationality	AttributeRequestType
BirthName	AttributeRequestType
PlaceOfResidence	AttributeRequestType
ResidencePermitI	AttributeRequestType
RestrictedID	AttributeRequestType
AgeVerification	AttributeRequestType
PlaceVerification	AttributeRequestType

Fig. 1. Data fields of the German e-ID card (Source: [17], Figure. 13)

Furthermore, the German e-ID card supports age verification, a query of the place of residence and a pseudonymisation (Restricted-ID). These functionalities could be used for checking the eligibility to vote as they provide the necessary data, which can be compared to the corresponding personal data stored in the electoral register. Figure 2 shows an abstract infrastructure and the interaction between the involved components.

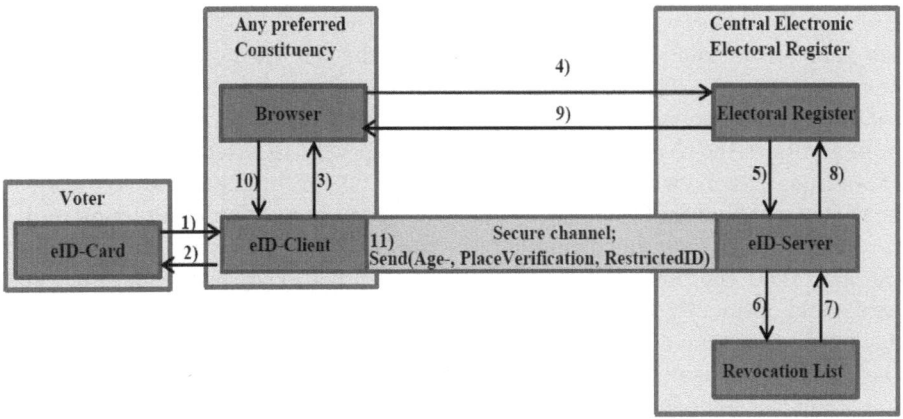

Fig. 2. Abstract Infrastructure and Interaction between involved Components

By using the Restricted-ID functionality, neither the PC of the electoral committee[4] nor the electoral register would know for which voter the eligibility to vote is being checked. The electoral register can respond to the request, if a Restricted-ID (voter) is eligible to vote or not, without knowing the particular voter behind the Restricted-ID. However, the identity of the voter could be revealed in case the cryptographic algorithms, which are used for the generation of the Restricted-ID and for securing the Internet communication, are broken. Besides intercepting the data transferred over the network to the electoral register, an attacker also needs to know the public key of each German e-ID card and the public key of the electoral register (eID-Server) [17].

Furthermore, if the electoral register (eID-Server) and the Certification Authority of the German e-ID cards cooperate, even today they can assign each Restricted-ID stored on the electoral register to the identity of the voter [4]. Therefore, storing the Restricted-IDs on the electoral server permanently must be forbidden and the deletion of the stored Restricted-IDs must be verified by the corresponding data protection expert. A long-term storage of data might only be acceptable in case of a pending complaint requesting the scrutiny of an election. However, the storage must be set up by the Federal Returning Officer and controlled by the responsible data protection expert.

---

[4] In Germany the authorisation of voters and the tallying of votes is carried out at the constituency where votes have been cast.

The authentication with the German e-ID card has a number of advantages with respect to data privacy in comparison with the classical approach. Instead of the voter's personal data a pseudonym is transferred over the network. As the Restricted-ID is unique in the context of the election, a voter trying to vote more than once will easily be detected. Furthermore, citizens who have lost their right to vote according to § 13 of the Federal Electoral Act can easily be identified as well. Therefore, the so-called Country Verifying Certificate Authority (CVCA) can publish a corresponding revocation list, which contains all election-specific Restricted-IDs that are not allowed to exercise their right to vote. Depending on the implementation, the successful checking of the eligibility to vote could either be accepted by the electoral committee or by a voting machine which then might enable the voter to start the vote casting process.

In addition, the electoral committee is not expected to enter the personal data of voters manually, which is error prone and time consuming. However, it must be considered that currently not all citizens are in possession of a German e-ID card and therefore not all citizens can use the German e-ID card in the context of checking their eligibility to vote. But the authentication with the German e-ID card could optionally be offered to those eligible voters, who already possess this document and have activated the eID-Functionality. Although, the principle of the equal elections requires that every citizen shall be able to exercise his right to vote in the same formal way (besides the equality of counter value and result value), this does not mean that there can be only one option for vote casting. In that regard, postal voting provides a different way of voting too but it is constitutionally compatible since it is offered as an option and it strengthens the principle of universal elections (ref. to page 125 in [13]). Finally, it has to be said that since 11/1/2010 citizens applying for an identification document only receive the German e-ID card. However, there is no obligation to exchange the "old" identity card. According to identity card law (ref. to § 6.1 in [22]), German identity cards are valid for ten years. Therefore, "old" identity cards will be present until 10/31/2020. After this date, all eligible voters shall possess a German e-ID card and could subsequently use it for authentication, if the eID-Functionality has been activated. However, even after 10/31/2020, an additional option besides the German e-ID card must be provided for identification and authentication.

A regulation, which requires that voters can only be identified by providing the German e-ID card, is not compatible with Article 38.1 sentence 1 Basic Law because it violates the principle of universal elections. Thus, it is possible that voters lose their German e-ID card just before the election or the German e-ID card is stolen or missing. Therefore, the submission of another official document which is suitable and intended for proving the identity of the owner shall be considered. Since the election technique proposed in this work allows vote casting in any preferred constituency within the electoral area, the identification document must contain the place of residence of the voter as well. This is necessary in order to identify the corresponding electoral district, thus the votes will count for the intended candidates. In this context, a German driving license is not appropriate because it does not provide information of the place of residence of the owner. Thus, the election notification could still be sent to all eligible voters in order to enable identification and authentication. The personal data of voters on the election notification could be entered manually into the system by the electoral committee. This is not objectionable from a legal point of view, because according to § 14.1 sentence 2 Federal Electoral Code, the electoral register can be maintained through an automatic process. Thereby, it must be ensured that necessary data for checking the eligibility to vote is used only for the intended purpose and can be transferred securely, for instance, by using cryptography.

Table 1 summarizes the advantages and disadvantages of using manual (Poll Workers) or automatic (German e-ID card) electronic voters' identification and authentication.

Table 1. Manual v.s. automatic electronic voters' identification and authentication

Manually (Poll Workers)	Automatically (German e-ID)
Advantages	*Disadvantages*
Compliant with the principle of universal elections	- (not all citizens posses it)
Disadvantages	*Advantages*
Not long-term secure	+ (adversary needs more effort)
Error prone	+
Time consuming	+
−	Transmit a pseudonym instead of voter's identity
−	Neither the PC of the electoral committee nor the electoral register knows the voter's identity
−	Eligibility check can be performed by the electronic voting machine

4   Vote Casting and Tallying

While maintaining the current election system and providing vote casting in any preferred constituency, it must be ensured that each voter is provided with the corresponding ballot of her constituency and that her vote is also counted in her constituency.

4.1   Paper Ballot

In case vote casting is still done with paper ballots, there are two possibilities to provide the corresponding voting ballot: either each constituency keeps enough paper ballots from all electoral districts or the electoral committee prints the corresponding paper ballot on demand. The first approach requires that each constituency provides enough paper ballots from all electoral districts in order to enable vote casting for all eligible voters. This approach appears impractical, because in Germany there are approximately 299 different ballots, and therefore not further considered. The tallying of votes can take place either in the constituency, where the voter casts her vote or in the constituency the voter is registered in. The first option violates the principle of the secret ballot in case only one voter (or few voters) casts her vote in a foreign constituency. In this case, the electoral committee knows what the respective voter voted for. The second approach requires that the paper ballot is sent to the constituency the voter is assigned to. Sending the paper ballot by post is not recommended because of the associated time delay. Another possibility would be to transfer the paper ballot electronically over the Internet. In that regard, the only remaining option is to scan and subsequently transfer the paper ballot to the respective constituency. In order to ensure the principle of free and secret elections the paper ballots would have to be scanned and transferred by the voter personally. Afterwards, the electronically recorded ballot must be encrypted right after scanning and transferred to the respective constituency over a secure channel, e.g. using standard cryptographic protocols for secure communication over the Internet, like SSL/TLS[5]. The votes (cast paper ballots) of other constituencies must finally be sent to a central location, whereas ballot secrecy must be ensured, for instance similar to postal voting.

This approach can be implemented in two ways: either using canonical ballots or encoded ballots, like in [27], [23], and [10]. In the canonical ballot approach, two major disadvantages are identified: First, electronic emissions might leak the voter's choice, thereby violating ballot secrecy. Second, it is technically not possible for the voter to verify, if the scanner has encrypted and sent her cast vote without changing it. The major disadvantage in the encoded ballot approach are the costs for special purpose equipment, special printers that are able to print scratch fields, like in [27], or two layered paper ballots, like in [23]. Furthermore, the verifiability of the proper ballot encoding is difficult to implement, as poll workers must have access to the corresponding private key(s) of foreign constituencies.

4.2   Electronic Ballot

As an alternative, voters could cast their vote electronically, directly on an electronic voting machine. In this case, the electronic vote could be transferred to the respective constituency just at the point of voting or afterwards. In order to ensure the principle of free and secret elections, the cast vote must be encrypted subsequently. For the sake of not interfering with ballot secrecy, two different machines should be used for voter authentication and vote casting and transmission.

---

[5] In this context, tow technical "unresolved" issues must be considered: First, poll workers must be able to check the SSL/TLS server's certificate. Second, secrecy is provided only as long as the used cryptographic mechanisms remain unbroken.

A number of technical proposals for end-to-end verifiable electronic voting schemes/systems, which enable electronic vote casting, can be considered for directly implementing this approach, for example [5], [18], and [28].

In section 4.1, electronic emissions are an issue with respect to ballot secrecy. Furthermore, costs for the provision and maintenance of electronic voting machines arise.[6] However, end-to-end verifiable electronic voting schemes/systems provide an increased level of verifiability in comparison with postal voting and the traditional voting in the "home constituency". By using electronic voting ballots, voters could also comprehend the impact of their cast vote much better as the system provides appropriate feedback (e.g. regarding invalid votes). Furthermore, this approach enables visually impaired people to cast their vote personally. This strengthens the principle of direct elections as well as the principle of secret elections, because these voters - in contrast to the regulations in § 57 of the Federal Electoral Code - do not need to take an auxiliary person into the voting booth. Thus, they can cast their vote secret and personally. Thus, it is conceivable that voters are informed about the validity of their vote.

Table 2 summarizes the advantages and disadvantages of using canonical paper ballots or electronic ballots on electronic voting machines for vote casting.

Table 2. Canonical paper v.s. electronic ballot on electronic voting machine

Canonical Paper Ballot (on demand)	**Electronic Ballot**
Advantages	*Disadvantages*
Established method	−
+	Costs for the provision and maintenance of electronic voting machines
Disadvantages	*Advantages*
−	Provides an increased level of cryptographic verifiability
−	Enables visually impaired people to cast their vote personally
Time for returning the ballots to the appropriate constituency	+
−	Voters can comprehend the impact of their cast vote much better

Table 3 summarizes the advantages and disadvantages of using encoded paper ballots or electronic ballots on electronic voting machines for vote casting.

The comparisons in table 2 and 3 show that electronic ballots on electronic voting machines have more advantages, especially with respect to cryptographic verifiability.

---

[6] Note, these costs are lower than the one for special printers.

Table 3. Encoded paper v.s. electronic ballot on electronic voting machine

Encoded Paper Ballot (on demand)	Electronic Ballot
Advantages	*Disadvantages*
Electronic emissions do not endanger ballot secrecy	−
Disadvantages	*Advantages*
Cryptographic verifiability is difficult to implement	+
−	Enables visually impaired people to cast their vote personally
Higher costs for special printers	+ (less costs for electronic voting machines)
−	Voters can comprehend the impact of their cast vote much better

5   Summary and Discussion

In this paper we have analysed the application of vote casting in any preferred constituency using the German parliamentary elections as an example. Thereby, we have shown that a centralised electoral register cannot be declined in general. Different approaches of voter identification and authentication, and checking the eligibility to vote were discussed. The ballot record and the telephone are no adequate solutions, while the manual input of personal data and the use of the German e-ID card have both their advantages and disadvantages. With regard to the vote casting and tallying, we have shown that both processes shall be carried out electronically in order to provide vote secrecy towards the electoral committee or any third party (e.g. an eavesdropping attack over the Internet) in the best way. In this case cryptographic mechanisms are essential. This means that the cast votes must be transferred in an encrypted form. Thus, the question remains whether this approach complies with the principle of the public nature of elections which has been modified by the Federal Constitutional Court of Germany in 2009. Thereafter, it must be possible for the citizen to check the essential steps in the election act and in the ascertainment of the results reliably and without special expert knowledge [14].

Cryptography is based on mathematical processes, which can be visualized to some extent, but until now these processes cannot be illustrated in a way that everyone is able to understand them, regardless of expert knowledge. Thus, the principle of the public nature of elections - just as the election principles in Article 38.1 sentence 1 Basic Law - is guaranteed without any reservation. However, the nature of things entails that not all election principles can be fulfilled in total purity (ref. to page 124 in [13]). Insofar, the restriction of one election principle is not unconstitutional per se, but may be justified as long as the constitution contains a respective authorisation, the deviation ensures the national political objectives or if the restriction is necessary in the interests of another election principle (ref. to page 369) in [15]). Vote casting in any preferred constituency could strengthen the principle of universal elections significantly. Thereby, those people, who decided to travel on Election Day in the short term or to be absent because of any other reason, are given the opportunity to participate in the election. Postal voting cannot provide this opportunity, as it requires an early application for a ballot paper. Furthermore, in contrast to postal voting, the moment of casting a vote would not be carried out in a private environment, but would remain in a controlled environment.[7] While voting in any preferred constituency, the compliance with all election principles could be ensured and controlled by the public, because everyone can see that the voter enters and leaves the polling booth alone. Although postal voting is an indispensable voting channel for all citizens who are not able to visit a constituency within the electoral area, it can be assumed based on the increasing number of postal voters, that this voting channel is also used by citizens who would not actually need it. However, in order to ensure the election principles in the best possible way, vote casting in any preferred constituency should be considered as an additional voting channel.

In future work we will further analyse, if its application is constitutionally compliant also in the context of regional and local elections. In that regard it needs to be said that German states often establish the active right to vote with a certain period of residence in the particular state.[8] Furthermore, it must be noticed that regional and local elections do not take place at the same time. Therefore, vote casting outside the corresponding federal state or municipality is only possible with very large organisational effort. Based on the findings of this work, we aim to concretise the legal requirements for the establishment of a centralised electoral register and to provide a practical solution for accessing the currently distributed electoral register infrastructure. Thereby, we will focus on both options for identification and authentication of voters, namely by using the election notification, the German e-ID card or a combination of both. Finally, we will analyse, if existing proposals for end-to-end verifiable electronic voting schemes/systems, namely [5], [18], and [28] that could implement the approach treated in section 4.2, comply with the findings of this work and fulfill the technical and legal requirements for electronic voting in Germany.

Acknowledgments. This paper has been developed within the project 'VerkonWa' - Verfassungskonforme Umsetzung von elektronischen Wahlen - which is funded by the Deutsche Forschungsgemeinschaft (DFG, German Science Foundation).

References

1. Austrian Ministry for Science and Research: Evaluierungsbericht: E-Voting bei den Hochschülerinnen- und Hochschüler-schaftswahlen 2009, E-voting evaluation report, Wien (2010) (in German)

---

[7] This criticises Richter [25].

[8] For example § 2.1 No. 3 Electoral Act for the parliament of the State of Hessen.

2. Briefwahl, http://www.bundeswahlleiter.de/de/glossar/texte/
   Briefwahl.html (online: accessed May 10, 2013) (in German)
3. Bräunlich, K., Kasten, A., Grimm, R.: Der neue Personalausweis zur Authentifizierung bei elektronischen Wahlen. In: Der 12. Deutsche IT-Sicherheitskongress
   - Sicher in die digitale Welt von morgen, pp. 211–225 (2011) (in German)
4. Bräunlich, K., Grimm, R., Kasten, A., Vowé, S., Jahn, N.: Der neue Personalausweis zur Authentifizierung von Wählern bei Onlinewahlen (2011) (in German)
5. Budurushi, J.: End-to-End Verifiable and Coercion Resistant Electronic Voting
   Protocol for Distributed Voting Machines in Polling Stations. Master thesis. Darmstadt (2012)
6. Budurushi, J., Neumann, S., Volkamer, M.: Smart Cards in Electronic Voting:
   Lessons Learned from Applications in Legally binding Elections and Approaches
   Proposed in Scientific Papers. In: Kripp, M.J., Volkamer, M., Grimm, R. (eds.)
   5th International Conference on Electronic Voting 2012, vol. 205, pp. 257–270.
   Gesellschaft für Informatik, Bregenz (2012)
7. Bundesgesetzblatt I, No. 21, pp. 383–388 (May 9, 1956),
   http://www.bgbl.de/Xaver/start.xav?startbk=Bundesanzeiger_BGBl&bk=
   Bundesanzeiger_BGBl&start=//*%5B@attr_id=%27bgbl156s0383.pdf%27%5D
   (online: accessed May 10, 2013) (in German)
8. Bundesgesetzblatt I, No. 26, pp. 1342–1350 (April 26, 2002),
   http://www.bgbl.de/Xaver/start.xav?startbk=Bundesanzeiger_BGBl&bk=
   Bundesanzeiger_BGBl&start=//*%5B@attr_id=%27bgbl102s1342.pdf%27%5D
   (online: accessed May 10, 2013) (in German)
9. Carracedo Gallardo, J., Belleboni, P.E.: Use of the New Smart Identity Card to Re-
   inforce Electronic Voting Guarantees. In: 4th International Conference for Internet
   Technology and Secured Transactions, pp. 1–6. IEEE Press, London (2009)
10. Chaum, D., Essex, A., Carback, R., Clark, J., Popoveniuc, S., Sherman, T.A.,
    Vora, L.P.: Scantegrity: End-to-End Voter-Verifiable Optical-Scan Voting. IEEE
    Security & Privacy, 40–46 (2008)
11. Deutscher Bundestag, Drucksache 17/10158,
    http://dipbt.bundestag.de/dip21/btd/17/101/1710158.pdf (online: accessed
    May 10, 2013) (in German)
12. Estonian National Electoral Committee: E-voting System General Overview,
    http://www.vvk.ee/public/dok/General_Description_E-Voting_2010.pdf
    (online: accessed May 10, 2013)
13. Federal Constitutional Court of Germany: Entscheidungen des Bundesverfassungs-
    gerichts (BVerfGE) 59, pp. 119–128 (1981)
14. Federal Constitutional Court of Germany: Entscheidungen des Bundesverfassungs-
    gerichts (BVerfGE) 123, pp. 39–88 (2009)
15. Federal Constitutional Court of Germany: Entscheidungen des Bundesverfassungs-
    gerichts (BVerfGE) 95, pp. 335–407 (1996)
16. Federal Office for Information Security: Advanced Security Mechanism for Machine
    Readable Travel Documents - Part 2. Technical report, BSI-TR-03110-2 (2012)
17. Federal Office for Information Security: Functional Specification eID-Server - Part
    1. Technical report, BSI-TR-03130-1 (2012)
18. Gibson, J.P., Lallet, E., Raffy, J.-L.: Engineering a Distributed e-Voting System
    Architecture: Meeting Critical Requirements. In: Giese, H. (ed.) ISARCS 2010.
    LNCS, vol. 6150, pp. 89–108. Springer, Heidelberg (2010)
19. Internet X.509 Public Key Infrastructure Certificate and Certificate Revocation
    List (CRL) Profile, http://tools.ietf.org/html/rfc5280 (online: accessed May
    10, 2013)

20. Meister, G., Hühnlein, D., Araujo, R.: eVoting with the European Citizen Card. In: Brömme, A., Busch, C., Hühnlein, D. (eds.) Proceedings of the Special Interest Group on Biometrics and Electronic Signatures, vol. 137, pp. 67–78. Gesellschaft für Informatik, Darmstadt (2008)

21. Mishra, A., Gupta, B.B., Joshi, R.C.: A Comparative Study of Distributed Denial of Service Attacks, Intrusion Tolerance and Mitigation Techniques. In: European Intelligence and Security Informatics Conference (EISIC), pp. 286–289 (2011)

22. Personalausweisgesetz (PAuswG),
    http://www.gesetze-im-internet.de/pauswg/BJNR134610009.html (online: accessed May 10, 2013) (in German)

23. Popoveniuc, S., Hosp, B.: An Introduction to PunchScan. In: Chaum, D., Jakobsson, M., Rivest, R.L., Ryan, P.Y.A., Benaloh, J., Kutylowski, M., Adida, B. (eds.) Towards Trustworthy Elections. LNCS, vol. 6000, pp. 242–259. Springer, Heidelberg (2010)

24. Referentenentwurf Bundesmeldegesetz (MG),
    http://philipbanse.de/docs/Referenenentwurf_Meldegesetz.pdf (online: accessed May 10, 2013) (in German)

25. Richter, P.: Briefwahl für alle? - Die Freigabe der Fernwahl und der Grundsatz der Öffentlichkeit der Wahl. In: Die Öffentliche Verwaltung, pp. 606–610. W. Kohlhammer GmbH (2010) (in German)

26. Rössler, T.: Electronic Voting Using Identity Domain Separation and Hardware Security Modules. In: Godart, C., Gronau, N., Sharma, S., Canals, G. (eds.) I3E 2009. IFIP AICT, vol. 305, pp. 1–12. Springer, Heidelberg (2009)

27. Ryan, Y.A.P., Bismark, D., Heather, J., Schneider, S., Xia, Z.: Prêt à voter: a voter-verifiable voting system. IEEE Transactions on Information Forensics and Security, 662–673 (2009)

28. Sandler, D.R., Wallach, D.S.: The case for networked remote voting precincts. In: Proceedings of the 3rd USENIX/ACCURATE Electronic Voting Technology Workshop, San Jose, CA (2008)

29. Schreiber, W.: Bundeswahlgesetz: Kommentar. Carl Heymanns Verlag, Köln (2009) (in German)

30. Subramani, S.: Denial of Service attacks and mitigation techniques: Real time implementation with detailed analysis. SANS Institute InfoSec Reading Room,
    http://www.sans.org/reading_room/whitepapers/detection/denial-service-attacks-mitigation-techniques-real-time-implementation-detailed-analysi_33764 (online: accessed May 10, 2013)

31. The Transport Layer Security (TLS) Protocol Version 1.2,
    http://tools.ietf.org/html/rfc5246 (online: accessed May 10, 2013)

Attacking the Verification Code Mechanism in the Norwegian Internet Voting System

Reto E. Koenig, Philipp Locher, and Rolf Haenni

Bern University of Applied Sciences, CH-2501 Biel, Switzerland
{reto.koenig,philipp.locher,rolf.haenni}@bfh.ch

Abstract. The security of the Norwegian Internet voting system depends strongly on the implemented verification code mechanism, which allows voters to verify if their vote has been cast and recorded as intended. For this to work properly, a secure and independent auxiliary channel for transmitting the verification codes to the voters is required. The Norwegian system assumes that SMS satisfies the necessary requirements for such a channel. This paper demonstrates that this is no longer the case today. If voters use smartphones or tablet computers for receiving SMS messages, a number of new attack scenarios appear. We show how an adversary may exploit these scenarios in systems providing vote updating and point out the consequences for the vote integrity in the Norwegian system. We also give a list of possible counter-measures and system enhancements to prevent and detect such attacks.

1 Introduction

In the design and implementation of secure Internet voting systems, the *secure platform problem* is one of the most challenging obstacles to overcome [23]. Given the manifold vulnerabilities of today's computers, particularly those caused by malicious software, it is inappropriate to assume that voters will have access to a reliable machine that works correctly under all possible circumstances. Voting protocols must therefore be designed to deal with the possibility that some voters will use machines that are infected by various types of possibly very sophisticated malware. In a worst-case scenario, the malware is designated to attack particular voting events, while remaining completely silent and therefore hard to detect at other times. Attacks of such a type can be launched with a few mouse clicks. Since the correct outcome of an election is of great significance for the whole electorate, infected computers become immediately a problem for everybody.

Recent malware attacks in other application areas have demonstrated that they represent a real and serious threat today. In 2012, for example, estimated 36 million Euros were stolen from several ten thousand bank customers all across Europe by a smart Trojan called *Eurograbber* [14]. In a recent report, the number of new Windows-based malware in 2012 is estimated as almost 1.4 million [2]. Increasing numbers of new malware are reported for other platforms, in particular in the emerging area of mobile devices (smartphones and tablet computers).

J. Heather, S. Schneider, and V. Teague (Eds.): VoteID 2013, LNCS 7985, pp. 76–92, 2013.

1.1   Existing Approaches

A malware attack against an Internet voting system may aim at violating either the secrecy or the integrity of the vote (or both). Full protection against both types of attacks is very hard to achieve. Possible full protection approaches are based on distributing trustworthy hardware devices to the voters, but this is very expensive [8]. Some other approaches suggest using trusted out-of-band channels such as regular postal mail. The idea is to securely exchange additional information between the voting system and the voters, which allows them to protect the privacy or to verify the integrity of the vote. There are two related ways of using such an auxiliary channel, each of which with its own pros and cons.

Code Voting [10,13,19,22]. The idea of code voting is to enter candidate codes instead of candidate names when casting a vote. These codes are distributed over a separate secure channel in form of personalized code sheets and differ from voter to voter. This prevents the voter's insecure platform from learning the actual candidate choice and from guessing the codes of other candidates. This simple mechanism thus provides privacy and integrity in the presence of designated malware, but it does not prevent the malware from not casting the vote at all or from casting votes with invalid codes. Another major problem of code voting is the restricted usability.

Verification Codes [3,9,11,16,21]. The setting here is similar to code voting, but instead of entering the codes of the selected candidates as printed on the personalized code sheet, voters only need to check if the codes match with what is displayed by the voting system after casting the vote. If the codes match, the voter has a strong indication that the vote has been cast and recorded as intended.[1] Since verifying the codes is an optional step, usability is not so much of an issue as in code voting. On the other hand, verification codes alone cannot prevent malware from breaking the secrecy of the vote.

Code voting and verification codes can be applied separately or in combination. If applied in combination, the vote secrecy is protected and a strong indication is given that the vote has been cast and recorded as intended. A general problem that affects all possible scenarios is the secure printing of the code sheets. It is usually solved by organizational and non-cryptographic technical measures. Another general problem is the possibility that malware can learn the codes in a system that supports vote updating. As soon as several codes are known to the malware, it can start fooling the voter and possibly cast a final vote that is different from the voter's intention.

---

[1] Some existing systems, for example the system used in the canton of Geneva in Switzerland [4, 27], use a simplified type of verification code in form of a picture, which differs from voter to voter, but not from candidate to candidate. In such a case, a correct verification code only implies that some vote has reached the voting server, but it does not guarantee its integrity.

The Norwegian Internet voting system is based on verification codes and supports vote updating [7, 18, 25].[2] To avoid that malware learns the verification codes, the existence of two separate out-of-band channels is assumed: Initially, the code sheets are sent by postal mail to the voter's home address (pre-channel), and after vote casting, an SMS message with the verification codes of the selected candidates is sent to the voter's mobile device (post-channel). This introduces additional trust assumptions, for example that SMS provides a sufficiently secure and truly out-of-band channel, which is strictly detached and completely independent from the Internet (voting channel). Since SMS-based one-time passwords are used for voter authentication, these assumptions are even more critical and may have much farther-reaching consequences when violated.

1.2   Contribution and Overview

In this paper, we provide evidence that SMS is no longer a sufficiently secure candidate for the out-of-band post-channel in the Norwegian Internet voting system. The main problem is the widespread use of smart mobile devices today, which provide all sorts of new attack scenarios. Eurograbber is a prominent example that illustrates the practicability and efficiency of such attacks. In a recent report [15], two students of ours demonstrated that such attacks can be executed using even less infrastructure than was required by Eurograbber. Not surprisingly, the attacks presented in the report are directly transferable to the Norwegian system, as they rely on equivalent trust assumptions.

Based on these findings, we provide a systematic overview and detailed description of the attacks that result from using the SMS channel—as proposed in the Norwegian system—in combination with vote updating. Our analysis gives enough technical detail to understand the attacks not only from a conceptual point of view, but also from the perspective of implementing corresponding malware. For each attack scenario discussed in our overview, we point out the consequences with respect to the secrecy and integrity of the vote. We also discuss the effectiveness of each attack in terms of practicability, scalability, and detectability. Finally, we propose some counter-measures for preventing or detecting such attacks, and therefore contribute to the improvement of the Norwegian system.

2   The Norwegian E-Voting System

In this section, we provide a high-level description of the Norwegian voting system as described in the available literature [5–7, 9, 25]. The system overview is given from the voter's perspective, as the attacks presented in Section 3 are not targeted towards the server infrastructure. Then we explain precisely the role of the verification codes and the underlying trust assumptions.

---

[2] In the available documents about the Norwegian system, verification codes are called *return codes* [6] or *receipt codes* [7]. To avoid any ambiguity with the concept of a receipt in the sense of receipt-free voting systems, we prefer to call them verification codes. Furthermore, code sheets are called *poll cards* [6] or *voting cards* [7]. We prefer to call them code sheets, as it is common in the code voting literature.

2.1   Overview of the Voting Process

According to the analysis of the Norwegian system in [7], the main actors involved in the vote casting process are the voter V, the voter's computer P, the ballot box B, the receipt generator R, the decryption service D, and the auditor A. It is assumed that they communicate over secure, authenticated channels, as shown in Figure 1 (or in [7]). Unidirectional channels are represented by single-ended arrows. All other channels are bidirectional. The offline pre-channel for sending the personalized code sheets to the voters by postal mail is not shown. In this paper, we adopt the assumptions that both the printing service and postal mail are sufficiently reliable and secure, i.e., we presume that voters receive their code sheet before the voting period begins, and that the candidate codes remain secret during the printing and transmission process.

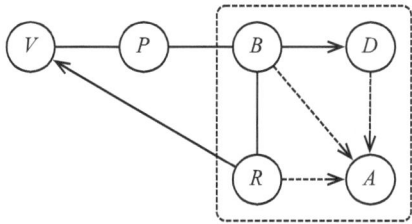

Fig. 1. The simplistic view of the communication channels of the Norwegian system as presented in [7]. This picture ignores the fact that most voters today receive SMS messages on smartphones or other mobile devices, which may be infected by malware. The direct arrow from the receipt generator to the voter is therefore an oversimplification of today's reality.

During the voting period, the voter first initiates the voter authentication mechanism provided by MinID, a two-level authentication service that was created to offer standardized authentication for various governmental services in Norway.[3] For this, the voter enters the personal credentials consisting of an identification number and a secret password. The MinID server then generates a one-time password (a five-digits code called *SMS code*) and sends it to the voter by SMS.[4] Finally, if the voter enters the correct SMS code, the authentication process succeeds.

After authentication, the voter selects the voting options using the computer and submits the vote. The submitted vote is encrypted and signed by the computer and sent to the ballot box. The ballot box blinds the vote and passes the blinded vote together with voter's personal identification number to the receipt generator. Based on the identification number the receipt generator computes the personalized verification codes of the blinded vote and sends them back to

---

[3] In upcoming Internet voting pilots, additional external authentication mechanisms will be supported (BankID, Buypass, Commfides).

[4] MinID users can order a sheet with multiple one-time passwords by postal mail.

the voter by SMS. Finally, the voter checks the received verification codes with those on the code sheet. At the end of the voting period, all encrypted votes are sent to the decryption service, where the votes are mixed and decrypted and the final tally is calculated. An auditor supervises the entire process.

Since vote updating is allowed in the Norwegian system, voters can repeat the above vote casting procedure multiple times, in the same or in different MinID sessions.[5] It is also possible to cast a final paper vote at the polling station, where any electronic vote is overridden. Note that vote updating provides some protection against vote buying and coercion.

2.2   Adversary Model and Trust Assumptions

The main purpose of the verification code mechanism is to give voters some feedback on whether the vote has been cast and recorded as intended. Matching verification codes should provide voters with strong evidence that everything worked properly, at least with very high probability, whereas non-matching or missing verification codes should provide strong evidence that something went wrong somewhere, which should then encourage voters to vote again, possibly on paper. For this mechanism to work—in addition to the assumption that the code sheets were generated, printed, and mailed securely—it is necessary to assume that the adversary's capabilities are restricted as follows [1, 7]:

1. The server infrastructure is not under the adversary's control, in particular
   - the MinID authentication service,
   - the ballot box,
   - the receipt generator.
2. The SMS post-channel cannot be intercepted, interrupted, or manipulated by the adversary.
3. The component on the voter's device used to receive and display SMS messages is not compromised or controlled by the adversary.
4. The adversary is polynomially bounded and thus incapable of breaking cryptographic primitives.

Otherwise, we consider an external adversary capable of controlling the Internet voting channel and compromising an arbitrary number of voting computers. Internal adversaries are excluded by the first assumption in the above list.

As the security of the Norwegian Internet voting system depends strongly on the verification code mechanism, any violation of the above assumptions may potentially lead to incorrect votes and thus to an incorrect election outcome. Of particular importance is the assumed security and independence of the SMS post-channel, over which the verification codes are transmitted to the voters. Accordingly, the post-channel as shown in Figure 1 goes from the receipt generator directly to the voter. Note that this is clearly a simplistic view, which does not

---

[5] The available protocol specification does not define whether vote updating in the same MinID session is supported or not [6,7]. Therefore, we take this possibility into account in our analysis.

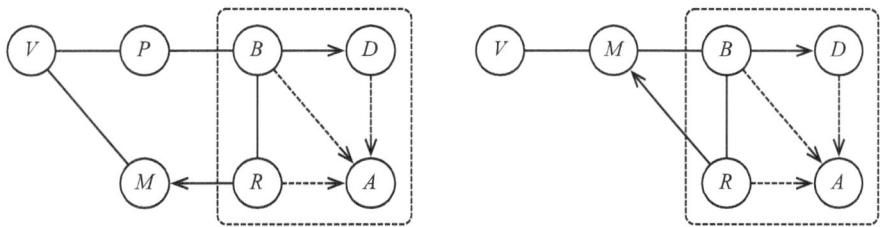

Fig. 2. A more complete picture of the communication channels in the Norwegian system: With two separate devices, a computer P and a mobile device M (left), or with a single mobile device M (right)

take into account that most users today use smartphones or tablet computers for sending and receiving SMS messages. Since these device are more and more comparable to ordinary computers, it is no longer legitimate to consider them immune against malware or other types of external attacks. Figure 2 shows two updates of Figure 1, one with an additional mobile device M and one with M replacing the voter's computer (e.g., when using a tablet computer for vote casting and as an SMS receiver). In comparison with Figure 1, this obviously creates a number of additional attack scenarios. We will discuss them in detail in the following section.

3   Attacking the SMS Channel in the Norwegian System

The verification mechanism in the Norwegian Internet voting system is thought to be a solution for the secure platform problem. It does not prevent malware from taking full control over the voter's computer or its web browser, but it aims at making such an attack detectable. In this section, we assume that the voter's computer is infected by malware, but that the voter is not aware of the infection. We suppose that the malware mainly resides inside the voter's web browser and is therefore capable of launching all sorts of *man-in-the-browser* (MITB) attacks against arbitrary web applications, including the web application of the Norwegian system. It may therefore modify the content of the displayed web pages, modify incoming or outgoing transactions, insert additional transactions, communicate with other computers over the network, or even use the computer's local WLAN, Bluetooth, IrDA (infrared communication), or audio interfaces. This can all happen in a completely covert fashion invisible to both the voter and the web application.

If such an MITB malware resides on the voter's computer, it can easily break the secrecy of the vote, for example by observing the voter's interaction with the web application and by transmitting a transcript to a remote computer. But this is not what the vote verification mechanism tries to avoid, its goal is only to protect the integrity of the vote. For this, the verification codes cannot simply be displayed on the screen of the voter's computer, because this would allow the malware to silently submit a vote update without the voter noticing. This is why the codes need to be delivered out-of-band.

In this section, we discuss three different attack scenarios for breaking the vote integrity in the Norwegian system. They correspond to the three pictures shown in Figures 1 and 2. In the first scenario, the SMS channel is attacked directly, by operating a fake GSM base transceiver station in the voter's proximity. In the second and third scenario, the mobile device used to receive SMS messages is attacked with additional malware. The practicability, scalability, and detectability of corresponding attacks is different in each scenario.

3.1   Attacking the Security of the SMS Channel

There are two different ways of attacking the SMS channel by an external adversary. Since SMS messages are transmitted over the GSM network, the airway traffic between the closest base transceiver station (BTS) and the mobile device is (optionally) encrypted with the weak and broken stream cipher A5/1 or A5/2. A *passive* attack consists in intercepting this traffic and by decrypting the A5-encrypted content. This attack requires only low-budget hardware (less than $100) and open-source software such as AirProbe and OsmocomBB.[6]

The practicability of an *active* attack with a fake GSM base transceiver station (also called *IMSI catcher*) has been shown by Chris Paget during a live demonstration at the Defcon conference in 2010 with a $1500 device made from of-the-shelf hardware and an open-source software called OpenBTS.[7] Once such a fake BTS is operating, it can serve as a proxy between the real GSM network and the GSM phones of any kind, covering an area of up to 35km radius. As GSM does not provide any kind of sender authentication, it is a simple task for a proxy to intercept, block, or fabricate SMS messages [12, 17, 20, 24, 26].

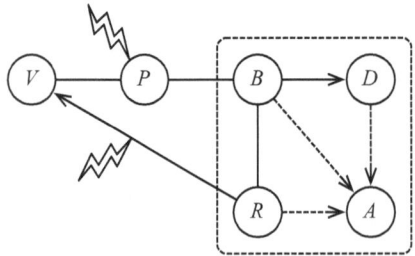

Fig. 3. A combined and synchronized attack against the voter's computer and the SMS channel

If the SMS post-channel in the Norwegian system is attacked as explained above, it can no longer protect the integrity of the vote, even if the SMS verification codes obtained after vote casting match. The attack scenario in Figure 3

---

[6] See http://bb.osmocom.org and https://svn.berlin.ccc.de/projects/airprobe.
[7] See http://wush.net/trac/rangepublic.

shows a situation where both the voter's computer and the SMS post-channel are under attack. If these attacks are coordinated by the same adversary, it is easy to bypass the verification code mechanism in the following way.

Attack 3.1. *Silent vote updating with blocked verification codes by fake BTS.*

1. *When a vote is cast, the MITB malware informs the fake BTS to withhold the second next SMS message from the receipt generator.*
2. *The fake BTS transmits the first SMS message from the receipt generator to the voter's mobile phone.*
3. *Within the same MinID session, but possibly with some delay to not attract too much attention, the MITB malware silently casts a second vote (vote updating).*
4. *The fake BTS blocks the second SMS message from the receipt generator.*

This attack is executed every time the voter casts a vote. The confirmation codes obtained over the SMS channel will always match and thus let the voter think that everything worked properly. As nothing suspicious happens on either side, except maybe for an increased percentage of vote updates, the attack is likely to remain unnoticed by both the voter and the voting system. However, the presence of a fake BTS is something that will draw somebody's attention sooner or later. In such a case, determining the location of the fake BTS is clearly not very difficult.

This attack clearly violates the vote integrity of the voters under attack, and thus leads to an incorrect election outcome. It is thus a serious security problem for the Norwegian Internet voting system. On the other hand, as the attack requires hardware infrastructure and maintenance from the adversary, and is geographically limited to the signal perimeter of the fake BTS, it has a very limited scalability and is therefore mainly applicable to local municipality elections.

3.2   Attacking the Independence of the SMS Channel

The key of the attack in the previous section is the adversary's ability to block the SMS message with the verification codes. This allows the MITB malware to silently submit a second vote without any noticeable consequences. The two attacks presented in this section are based on the same idea, but they do not require any hardware infrastructure to interrupt the SMS channel between the receipt generator and the voter. Figure 4 shows two different attack scenarios in which the required independence between the voting channel and the SMS post-channel is violated. This means that verification codes can no longer be transmitted out-of-band. In the first scenario, the adversary controls both the voter's computer P and the SMS-receiving mobile device M. In the second scenario, the adversary controls the single mobile device M used for casting votes and receiving SMS messages.

Attacking Two Devices. We consider now a combined attack against both the voter's computer and the voter's mobile device. Installing respective malware

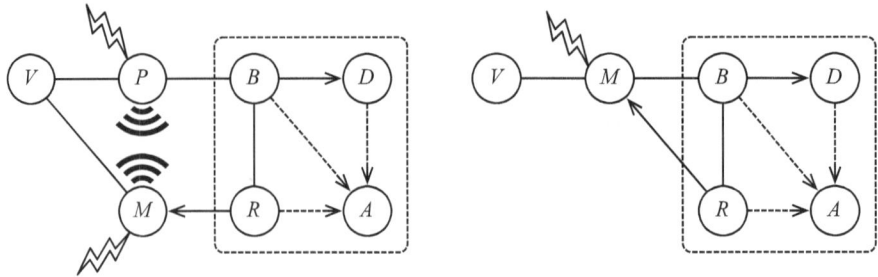

Fig. 4. Two attack scenarios of blocking the SMS post-channel for voters using a smart mobile device

on two different devices may appear nearly impossible, but one can easily think of a sophisticated social engineering attack, possibly launched by the malware of the first infected device to finally infect the other device with its malicious counterpart. For example, suppose the MITB malware on the voter's computer gets into possession of the voter's mobile phone number. Then it can send an SMS message to the voter's mobile device with a download invitation for a seemingly useful free app, for instance one the presents the political profiles of the candidates in the forthcoming election. If the voter follows the instructions, the double infection is established. The infection in the Eurograbber attack, where an SMS message instructed the victims to install a security update on their mobile device, was a social engineering attack of that type [14].

Recent technology advances may allow even simpler ways of infecting two devices simultaneously. A general trend pushed by the major technology providers today is to offer a uniform user experience on multiple devices with cloud-based synchronization of personal data and apps. Already today, both the Android and the iOS operating systems allow automatic app installation across multiple devices. The MITB malware on the voter's computer could therefore silently select its free malicious counterpart in the app store and therefore initiate the installation on the mobile device with ease, and without attracting too much attention.

If we suppose that both involved devices are infected by malware and thus controlled by the adversary, the attack is almost straightforward.

Attack 3.2. *Silent vote updating with blocked verification codes on the voter's mobile device.*

1. *When a vote is cast, the MITB malware informs its counterpart on the mobile device to withhold the second next SMS message from the receipt generator.*
2. *When the first SMS message from the receipt generator arrives, it is stored and displayed as usual on the mobile device.*

3. *Within in the same MinID session, but possibly with some delay to not attract too much attention, the MITB malware silently casts a second vote (vote updating).*
4. *When the second SMS message from the receipt generator arrives, it is blocked and immediately deleted by the malware on the mobile device.*

In Step 1 of this attack, the two malware counterparts need to setup a unidirectional communication channel from the voter's computer to the mobile device. We consider four attack options for doing so:

a) One of the simplest options is Bluetooth. Provided that the two devices are already paired, a Bluetooth connection can be established very easily and without the user noticing. Since Bluetooth connections are point-to-point, no traces are left on devices other than the ones involved in the attack. Sophisticated malware takes care of removing all possible local traces such as entries in log files or in the device's usage history.
b) A standard TCP/IP network connection is another simple option, provided that the mobile device is connected at the time of the attack. If both devices are connected to the same LAN, 'finding' each other is rather simple, for example by locally broadcasting an inconspicuous handshake message. If they are not connected to the same LAN, for instance if the mobile device is connected over a cellular data network (GPRS, UMTS, EDGE, LTE), then a remote server to which each malware connects is needed to establish the connection. In both cases, some inevitable traces are left along the path that the message has taken in the network. These traces may help to uncover the attack in suspicious cases.
c) If the malware on the voter's computer knows the mobile device's phone number, then sending an SMS message or making a call to alert the mobile device might be another easy-to-implement option. When the mobile phone receives such an alert SMS, it silently blocks and immediately deletes the message. If it receives a call, the call is suppressed and deleted from the list of incoming calls. Traces are only left at the voter's mobile network carrier, through which the SMS message or call is delivered.
d) Another interesting option is to use the audio output of the voter's computer to emit a ultrasonic audio signal (>20kHz), which is not audible by humans, but which can be captured by the mobile device's microphone.[8] This leaves no traces at all on both sides.

The fact that most of these options leave almost no evident traces, they are very hard to detect in real-time and almost impossible to uncover in retrospect. Furthermore, as no external command-and-control mechanism is needed in order to execute the attack on the voter's side, there is no channel back to the adversary.

---

[8] While almost all microphones are capable of capturing ultrasonic signals, only so-called *piezoelectric loudspeakers* are able to emit them. If no piezoelectric loudspeakers are available at the voter's computer, an audible acoustic signal could be used to carry out the attack. This may attract the voter's attention, but not necessarily raise much suspicion if obfuscated properly.

This simplifies the preparation and execution of the attack and decreases the chance of being detected.

Several of the above attack options have been implemented in the attack against mTAN-based online banking applications as presented in [15]. This report demonstrates that implementing such an attack is surprisingly simply and only requires basic knowledge in IT security and limited skills in programming mobile devices. For example, taking full control over the SMS functionality in the Android operating system is done in a few lines of code, including the deletion of corresponding log file entries.[9] Even sending and receiving messages over an ultrasonic channel is just a matter of using the right software libraries.[10]

Attacking a Single Device. Finally, we suppose that the voter uses the same device for casting the vote and for receiving the verification code. Today's tablet computers provide both a full-featured web browser with a sufficiently large display and GSM communication for sending and receiving SMS messages. This attack scenario with a single mobile device M is shown on the right hand side of Figure 4. Among the scenarios discussed in this section, it is clearly the simplest one. Compared to Attack 3.1, no additional hardware equipment is needed to execute the attack. Compared to Attack 3.2, only a single device needs to be infected by malware and no additional communication channel needs to be established. As the malware needs to control both the web browser and the SMS component of the voter's mobile device, it must be slightly more powerful than a simple MITB malware. The concrete steps for the malware to execute the attack are the following.

Attack 3.3. *Silent vote updating with blocked verification codes on a single mobile device.*

1. *When a vote is cast, the malware on the voter's mobile device starts monitoring the incoming SMS messages.*
2. *When the first SMS message from the receipt generator arrives, it is stored and displayed as usual on the mobile device.*
3. *Within in the same MinID session, but possibly with some delay to not attract too much attention, the malware silently casts a second vote (vote updating).*
4. *When the second SMS message from the receipt generator arrives, it is blocked and immediately deleted.*

Besides its simplicity, this attack has the advantage of only affecting the voter's mobile device and thus not leaving any traces at all at other places. Even the traces left on the infected device can be entirely removed, if the malware is sophisticated enough to delete all entries in corresponding log files, in the device's usage history, or in the list of notifications. Therefore, the adversary's risk of being detected is even smaller than in the two attacks presented before. On the

---

[9] *SMS Popup* provides free source code for programming SMS applications in the Android operating system, see http://code.google.com/p/android-smspopup.

[10] *SSCConnect* is an example of an ultrasonic communication tool for both the Android and the iOS operating systems, see
http://www.sonicom.co.kr/main_eng/m_3_1.php.

other hand, as long as only a minority of voters is using a single mobile device for both vote casting and verification, the scalability of the attack is fairly limited.

3.3   Attacking the MinID Authentication Service

All three attacks presented so far are based on the assumption that the SMS post-channel is under the adversary's control. If this is actually the case, a more general attack with much farther-reaching consequences can be launched in a very similar way against the MinID authentication service. It is also based on blocking incoming SMS messages, the ones that contain the one-time passwords from the MinID authentication server. The attack scenario here is identical to the online banking attacks presented in [15].

The attack works in all three scenarios presented so far. As an example, we consider here the scenario with two devices, one for accessing the MinID-based web application and one for receiving the SMS message with the one-time password. As before, we suppose that both devices are infected by malware from the same adversary. To prepare an attack, the MITB malware intercepts the victim's MinID credentials during the login process of a MinID-based service. The credentials are either stored locally on the victim's computer, sent over the network to a remote server, or transmitted to the malware's counterpart on the victim's mobile device (using one of the unidirectional communication channels proposed in Attack 3.2). The place where the credentials are stored or sent to determines the location from where the actual attack will be launched.

The simplest possibility for executing the attack is the third one. In that case, the malware on the mobile device knows the MinID credentials and is able to block incoming SMS messages. It can then initiate the MinID login process, submit the victims's correct credentials, retrieve the one-time password from the incoming SMS message, block the SMS message from being displayed to the user, and finally submit the one-time password to complete the authentication process. The web application will then accept the malware as a legitimate user and give access to its resources and functionalities. All this happens silently in the background, possibly while the user is not using the device.

All MinID-based applications are affected equally by this attack. In an attack against the Norwegian voting system, it could be used to postpone the final vote cast to a different MinID session, which obfuscates the attack further. Note that the attack is even easier to implement in the scenario with a single device.

4   Preventing and Detecting the Attack

What should the people behind the Norwegian system do in the light of the attacks presented in the previous section? In this section, we suggest some countermeasures and enhancements, which may help detecting or even preventing such attacks. Recall that all attacks depend on the vote updating feature of the Norwegian system and on the adversary's ability to silently block and discard incoming SMS messages from the receipt generator. The proposition listed below can be implemented separately or in combination.

No Vote Updating. The simplest but most radical counter-measure against all proposed attacks is to discard vote updating on the electronic channel. This feature offers some protection against vote buying and coercion, but it is also responsible for undermining the verification code mechanism in the proposed attacks. Without vote updating, the first submitted vote is the one that counts. This does not prevent the malware on the voter's computer from submitting a different vote, but then the verification codes will no longer match. The malware on the voter's mobile device could also try to block the SMS message from the receipt generator, but this would immediately make the voter suspicious. In both cases, voters are instructed to cast a final vote on paper. This shows that the verification code mechanism perfectly works without vote updating. To allow or to discard vote updating is therefore a trade-off between solving the secure platform problem or preventing vote buying and coercion.

Vote Updating in Different Sessions. A less drastic counter-measure is to allow vote updating, but to require different MinID sessions for doing so.[11] This would clearly prevent the malware from executing the third step in each of the Attacks 3.1 to 3.3, but the adversary would still have the option of attacking the MinID authentication service as presented in Section 3.3. The people behind the Norwegian system could then argue that they are not responsible for the MinID security, but this does not solve the problem. Note that the MinID security could be improved by delivering multiple one-time passwords beforehand by postal mail (which is currently an option for users with no registered phone number) or on a secure hardware token.

Voting TAN. Another possible counter-measure is based on the fact that a secure pre-channel already exists for delivering the code sheets to the voters by postal mail. This channel could therefore be used for other purposes without much additional effort. We propose to include an indexed list of additional one-time passwords. Such a password plays the role of a *transaction authentication number* (TAN), which voters need to enter for casting a vote. As the malware will always be unaware of the correct next voting TAN, this would again prevent the third step in each of the Attacks 3.1 to 3.3. The adversary could then try to get into possession of some voting TANs with a phishing attack, but this would clearly lower the overall effectiveness of the attack. Enhancing the Norwegian voting system with voting TANs seems therefore to be a viable solution, even if it slightly decreases the usability. Note that it also restricts the number of vote updates, which could be exploited by a vote buyer or a coercer.

CAPTCHA. Each attack presented in this paper exploits the fact that the voting servers cannot distinguish if a vote has been cast by the voter or by the malware on the voter's computer. CAPTCHA is a widely applied challenge-response test to prevent automated software from performing actions in behalf

---

[11] From showing a draft of this paper to Christian Bull, the Chief Security Officer of the Norwegian e-voting project, we have learned that the actual implementation already prevents vote updating within the same MinID session.

of humans. Voters could therefore be asked to solve a CAPTCHA when casting a vote. Under the assumption that CAPTCHAs cannot be solved automatically by the malware (using sophisticated OCR software or cheap human labor), this would again prevent the execution of the third step in each of the Attacks 3.1 to 3.3. Note that enhancing the Norwegian system with CAPTCHAs is very easy to implement, but it would decrease the overall usability.

Trusted SMS Receiver. If we neglect the threat of Attack 3.1, in which a hardware infrastructure is needed to interrupt the SMS post-channel, we can assume that the SMS message from the receipt generator reaches the mobile device to which it is sent. The remaining problem then is the malware's ability to block the SMS message from being displayed, as proposed in Attack 3.2 and Attack 3.3. To solve this problem, voters could be equipped with a trusted tiny SMS receiver, which does nothing else than displaying incoming SMS messages from a dedicated set of certified senders (receipt generator, MinID authentication service). If produced in large numbers, we expect the price for such tiny SMS receivers with a small display and an integrated SIM card to be reasonably small.

An additional measure to prevent Attack 3.1 is to attach a one-time password to the SMS message from the receipt generator. After checking the verification codes, the voter needs to enter the password to finalize the vote cast. To prevent the adversary from intercepting this password when the SMS message passes through the fake BTS, it must be encrypted by the receipt generator and decrypted by the trusted SMS receiver. Another possible counter-measure against Attack 3.1 is to let the trusted SMS receiver automatically send a digitally signed SMS acknowledgment back to the receipt generator.

Trusted Hardware Token. In the previous solution with the trusted SMS receiver, we suggested a digitally signed SMS acknowledgment as an ultimate measure to prevent Attack 3.1. Note that the same idea works independently of using SMS as transmission channel. The SMS receiver could therefore be replaced by a trusted hardware token with the ability to receive and display encrypted messages and to return a signed acknowledgment to the receipt generator. Such devices are available on the market, for example the *Zone Trusted Information Channel* (ZTIC), which establishes an end-to-end TLS connection via the user's untrusted computer to a remote server [28,29]. Under the assumption that such devices are trustworthy in displaying all incoming messages, the MITB malware could still block the final acknowledgment message, but this would attract attention on the server side where the acknowledgment is expected.

Analyzing Vote Update Patterns. The common denominator of the attacks presented in this paper is that they all exploit the vote updating feature of the Norwegian system. Shortly after a vote has been cast from an infected computer, a vote update from the same voter is initiated by the malware. This obviously generates statistical patterns in the electronic ballot box, which differ from normal usage patterns. Even the vote updating frequency may already be a good

Table 1. Overview of the strengths and weaknesses of the three attacks and corresponding options presented in this paper

		Practicability	*Scalability*	*Non-Detectability*	*Overall Risk*
Attack 3.1		low	low	low	low
Attack 3.2	a.	medium	medium	high	medium
	b.		high	medium	medium
	c.		high	medium	medium
	d.		high	high	high
Attack 3.3		high	medium	high	high

indicator for detecting an attack on a statistical basis. Corresponding plausibility tests could be added to the Norwegian system.[12]

5   Conclusion

In this paper, we analyzed the security of the verification code mechanism in the Norwegian Internet voting system. Our analysis takes the perspective of an adversary, who tries to interrupt the SMS post-channel, which is needed to transmit the verification codes to the voter after casting a vote. We investigated three different attack scenarios, in which the adversary is able to submit a fake vote update in the name of an eligible voter. The key for the adversary to execute such an attack is to block the SMS message from the receipt generator, which would make the voter suspicious when delivered. In each attack scenario, the interruption of the SMS channel is achieved in a different way.

In Table 1, we summarize the three attack scenarios by rating them with respect to the most relevant criteria: practicability, scalability, non-detectability. Attack 3.1 is clearly the least practical and scalable one, and the presence of a fake BTS is likely to attract attention. Hence, it receives our weakest overall rating. Much more practical and scalable is Attack 3.2, even if infecting two devices simultaneously with malware poses a supplementary challenge to get started. In Attack 3.3, only a single device needs to be infected, but the scalability is limited to the percentage of voters to which this attack scenario applies. Since Attack 3.2 (depending on the chosen option) and Attack 3.3 are also very hard to detect, we evaluate them both as highly risky for the Norwegian system.

Our final conclusion and general recommendation for the persons in charge of the Norwegian system is not to underestimate these types attacks. Similar attacks against online banking services have already demonstrated that they represent a real threat, and we know from our students that they are not very difficult to implement. Therefore, we recommend making the Norwegian system more resistant against these types of attack, for example by implementing some of the proposed counter-measures.

---

[12] In the 2011 pilots of the Norwegian Internet voting system, 3.6% of the voters eligible to vote electronically submitted multiple votes.

As a final note, we want to emphasize that the main threat results from the smartphone, which is an insecure platform per se. Implementing the verification code mechanism as a smartphone app is therefore not a viable solution.[13]

Acknowledgments. We thank the anonymous reviewers for their thorough reviews and appreciate the comments and suggestions. This research has been supported by the Swiss National Science Foundation (project No. 200021L_140650).

References

1. Ansper, A., Heiberg, S., Lipmaa, H., Øverland, T.A., van Laenen, F.: Security and trust for the Norwegian e-voting pilot project E-Valg 2011. In: Jøsang, A., Maseng, T., Knapskog, S.J. (eds.) NordSec 2009. LNCS, vol. 5838, pp. 207–222. Springer, Heidelberg (2009)
2. Benzmüller, R.: MalwareReport: Half-yearly report (January-June 2012). Tech. rep., G Data SecurityLabs (2012)
3. Chaum, D., Carback, R., Clark, J., Essex, A., Popoveniuc, S., Rivest, R.L., Ryan, P.Y.A., Shen, E., Sherman, A.T., Vora, P.L.: Scantegrity II: End-to-end verifiability by voters of optical scan elections through confirmation codes. IEEE Transactions on Information Forensics and Security 4(4), 611–627 (2009)
4. Chevallier, M., Warynski, M., Sandoz, A.: Success factors of Geneva's e-voting system. Electronic Journal of e-Government 4(2), 71–78 (2006)
5. Cortier, V., Wiedling, C.: A formal analysis of the Norwegian E-voting protocol. In: Degano, P., Guttman, J.D. (eds.) POST 2012. LNCS, vol. 7215, pp. 109–128. Springer, Heidelberg (2012)
6. Gebhardt Stenerud, I.S., Bull, C.: When reality comes knocking–Norwegian experiences with verifiable electronic voting. In: 5th International Workshop on Electronic Voting, EVOTE 2012, Bregenz, Austria, pp. 21–33 (2012)
7. Gjøsteen, K.: Analysis of an internet voting protocol. IACR Cryptology ePrint Archive 2010/380 (2010)
8. Haenni, R., Koenig, R.E.: Voting over the Internet on an insecure platform. In: Design, Development, and Use of Secure Electronic Voting Systems. IGI Global (accepted, 2013)
9. Heiberg, S., Lipmaa, H., van Laenen, F.: On e-vote integrity in the case of malicious voter computers. In: Gritzalis, D., Preneel, B., Theoharidou, M. (eds.) ESORICS 2010. LNCS, vol. 6345, pp. 373–388. Springer, Heidelberg (2010)
10. Helbach, J., Schwenk, J.: Secure internet voting with code sheets. In: Alkassar, A., Volkamer, M. (eds.) VOTE-ID 2007. LNCS, vol. 4896, pp. 166–177. Springer, Heidelberg (2007)
11. Helbach, J., Schwenk, J., Schäge, S.: Code voting with linkable group signatures. In: Krimmer, R., Grimm, R. (eds.) 3rd International Workshop on Electronic Voting, EVOTE 2008. Lecture Notes in Informatics, vol. P-131, pp. 209–222. Gesellschaft für Informatik E.V., Bregenz (2008)
12. Hubacher, I.: Management Demo: Intercepting SMS. Bachelor thesis, Bern University of Applied Sciences, Biel, Switzerland (2011)

---

[13] In a recent talk at the *Verifiable Voting Schemes Workshop* in Luxembourg on March 22nd, 2013, Jan Willemson suggested such a solution for the Estonian system.

13. Joaquim, R., Ribeiro, C., Ferreira, P.: Improving remote voting security with code-Voting. In: Chaum, D., Jakobsson, M., Rivest, R.L., Ryan, P.Y.A., Benaloh, J., Kutylowski, M., Adida, B. (eds.) Towards Trustworthy Elections. LNCS, vol. 6000, pp. 310–329. Springer, Heidelberg (2010)
14. Kalige, E., Burkey, D.: A case study of Eurograbber: How 36 million euros was stolen via malware. Tech. rep., Versafe & Check Point Software Technologie (2012)
15. Klaus, S., Brei, D.: Sicherheit von E-Banking auf Smart-Platforms. Bachelor thesis, Bern University of Applied Sciences, Biel, Switzerland (2013)
16. Lipmaa, H.: Two simple code-verification voting protocols. IACR Cryptology ePrint Archive 2011/317 (2011)
17. Meyer, U., Wetzel, S.: On the impact of GSM encryption and man-in-the-middle attacks on the security of interoperating GSM/UMTS networks. In: 15th IEEE International Symposium on Personal, Indoor and Mobile Radio Communications, PIMRC 2004, Barcelona, Spain, vol. 4, pp. 2876–2883 (2004)
18. Øberg, M.W.: Improving the Norwegian Internet Voting Protocol. Master's thesis, Norwegian University of Science and Technology (2011)
19. Oppliger, R., Schwenk, J., Helbach, J.: Protecting code voting against vote selling. In: 4. Jahrestagung des Fachbereichs Sicherheit der Gesellschaft für Informatik e.V., Sicherheit 2008, Saarbrücken, Germany, pp. 193–204 (2008)
20. Perez, D., Pico, J.: A practical attack against GPRS/EDGE/UMTS/HSPA mobile data communications. White paper, Taddong S.L. (2011)
21. Ryan, P.Y.A.: Prêt à voter with confirmation codes. In: Shacham, H., Teague, V. (eds.) Electronic Voting Technology Workshop/Workshop on Trustworthy Elections, EVT/WOTE 2011, San Francisco, USA (2011)
22. Ryan, P.Y.A., Teague, V.: Pretty good democracy. In: Christianson, B., Malcolm, J.A., Matyáš, V., Roe, M. (eds.) Security Protocols 2009. LNCS, vol. 7028, pp. 111–130. Springer, Heidelberg (2013)
23. Schläpfer, M., Volkamer, M.: The secure platform problem: Taxonomy and analysis of existing proposals to address this problem. In: 6th International Conference on Theory and Practice of Electronic Governance, ICEGOV 2012, Albany, USA (2012)
24. Song, Y., Zhou, K., Chen, X.: Fake BTS attacks of GSM system on software radio platform. Journal of Networks 7(2), 275–281 (2012)
25. Spycher, O., Volkamer, M., Koenig, R.: Transparency and technical measures to establish trust in Norwegian Internet voting. In: Kiayias, A., Lipmaa, H. (eds.) VoteID 2011. LNCS, vol. 7187, pp. 19–35. Springer, Heidelberg (2012)
26. van den Broek, F.: Catching and Understanding GSM-Signals. Master's thesis, Radboud University Nijmegen (2010)
27. von Bergen, P.: Analyse du code source de l'application d'e-voting de Genève. Project report, Bern University of Applied Sciences, Biel, Switzerland (2013)
28. Weigold, T., Hiltgen, A.: Secure confirmation of sensitive transaction data in modern Internet banking services. In: World Congress on Internet Security, WorldCIS 2011, London, U.K., pp. 125–132 (2011)
29. Weigold, T., Kramp, T., Hermann, R., Höring, F., Buhler, P., Baentsch, M.: The Zurich Trusted Information Channel – An efficient defence against man-in-the-middle and malicious software attacks. In: Lipp, P., Sadeghi, A.-R., Koch, K.-M. (eds.) Trust 2008. LNCS, vol. 4968, pp. 75–91. Springer, Heidelberg (2008)

A Formal Model for the Requirement of Verifiability in Electronic Voting by Means of a Bulletin Board

Katharina Bräunlich and Rüdiger Grimm

University of Koblenz-Landau, Department of Computer Science, Koblenz, Germany
{hupfi,grimm}uni-koblenz.de

Abstract. Trust in an electronic voting system is an essential premise for electronic elections. Trust in a system can be strengthened by controlling its correct functioning. There are two ways to assure the correct functioning of a system. Firstly, before using a system, neutral experts can evaluate and certify the security of its implementation. Secondly, while using the system, its users can verify its outcome by appropriate verification tools. Verifiability is a specific security function, which is subject to certification itself. This paper presents a formal security requirements model for the verifiability of electronic voting systems by means of a Bulletin Board that publishes all important communication steps without violating the secrecy of voting.

Keywords: Electronic Voting, Verifiability, Formal Specification, Common Criteria, IT System Evaluation and Certification, Bulletin Board.

1 Introduction

Trust in the electronic voting system is an essential premise for electronic voting. One way to strengthen the trust of the voters in the electronic voting system, is the assurance of system security by means of verifiability. In order to grant *end-to-end-verifiability* [1], the essential steps of the election have to be retraceable by the voters. The essential steps of the election are the marking and encryption of the vote, the casting of the encrypted vote (=ballot)[1] and the counting of the ballots from the ballot box. Thus, the success of the following steps has to be verifiable:

(V1) *Cast-as-intended*

The voter can ascertain himself that the ballot is correctly encrypted and thus, represents his voting decision correctly. In order to protect ballot secrecy, cast-as-intended can only be verified by the voter himself. Furthermore, the voter can only verify cast-as-intended *before* the ballot has been cast into the ballot.[2]

---

[1] In traditional paper-based voting, a ballot is a vote sheet covered by an envelope against unauthorized eyes. Encryption is a cryptographic means to cover the electronic vote against unauthorized eyes.

[2] Due to this restriction, the use of decoy credentials or decoy receipts is not covered in this paper.

J. Heather, S. Schneider, and V. Teague (Eds.): VoteID 2013, LNCS 7985, pp. 93–108, 2013.

(V2) *Recorded-as-cast*

The voter can retrace that his ballot is correctly transmitted and stored in the ballot box. In order to protect receipt-freeness, recorded-as-cast has to be implemented such that the voter cannot prove his voting decision (to others). The verification of recorded-as-cast can take place directly after the ballot casting or after the voting phase.

(V3) *Counted-as-recorded*

The voter as well as the broad public can verify the election result. I.e. it has to be verifiable that all ballots from the ballot box are counted-as-recorded.

End-to-end-verifiability as described above is one way to assure system security and thus, to strengthen the trust of the voters in the electronic voting system. Another way is the certification of the electronic voting system. As discussed in [2], these approaches are not exclusive but should be combined in order to obtain the best possible result.

The *Common Criteria for Information Technology Security Evaluation (CC)* [3] are a common standard to evaluate and certify the security of IT systems while the *Common Evaluation Methodology (CEM)* [3] specifies the framework for the evaluation of such systems. An advantage of the CC is the structured and systematic specification of security requirements for an IT system in terms of Protection Profiles or Security Targets. A *Protection Profile (PP)* specifies a product-independent description of security requirements in a group of products, e.g. online voting products in general. A *Security Target (ST)* represents a product-specific and thus, implementation-dependent specification of security requirements for a specific product, e.g. an implemented online voting system. The CC allows to evaluate (and then, to certify) a PP or the implemented security functions of a product against a specified ST. The ST may refer to a certified PP.

A PP is evaluated with respect to its completeness and consistence. It has to be proven that the identified threats, assumptions and security policies are completely covered by the security objectives of the system or its operational environment. Furthermore, the CC define seven *Evaluation Assurance Levels (EAL)*. These EAL indicate the evaluation depth from EAL 1 'functional tested' to EAL 7 'formally verified and tested'. They are hierarchically ordered such that each EAL represents more assurance than all lower EALs. The increase in assurance is not only achieved by an increasing evaluation depth but also by an increasing scope of the evaluation, i.e. which documents are required and included in the evaluation (from software and documentation to a formal model). For instance, the CC Protection Profile 0037 [4] defines a basic set of security requirements for online voting products and requires an evaluation according to EAL2+ (structural tested). EAL2+ seems to be sufficient for non-parliamentary elections. However, parliamentary elections demand a evaluation depth of EAL 5 or higher. A CC evaluation according to EAL 5 or higher claims for the application of formal methods [3] and requires the proof that the security functions enforce the security properties [5].

This paper presents a formal model for the requirement of verifiability in electronic voting. We do not describe verifiability as an abstract property of a voting system. Instead we select a bulletin board as a concrete verification mechanism and specify verifiability as a security property of the bulletin board. A bulletin board is a public channel like, for example, a website [6]. Information (e.g. ballots) are published on the bulletin board such that the voter and the public can verify the election without losing ballot secrecy.

The formalization of verifiability in this paper helps to clarify and better understand the requirement of verifiability. It can also serve as a formal security model for electronic voting systems which enables the CC evaluation of online voting products according to EAL5 or higher.

This paper is organized as follows: In section 2 related work is discussed. In section 3 the formal basics that are needed for the formalization of verifiability are explained. In section 4 a formal security model for electronic voting systems concerning verifiability is presented. For a better readability, the formalisms in section 3 and 4 are enriched with examples. In terms of the CC, the formal model in this paper addresses the PP and thus, the implementation-independent requirements. Due to the implementation-independent und universal character of the PP, the examples are chosen from different products/protocols. In section 4.4 it is described how our formal model guarantees end-to-end-verifiability. This description is complemented with an example. Section 5 presents a conclusion and future work.

2   Related Work

The following related work is (according to the focus of this paper) restricted to the formal specification of the requirement of verifiability in electronic voting, particularly with regard to a CC evaluation according to EAL 5 or higher.

There exist several works concerning the formal specification of privacy properties as for example [7],[8],[9],[10]. While the authors in [11] give a formalization of fairness and eligibility, [12] presents a formalization of eligibility, vote integrity and nonreuseability. Furthermore, [13] and [14] define eligibility and protection against precipitance (haste) of the voter in a formal way. But none of these works considers vote verifiability.

Indeed, the concept of verifiability or the development of voter verifiable voting schemes is subject to many publications in the academic literature as for example [1],[6],[15], [16],[17], [18]. However, only few works address the formalization of verifiability. In [19] and [20] a formalization of individual and universal verifiability is applied to a concrete protocol, namely the protocol by Fujioka et al. [21]. But these two works do not provide a generic approach to verify security properties in the sense of a CC evaluation.

In [22] a bulletin board for electronic voting systems is modelled. However, this formal framework is used to specify privacy issues as coercion-resistance and forced vote spoiling but do not address verifiability.

[23] presents a formalization of verifiability in the applied pi calculus and thus, in a process-oriented formalism. According to [5], it has to be proven in

the course of a CC evaluation (a) that the security functions enforce the security properties and (b) that the evaluated product conforms to the formal model. Compliance of the product with the formal model (b) is verified by analyzing the product's implementation of the security functions with respect to the formal model. Thus, a formal security model for a CC product evaluation requires the specification of state transition rules. A process-oriented formalization like [23] is suitable to verify properties of protocols. However, it is unsuitable to evaluate concrete electronic voting products according to the CC.

In this work a state-oriented formal security model w.r.t. verifiability is presented which provides with the security theorem (sec. 4.3) a proof of the enforcement of the security properties (see (a) above) as demanded for the CC evaluation.

3   Formal Basics

The formalization of verifiability requires some formal basics which are described in this section.

Let *Agents* be the set of all communication partners who communicate with each other by exchanging messages. *Messages* denote the set of all messages like for example *startElection, stopElection* or *castBallot*.

According to the Dolev-Yao model [24], we assume that an attacker has full control of the public network. Thus, we differentiate between messages that are sent via *public* or *private channels*. The attacker can read any message which is exchanged via a public channel, as, for example, a plaintext message which is transmitted over an insecure network. However, private channels are not under the control of the attacker. The attacker cannot read privately exchanged messages as, for example, an encrypted message which is transmitted between the voting server and the voting client.

Definition 1. *(Events)*
Let Channel := private, public. Then Events denotes the set of all possible events and is defined as:

$$Events \subseteq \pm Messages \times Agents \times Agents \times Channel$$

Let $m \in Messages$ and $a, b \in Agents$. A negative sign of a message m indicates that the associated event is being sent; a positive sign indicates the reception of an event. For instance, (m, a, b, pub) represents the event that a receives the message m from b via a public channel. Accordingly, $(-m, b, a, priv)$ specifies the event that b sends the message m to a via a private channel.

Definition 2. *(Projection)*
Let $1 \leq k \leq n$. Then π_k denotes the set-theoretic projection of a Cartesian product of n sets on its k-th component.

Let $x \in Events$. Then $\pi_1(x)$ returns the message m of the associated event, $\pi_2(x)$ returns a who is the sender of the message m if a negative sign is associated with

m or the recipient otherwise, $\pi_3(x)$ returns b who is the sender of the message m if a positive sign is associated with m or the recipient otherwise and $\pi_4(x)$ returns the type of the communication channel.

Definition 3. (Lists)
Let $\mathcal{L}_Q := \{(q_j \in Q)_{j \in \{1,\ldots,k\}} \mid k \in \mathbb{N}\}$ be the set of all possible lists (= tuples) whose elements are members of the set Q.

In this paper, we use lists to collect events. Let L be a list of elements of a set Q and $q \in Q$. Then we will use the following functions on lists: $set(L)$ denotes the (unordered) set that consists of all elements of L. $L \parallel q$ appends the element q at the end of the list L.

We now define the voting specific formalism. Let W_{total} be the set of all registered and eligible voters, where $W_{total} \subseteq Agents$ holds. We remark that each member of W_{total} or $Agents$ is considered as a potential attacker. Furthermore, let V be the set of all plaintext votes, representing the voting decisions of the voters. And let B be the set of all ballots, i.e. encrypted votes stored in the ballot box. We assume that the votes as well as the ballots are unique.

The formal model in this paper is based on a bulletin board [6]. A bulletin board is a public channel like for example a website. As the authors in [22] we focus on the communication between the bulletin board and its communication partners and do not specify its internal behavior. We assume, that it can be read by everyone, but it can only be written by authorized persons. Furthermore, we assume that all messages received by the bulletin board are automatically published, that only new messages can be added and old messages cannot be altered nor deleted.

The bulletin board is part of the electronic voting system. Thus, its formal definition is included in the definition of the state of the electronic voting system below.

Definition 4. (State of the electronic voting system)
An electronic voting system is driven by events e_1, e_2, e_3, ..., that carry the system through the states S_1, S_2, S_3, ... The state of the remote electronic voting system is a tuple $S_i = (B_i, V_i, W_i, BB_i)$ where

- B_i denotes the set of the ballots (=encrypted votes) in the ballot box.
- V_i denotes the set of plaintext votes which are used by the election authority for the tallying process. V_i are only taken from the ballot box B_i (see def. 13 below).
- W_i denotes the set of eligible voters, i.e. those voters who have not cast their ballot, yet.
- BB_i denotes the list of messages that are published on the bulletin board with $BB_i \in \mathcal{L}_{Messages}$. If the bulletin board receives a message via an event, the corresponding message will be appended to the end of the list. Or more formally: Let e_i be the last event which carried to state S_i and let $m_i = \pi_1(e_i)$ be the corresponding message that was exchanged by event e_i. Then

$$BB_i := \begin{cases} \emptyset & if \ i = 0 \\ BB_{i-1} \parallel m_i & if \ (\pi_2(e_i) = BB \ \wedge \ sign(m_i) > 0) \ or \\ & \quad (\pi_3(e_i) = BB \ \wedge \ sign(m_i) < 0) \\ BB_{i-1} & otherwise \end{cases}$$

The initial state is $S_0 := < B_0 = \emptyset, V_0 = \emptyset, W_0 = W_{total}, BB_0 = \emptyset >$.

In our model, the bulletin board is modeled as a list of received messages containing ballots and votes (see definition 12 and 14) or even more data that is needed for the verification process. Thus, we define *getVote* and *getBallot*. *getVote* extracts all plaintext votes from a set of messages, whereas *getBallot* extracts all ballots from a set of messages. These functions are used to filter information from the bulletin board.

Definition 5. *(choice)*
$$choice : W_{total} \cup \{\epsilon\} \to V \cup \{\epsilon\}$$

$$choice(a) = \begin{cases} \epsilon & if \ a = \epsilon \ or \ a \ has \ not \ voted \ yet \\ v \in V & if \ v \ is \ the \ vote \ of \ voter \ a \end{cases}$$

choice specifies how the voters vote. As soon as the voter has marked the voting form, *choice* returns the voter's voting decision v. Otherwise, it returns the empty word ϵ.

Definition 6. *(encrypt, decrypt)*
Let Params be the set of all (public and private) keys.
$$encrypt : V \times Params \to B$$
$$decrypt : B \times Params \to V$$

encrypt models the encryption of votes and maps a plaintext vote $v \in V$ and an encryption key $p \in Params$ onto a ballot $b \in B$. While *encrypt* models the encryption of the votes, *decrypt* models the decryption of the ballots. To ensure ballot secrecy, we demand that all ballots have the same size, i.e. the ballots do not allow any conclusions about the number of marks and/or their positions on the vote. Furthermore, we assume that $encrypt \circ decrypt = id_V$ and $encrypt \circ decrypt = id_B$ holds for a proper selection of the parameter. In addition, we assume that without knowledge of the proper $Params$ value, it is unfeasible to construct *encrypt* or *decrypt*. We also assume that there exists exactly one parameter $p \in Params$ which enables the decryption of a ballot.

In case of postal voting, *encrypt* corresponds to the inner envelope which hides the voter's voting decision and that does not contain any link to the voter.

Definition 7. *(ballot)*
$$ballot : W_{total} \to B \cup \{\epsilon\}$$
$$ballot(a) = \begin{cases} b & if \ choice(a) \neq \epsilon \wedge \exists p \in Params : b = encrypt(choice(a), p) \\ \epsilon & otherwise \end{cases}$$

ballot associates a voter with his ballot. If the voter has made his voting decision $(choice(a) \neq \epsilon)$, *ballot* returns the corresponding ballot $(b = encrypt(choice(a), p))$. Otherwise, *ballot* returns ϵ.

In case of postal voting, *ballot* complies with the identification of a voter's ballot by means of the outer envelope (which is labelled with the voter's name and address).

Definition 8. *(voter)*

$$voter : B \rightarrow W_{total} \cup \{\epsilon\}$$

$$voter(b) = \begin{cases} a & if \ b = ballot(a) \wedge b \notin B_i \\ \epsilon & otherwise \end{cases}$$

voter maps a ballot onto its producer. In order to ensure vote secrecy, the *voter* function has to be restricted. Only ballots that are not yet cast into the ballot box $(b \notin B_i)$ can be mapped onto their producers. Otherwise, *voter* returns ϵ. Thus, *voter* can only be applied to the ballot which is produced during the active state transition, namely $b \in B_{i+1} \setminus B_i$. This complies to traditional paper-based elections, where ballots from the ballot box are not linkable to their producers.

Definition 9. *(verifyEncryption)*

$$verifyEncryption_{a \in Agents} : B \rightarrow \{true, false\} \cup \{\epsilon\}$$

$$verifyEncryption_a(b) = \begin{cases} \epsilon & if \ a \neq voter(b) \\ true & if \ \exists p \in Params : decrypt(b, p) = choice(a) \\ false & if \ \forall p \in Params : decrypt(b, p) \neq choice(a) \end{cases}$$

verifyEncryption_a represents the verification that a ballot encodes the voting decision correctly. To guarantee ballot secrecy, only the producer of a ballot himself can verify the encryption of his vote. Thus, $a \in Agents$ only has access to function *verifyEncryption_a*. In case that the voter a himself invokes *verifyEncryption_a*, *verifyEncryption_a* returns *true* if the ballot encodes the voter's voting decision correctly. Otherwise, *verifyEncryption_a* returns *false*. If the function is invoked by a person who is not the producer of that particular ballot $(a \neq voter(b))$, it returns ϵ.

In order to ensure receipt-freeness, *verifyEncryption_a* does not return the plaintext vote. Though, implemented by an electronic voting system it must enable the voter to ascertain himself that the ballot is correctly encrypted. In case of Bingo Voting [15] *verifyEncryption_a* complies with the check if the number shown by the random number generator is equivalent to the number on the ballot that is associated with the chosen candidate or party, respectively. *verifyEncryption_a* is a mathematical function which returns a value independtly from the moment of its invocation. Implemented in an electronic voting system its invocation has to be restricted, in order to protect the voter from coercion.

$$invoke \_ verifyEncryption_a(S_i, b)$$
$$if(b \in B_i) \ then \ return \ \epsilon;$$
$$else \ return \ verifyEncryption_a(b);$$

If $verifyEncryption_a$ is invoked in a state S_i in which a ballot b is already stored in the ballot box ($b \in B_i$), the empty word ϵ is returned. If the ballot is not yet stored in the ballot box, $verifyEncryption_a$ is successfully applied. As soon as a ballot is stored in the ballot box it cannot longer be verified with respect to cast-as-intended. This complies to traditional paper-based elections where a ballot can only be unfolded and checked by the voter as long as it is not put into the ballot box.

Definition 10. *(tally)*
Let $k \in \mathbb{N}$ be the number of choices (candidates or parties). Then tally is defined as follows:

$$tally : 2^V \to \mathbb{N}_0{}^k$$

tally returns for a set of plaintext votes the number of marks for each choice. In analogy to *verifyEncryption*, the access to *tally* has to be controlled. I.e. implemented in an electronic voting system, it has to be restricted when *tally* can successfully be executed.

$$invoke \_ tally(S_i)$$
$$if(|B_i| = |V_i|) \ then \ return \ tally(V_i);$$
$$else \ return \ \epsilon;$$

This access control ensures completeness of the tally. Completeness means that all ballots which are cast into the ballot box are actually used to calculate the election result. Thus, *tally* can only be invoked if all ballots from the ballot box are decrypted at that particular moment ($|B_i| = |V_i|$). Otherwise, ϵ is returned, which means that no election result is obtained.

Note, that *invoke_tally* allows for intermediate results. If a legal system prohibits the calculation of intermediate results, the invocation of *tally* must be further restricted such that it can only be invoked after the official closing of the voting phase.

4   A Formal Security Model with Respect to Verifiability

Verifiability is some kind of "meta"-function which ensures the integrity of the election from beginning to end. In the context of electronic voting, it cannot be detached from ballot secrecy. Verifiability has to be provided without the violation of ballot secrecy. In practice, information (e.g. ballots or plaintext votes) are published on a public channel as a bulletin board. To preserve ballot secrecy, only some parts of the data are published, while others are kept secret. By all means, it has to be ensured that the plaintext vote cannot be mapped onto its producer/voter (directly or indirectly/transitively). Nonetheless, the logical chain of the published data has to provide full coverage of the voting procedure and exclude undetected manipulations with a probability bordering on certainty. In this paper, we do not model an abstract verification requirement but we model verifiability by means of a bulletin board.

4.1 Secure States

In this subsection we define secure states. For a better readability, we present the constraints one by one (def. 11-16). An electronic voting system is secure if and only if all constraints specified by def. 11-16 are fulfilled. Note, that in this subsection we define secure states, but not (yet) their enforcement. Enforcement of states security will be supported by the allowed state transitions in the following subsection 4.2.

Definition 11. *A state S_i is a secure state only if*
$$\forall b \in B_i : \exists j \leq i : verifyEncryption(b, voter_j(b)) = true$$

Explanation of the definition: The constraint above addresses the integrity of the ballot box. Thus, a state is secure only if all ballots from the ballot box ($\forall b \in B_i$) in some previous state ($\exists j \leq i$) would verify properly ($verifyEncryption(b, voter_j(b)) = true$) if this were attempted.

Definition 12. *A state S_i is a secure state only if*
$$B_i = getBallot(set(BB_i))$$

Explanation of the definition: The constraint above addresses the integrity and completeness of the ballots published on the bulletin board. It states that all ballots from the ballot box are published on the bulletin board. And vice versa, that no ballots are inserted nor manipulated. Remark that due to the unique character of the ballots (see p. 5) this definition does not allow more than one copy of one ballot in the ballot box as well as on the bulletin board. The same holds for the votes in definition 14.

Definition 13. *A state S_i is a secure state only if*
$$V_i \subseteq decrypt(B_i)$$

Explanation of the definition: This constraint addresses the integrity of the decryption process. It denotes that V_i is constructed only from encrypted votes from the ballot box B_i. Thus, no vote stuffing takes place. It allows, however, that some ballots are not yet decrypted, but not vice versa.

Lemma 1. *Let S_i be a secure state, then $encrypt(V_i) \subseteq B_i$ holds as well.*

According to definition 13 $V_i \subseteq decrypt(B_i)$ holds. Furthermore, ($encrypt \circ decrypt$) $(B_i) = B_i$ holds due to definition 6. Thus, lemma 1 holds as well.

Definition 14. *A state S_i is a secure state only if*
$$V_i = getVote(set(BB_i))$$

Explanation of the definition: The constraint above addresses the integrity and completeness of the plaintext votes published on the bulletin board. It states that all plaintext votes correspond to ballots from the bulletin board and the other way round, all published plaintext votes are actually contained in the set of plaintext votes. Thus, no plaintext vote has been deleted, inserted nor manipulated.

The constraints specified by definitions 11-14 ensure that all ballots are correctly cast, stored, decrypted and published and that no vote stuffing took place. However, these four constraints do not guarantee the completeness of the tally. Without further restrictions, ballots which have been cast into the ballot box could be deleted and thus, incomplete election results could be obtained. Nonetheless, the electronic voting system would remain in a secure state according to definitions 11-14, as long as the corresponding ballot would be deleted from the bulletin board as well. Therefore, the following definition 15 is added.

Definition 15. *A state S_i is a secure state only if*
$$\forall i, j \in \mathbb{N} : b \in getBallot(set(BB_i)) \Longrightarrow b \in getBallot(set(BB_{i+j}))$$

Explanation of the definition: The constraint above addresses the completeness of the ballots on the bulletin board. It ensures that once a ballot is published on the bulletin board it cannot be removed.

Note that the definition above does not address the ballots in the ballot box directly. This definition takes into account that the content of the bulletin board is publicly accessible while the content of the ballot box may not. However, in a secure state according to the property of definition 12 the set of ballots in the ballot box equals the set of ballots published on the bulletin board.

However, definition 15 does not rule out that ballots from the ballot box are not included in the tally. Therefore, definition 16 completes the definition of secure states.

Definition 16. *A state S_i is a secure state only if*
$$tally(decrypt(B_i)) = tally(getVote(set(BB_i)))$$

Explanation of the definition: The constraint above addresses the completeness of the tally. I.e. the result obtained from the ballots which are cast into the ballot box equals the result obtained from the plaintext votes which are published on the bulletin board.

Note a state is *secure* iff <u>all</u> constraints specified by definitions 11-16 hold and that the initial state is secure with respect to the definition of secure states above.

4.2   Allowed State Transitions

The rules for allowed state transitions represent the system's behavior and thus, the security functions that need to be implemented by the electronic voting system. In the following, three rules for allowed state transitions are specified to build up the content of the bulletin board and enforce the integrity and completeness of the bulletin board and thus, of the tally. A state transition is allowed if <u>one</u> of the three rules holds. For a better readability, we present these rules one by one.

Definition 17. *([Rule 1], no ballot is cast, no ballot is decrypted)*
A state transition from state S_i to state S_{i+1} by event t_{i+1} is permitted if:
$$B_{i+1} = B_i \ \wedge \ V_{i+1} = V_i \ \wedge \ W_{i+1} = W_i \ \wedge \ BB_{i+1} = BB_i$$

Explanation of the definition: This represents a state transition during which no ballot is cast into the ballot box nor decrypted. For example, this rule allows for the verification of the election or for the closing of the polling phase.

Definition 18. ([Rule 2], one ballot is cast, no ballot is decrypted)
A state transition from state S_i to state S_{i+1} by event t_{i+1} is permitted if:

$$V_{i+1} = V_i \quad \wedge \quad [\; \exists b \in B_{i+1} : \; B_{i+1} = B_i \cup \{b\} \quad \wedge \quad BB_{i+1} = BB_i \parallel b \quad \wedge$$
$$voter(b) \in W_i \quad \wedge \quad W_{i+1} = W_i \setminus \{voter(b)\} \quad \wedge$$
$$verifyEncryption(b, voter(b)) = true \;]$$

Explanation of the definition: This rule models a state transition during which a ballot is cast into the ballot box. In order to ensure that each eligible voter can cast exactly one vote, only eligible voters ($voter(b) \in W_i$) can cast a ballot into the ballot box ($B_{i+1} = B_i \cup \{b\}$) and then are eliminated from the list of eligible voters ($W_{i+1} = W_i \setminus \{voter(b)\}$). In addition, a ballot can only be cast into the ballot box if the voter was able to verify his ballot with respect to cast-as-intended ($verifyEncryption(b, voter(b)) = true$). Furthermore, this ballot is published on the bulletin board ($BB_{i+1} = BB_i \parallel b$)).

In this formal model, ballot casting and its publication on the bulletin board are defined as a closed transaction. I.e. it is assumed that both, storage and publication of a ballot, happen simultaneously during one atomic state transition. In practice storage and publication of a ballot may not be executed simultaneously but consecutively. However, then it has to be ensured that the execution of these two steps are performed directly one after the other and that they cannot be interrupted nor aborted.

Definition 19. ([Rule 3], no ballot is cast, one ballot is decrypted)
A state transition from state S_i to state S_{i+1} by event t_{i+1} is permitted if:

$$B_{i+1} = B_i \quad \wedge \quad [\; \exists v \in V_{i+1} \setminus V_i : V_{i+1} = V_i \cup \{v\} \quad \wedge \quad BB_{i+1} = BB_i \parallel v \quad \wedge$$
$$\exists p \in Params : encrypt(v, p) \in B_i \;]$$

Explanation of the definition: Typically this rule is applied after the voting phase is closed. It represents a state transition during which a ballot is decrypted. The decrypted ballot is added to the set of plaintext votes ($V_{i+1} = V_i \cup \{v\}$) and published on the bulletin board ($BB_{i+1} = BB_i \parallel v$). However, plaintext votes are only obtained from the ballot box ($encrypt(v, p) \in B_i$). Moreover, because *encrypt* and *decrypt* are injective functions, a new ballot must be taken for every invocation of *decrypt*. Otherwise, the obtained plaintext vote v was already in V_i and thus, $V_{i+1} \setminus V_i$ is empty. Therefore, no votes are inserted, double counted or manipulated.

As well as the ballot casting, the decryptiion of a ballot and its publication are modeled as a closed transaction. If the decryption of a ballot and the publication of the corresponding plaintext vote are not realized simultaneously in an electronic voting system, it has to be ensured that once a ballot is decrypted its publication on the bulletin board cannot be interrupted nor aborted.

4.3   Security Theorem

We now prove the security theorem that a permitted state transition always carries a secure state into another secure state.

Theorem 1. *If the state S_i of a voting system is secure and if the state transition t_{i+1} is permitted, then the succeeding state S_{i+1} is also secure.*

Proof

A state is secure, if <u>all</u> constraints specified by def. 11-16 are fulfilled. A state transition is permitted if <u>one</u> of the rules [Rule 1]-[Rule 3] specified by def. 17-19 holds.

If S_i is secure and the state transition t_{i+1} follows *[Rule 1]* then state S_{i+1} is obviously secure as well, because no ballot is cast, no vote is obtained nor is any information published on the bulletin board.

Let S_i be secure and t_{i+1} be a state transition according to *[Rule 2]*. Then the voting phase is still active and exactly one ballot b is cast into the ballot box and published on the bulletin board during state transition t_{i+1}.

- Since [Rule 2] demands $verifyEncryption_i(b, voter(b)) = true$, def. 11 is fulfilled in S_{i+1}.
- Due to [Rule 2] and the secure state property of S_i, $B_{i+1} = B_i \cup \{b\} = getBallot(set(BB_i \parallel b)) = getBallot(set(BB_{i+1}))$ holds. I.e. def. 12 is true in S_{i+1}.
- According to [Rule 2] $V_{i+1} = V_i$ holds. Because S_i was secure, $V_{i+1} = V_i \subseteq decrypt(B_i)$. Thus, $V_{i+1} \subseteq decrypt(B_i \cup \{b\}) = decrypt(B_{i+1})$ holds even more. Therefore, def. 13 is true in S_{i+1}.
- According to [Rule 2] one ballot and no plaintext vote is added on the bulletin board during t_{i+1}. Because S_i is secure, $V_i = getVote(set(BB_i))$ holds. Thus, $getVote(set(BB_i)) = getVote(set(BB_i \parallel b)) = getVote(set(BB_{i+1})) = V_i = V_{i+1}$ holds as well. Therefore, def. 14 is true in S_{i+1}.
- It has to be proven that no ballot is removed from the bulletin board during the active state transition. According to [Rule 2], $BB_{i+1} = BB_i \parallel b$ hold. Thus, $getBallot(set(BB_i)) \subset getBallot(set(BB_{i+1}))$ hold and therefore, def. 15 is fulfilled in S_{i+1}.
- If S_i is secure and t_{i+1} follows [Rule 2], then there are two possible options. $|B_i| = |V_i|$ holds in S_i. Then $|B_{i+1}| = |B_i \cup \{b\}| = |B_i| + 1 \neq |V_i| = |V_{i+1}|$. Thus, *tally* returns ϵ (see def. 10) and def. 15 is true in S_{i+1}.
  Let $|B_i| \neq |V_i|$ hold in S_i. Since S_i is secure, $V_i \subseteq decrypt(B_i)$ holds. Thus, $|B_i| > |V_i|$. Then $|B_{i+1}| = |B_i| + 1 > |V_i|$ holds even more. Thus, *tally* returns ϵ and the constraint specified by def. 16 is true in S_{i+1}.

This completes the proof that t_{i+1} according to [Rule 2] carries a secure state S_i into a secure state S_{i+1}.

Now let S_i be secure and t_{i+1} be a state transition according to *[Rule 3]*. Then exactly one ballot is decrypted and the obtained vote v is published on the bulletin board during state transition t_{i+1}.

- Due to [Rule 3] $B_{i+1} = B_i$ and $getBallot(set(BB_{i+1})) = getBallot(set(BB_i))$ hold. Thus, def. 11 and 12 both are fulfilled in S_{i+1}.
- Because S_i is secure, it is sufficient to prove that the new plaintext vote v is generated from a ballot in the ballot box, or more formally that $v \in decrypt(B_{i+1}) = decrypt(B_i)$. According to [Rule 3] for that particular ballot $encrypt(v) \in B_i$ holds. Based on Lemma 1 $v \in decrypt(B_i)$ holds as well. Thus, the constraints specified by def. 13 is fulfilled in S_{i+1}.
- Due to [Rule 3], $BB_{i+1} = BB_i \parallel v$ and $V_{i+1} = V_i \cup \{v\}$ hold. Thus, $getVote(set(BB_{i+1})) = getVote(set(BB_i \parallel v)) = getVote(set(BB_i)) \cup \{v\}$ holds as well. Because S_i is secure, $getVote(set(BB_i)) \cup \{v\} = V_i \cup \{v\} = V_{i+1}$ holds. Therefore, the constraint specified by def. 14 is true in S_{i+1}.
- According to [Rule 3], $getBallot(set(BB_i)) = getBallot(set(BB_{i+1}))$ holds. Because S_i was secure and def. 15 was fulfilled in S_i, def. 15 is fulfilled in S_{i+1} as well.
- Let S_i be secure and t_{i+1} a state transition according to [Rule 3].

  $|B_i| = |V_i|$ holds in S_i. Then [Rule 3] cannot be applied because all ballots from the ballot box are already decrypted. Or more formally, $V_{i+1} \setminus V_i = \emptyset$ Assume that $|B_i| > |V_i|$ holds in S_i and $|B_{i+1}| > |V_{i+1}|$ holds in S_{i+1} as well. Then, the decrypting process isn't completed yet. Thus, *tally* returns ϵ and the constraint specified by def. 15 is true in S_{i+1}.

  Let $|B_i| > |V_i|$ holds in S_i and let $v = decrypt(b)$ be the last ballot from the ballot box which is decrypted during the active state transition. Then $|B_{i+1}| = |V_{i+1}|$ holds in S_{i+1}. Based on that equality and the 1:1-mapping of *encrypt* and *decrypt*, then $V_{i+1} = decrypt(B_{i+1})$ holds. Due to def. 14 $V_{i+1} = getVote(set(BB_{i+1}))$ holds as well. Thus, the constraint specified by def. 16 is true in S_{i+1}.

This completes the proof that t_{i+1} according to [Rule 3], carries a secure state S_i into a secure state S_{i+1}.

Therefore, it has been proven that a permitted state transition carries a secure state always into another secure state.   □

4.4   Discussion of the Formal Model and Example Explanation

In this section it is explained how the constraints for secure states enable the retraceability of the election from beginning to end and an example is given.

Before a voter casts a ballot into the ballot box, he can check his ballot according to [Rule 2] such that it is *cast-as-intended* as specified by def. 11 (fig.1, step (1)). In case of Prêt-à-voter [18] the verification of cast-as-intended conforms to the check if the correct party or candidate is marked on the right side of the voting form, before the voting form is teared apart and the left side of the voting form (with the randomized candidate order) is destroyed.

As soon as the voter has cast his ballot into the ballot box, his ballot is published on the bulletin board according to [Rule 2] (fig.1, step (2)). The voter can identify his ballot on the bulletin board and verify that his ballot is *published-as-cast* according to def. 12. If the ballot was cast-as-intended and published-as-cast,

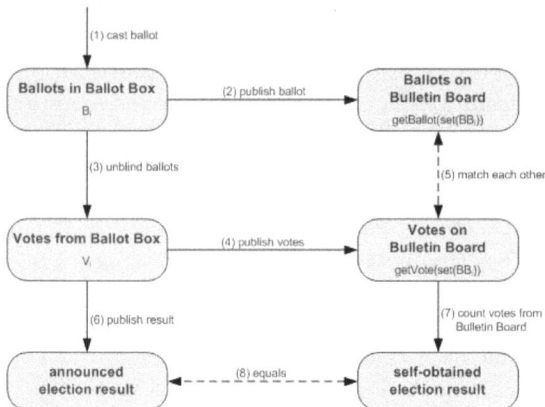

Fig. 1. Relationship between secure states and allowed state transitions w.r.t. verifiability

the voter can conclude that his ballot was *recorded-as-cast*. Prêt-à-voter does not publish the ballots immediately but after the voting is closed. But then the voter can identify his ballot by means of the ballot onion and verify that his ballot has been correctly transmitted and published.

Whenever a ballot is decrypted, the decryption process is executed according to [Rule 3] (fig.1, step (3)). Thus, the decryption is restricted to ballots from the ballot box as specified by def. 13 and enforced by [Rule 3]. Therefore, no vote stuffing or manipulation is possible.

To allow for public verification all obtained plaintext votes are published on the bulletin board (fig.1, step (4)). As specified by def. 14 and enforced by [Rule 3], all obtained plaintext votes are *published-as-decrypted*. If the ballots were recorded-as-cast and the plaintext votes were published-as-decrypted, the public as well as the individual voters can conclude that the ballots were *decrypted-as-recorded* (fig.1, step (5)).

However, this verification step is sensitive w.r.t. ballot secrecy. To ensure both, ballot secrecy and verifiability, the link between the encrypted and the corresponding plaintext vote has to be eliminated while the decryption has to be retraceable. For the calculation of the plaintext votes, Prêt-à-voter uses tellers to perform anonymising mixes and decrypt the ballots in order to eliminate the link between ballots and plaintext votes. The tellers can be audited using Randomized-Partial-Checking. Bingo Voting [15] accomplishs this verification step by means of Zero-Knowledge-Proofs.

Furthermore, the public can tally the votes from the bulletin board (fig.1, step (7)). If the votes are decrypted-as-recorded and published-as-decrypted and the announced election result equals the self-obtained election result, the public as well as the individual voters can conclude that *counted-as-recorded* holds as well.

5   Conclusion and Future Work

In this paper a formal IT security model specifying the requirement of verifiability by means of a bulletin board is presented. The security properties are specified by means of secure states (section 4.1) and enforced by rules for allowed state transitions (section 4.2). The security theorem in section 4.3 proves that by following the rules for allowed state transitions the system remains in secure states. In section 4.4 it is shown how verifiability is provided by the given definition of secure states.

The formal IT security model in this paper presents a formal sub model w.r.t. verifiability. It is a step towards the evaluation of online voting products against the CC Protection Profile [4] according to EAL5 or higher. The CC evaluation according to EAL5 or higher demands the application of formal methods. According to [5], this evaluation depth includes the verification (a) that the security functions enforce the security requirements and (b) that the electronic voting system complies with the formal model. The first part of the proof is presented in this paper with the security theorem. The second part of the proof addresses the compliance of a concrete electronic voting product with the formal model. This can be (manually or automatically) done by analyzing an electronic voting system whether or not it implements the security functions specified in our formal model by the rules for allowed state transitions.

Our next research step is the integration of receipt-freeness into our formal model and in case of a conflict between verifiability and receipt-freeness, the solution of this conflict. That way this formal security model can be evolved into a complete formal security model which covers all requirements for electronic voting and enables the evaluation of online voting products against the CC according to EAL5 or higher. Furthermore, as a proof of concept a case study concerning the application to a concrete voting protocol is desirable.

Acknowledgment. The research of this paper is funded by the Deutsche Forschungsgenmeinschaft (DFG) under the project 'Modellierung von Internetwahlen II' (ModIWa II).

References

1. Adida, B., Neff, C.: Ballot casting assurance. In: USENIX/Accurate Electronic Voting Technology Workshop, p. 7. USENIX Association, Berkeley (2006)
2. Volkamer, M., Schryen, G., Langer, L., Schmidt, A., Buchmann, J.: Elektronische Wahlen: Verifizierung vs. Zertifizierung. In: GI Jahrestagung, pp. 1827–1836 (2009)
3. Common criteria for information technology security evaluation, and common methodology for information technology security evaluation, version 3.1 (2006)
4. Volkamer, M., Vogt, R.: Common criteria protection profile for basic set of security requirements for online voting products. BSI-CC-PP-0037, Version 1.0 (April 18, 2008), https://www.bsi.bund.de/SharedDocs/Zertifikate/PP/aktuell/PP/aktuell/PP_0037.html (May 02, 2013)
5. Mantel, H., Stephan, W., Ullmann, M., Vogt, R.: Guideline for the development and evaluation of formal security policy models in the scope of itsec and common criteria. BSI, DFKI, Tech. Rep. (2004)

6. Benaloh, J.D.C.: Verifiable secret-ballot elections. Ph.D. dissertation, Yale University, Department of Computer Science, Technical Report number 561 (1987)
7. Bräunlich, K., Grimm, R.: Formalization of receipt-freeness in the context of electronic voting. In: ARES, pp. 119–126 (2011)
8. Delaune, S., Kremer, S., Ryan, M.: Verifying privacy-type properties of electronic voting protocols. Journal of Computer Security 17(4), 435–487 (2009)
9. Jonker, H.L., Pieters, W.: Receipt-freeness as a special case of anonymity in epistemic logic. In: Proc. IAVoSS Workshop on Trustworthy Elections (2006)
10. Jonker, H.L., de Vink, E.P.: Formalising receipt-freeness. In: Katsikas, S.K., López, J., Backes, M., Gritzalis, S., Preneel, B. (eds.) ISC 2006. LNCS, vol. 4176, pp. 476–488. Springer, Heidelberg (2006)
11. Kremer, S., Ryan, M.: Analysis of an electronic voting protocol in the applied pi calculus. In: Sagiv, M. (ed.) ESOP 2005. LNCS, vol. 3444, pp. 186–200. Springer, Heidelberg (2005)
12. Backes, M., Hritcu, C., Maffei, M.: Automated verification of remote electronic voting protocols in the applied pi-calculus. In: CSF, pp. 195–209 (2008)
13. Grimm, R., Hupf, K., Volkamer, M.: A Formal IT-Security Model for the Correction and Abort Requirement on Electronic Voting. In: EVOTE (2010)
14. Volkamer, M., Grimm, R.: Development of a formal it security model for remote electronic voting systems. In: Electronic Voting, pp. 185–196 (2008)
15. Bohli, J.-M., Müller-Quade, J., Röhrich, S.: Bingo voting: Secure and coercion-free voting using a trusted random number generator. In: Alkassar, A., Volkamer, M. (eds.) VOTE-ID 2007. LNCS, vol. 4896, pp. 111–124. Springer, Heidelberg (2007)
16. Chaum, D., Ryan, P.Y.A., Schneider, S.: A practical voter-verifiable election scheme. In: De Capitani di Vimercati, S., Syverson, P.F., Gollmann, D. (eds.) ESORICS 2005. LNCS, vol. 3679, pp. 118–139. Springer, Heidelberg (2005)
17. Popoveniuc, S., Hosp, B.: An introduction to punchScan. In: Chaum, D., Jakobsson, M., Rivest, R.L., Ryan, P.Y.A., Benaloh, J., Kutylowski, M., Adida, B. (eds.) Towards Trustworthy Elections. LNCS, vol. 6000, pp. 242–259. Springer, Heidelberg (2010)
18. Ryan, P.Y.A., Peacock, T.: Prêt-à-voter: A Systems Perspective. Technical Report CS-TR 929, School of Computing Science, Newcastle University (2005)
19. Baskar, A., Ramanujam, R., Suresh, S.P.: Knowledge-based modelling of voting protocols. In: TARK, pp. 62–71 (2007)
20. Talbi, M., Morin, B., Tong, V.V.T., Bouhoula, A., Mejri, M.: Specification of electronic voting protocol properties using ADM logic: FOO case study. In: Chen, L., Ryan, M.D., Wang, G. (eds.) ICICS 2008. LNCS, vol. 5308, pp. 403–418. Springer, Heidelberg (2008)
21. Fujioka, A., Okamoto, T., Ohta, K.: A practical secret voting scheme for large scale elections. In: Zheng, Y., Seberry, J. (eds.) AUSCRYPT 1992. LNCS, vol. 718, pp. 244–251. Springer, Heidelberg (1993)
22. Jonker, H., Pang, J.: Bulletin boards in voting systems: Modelling and measuring privacy. In: ARES. IEEE Computer Society Press (2011)
23. Kremer, S., Ryan, M., Smyth, B.: Election verifiability in electronic voting protocols. In: Gritzalis, D., Preneel, B., Theoharidou, M. (eds.) ESORICS 2010. LNCS, vol. 6345, pp. 389–404. Springer, Heidelberg (2010)
24. Dolev, D., Yao, A.C.: On the Security of Public Key Protocols. In: Proceedings of the 22nd Annual Symposium on Foundations of Computer Science, pp. 350–357. IEEE Computer Society, Washington, DC (1981)

Analysis of an Electronic Boardroom Voting System[*]

Mathilde Arnaud, Véronique Cortier, and Cyrille Wiedling

LORIA - CNRS, Nancy, France

Abstract. We study a simple electronic boardroom voting system. While most existing systems rely on opaque electronic devices, a scientific committee of a research institute (the CNRS Section 07) has recently proposed an alternative system. Despite its simplicity (in particular, no use of cryptography), each voter can check that the outcome of the election corresponds to the votes, without having to trust the devices.

In this paper, we present three versions of this system, exhibiting potential attacks. We then formally model the system in the applied pi-calculus, and prove that two versions ensure both vote correctness (even if the devices are corrupted) and ballot secrecy (assuming the devices are honest).

Keywords: Ballot Secrecy, Boardroom Voting, Correctness, Formal Methods.

1 Introduction

Electronic voting has garnered a lot of attention in the past years. Most of the results in this field have been focused on two main types of settings: distant electronic voting and voting machines. Distant electronic voting corresponds to systems where voters can vote from their own computers, provided they are connected to the Internet. Many systems have been devised, including academic ones (e.g. Helios [2], Civitas [5], or FOO [10]). Voting machines are used in polling stations and speed up the tally. Examples of voting machines are e.g. the Diebold machines [9] or the Indian voting machines [19], both of them having been subject to attacks [9,19].

Several security notions have been proposed for voting systems and can be split into two main categories: privacy [8] and verifiability [14]. Privacy ranges from ballot secrecy to coercion-resistance and ensures that no one can know how a particular voter voted. Verifiability enables voters to audit the voting process, e.g. by checking that their ballots appear on the bulletin board (individual verifiability), or checking that the outcome of the election corresponds to the ballots on the bulletin board (universal verifiability).

In this paper, we focus on a different and particular setting: boardroom meetings. Many committee meetings require their members to vote on several motions/decisions. Three techniques are typically used.

– Show of hands: this is a simple and cheap technique, which offers no privacy and requires to count the raised hands.

[*] The research leading to these results has received funding from the European Research Council under the European Union's Seventh Framework Programme (FP7/2007-2013) / ERC grant agreement no 258865, project ProSecure.

J. Heather, S. Schneider, and V. Teague (Eds.): VoteID 2013, LNCS 7985, pp. 109–126, 2013.

– Paper ballot: this solution offers privacy but may be tedious, in particular when there are several rounds of vote during a meeting.
– Use of electronic devices.

Electronic devices seem to offer both simplicity of use and privacy: committee members simply need to (privately) push a button corresponding to their choice on their own device and a central device computes and publishes the result. However, these systems are opaque: what if someone controls the central device and therefore falsifies the result of the election? In many committees such as boarding committees or scientific councils, controlling the result of the election (e.g. choice of a new president, decision on the future of a company, *etc.*) is even more important in terms of impact than breaking privacy. Even if the system is not malicious, it can simply dysfunction with no notifications, as witnessed e.g. by the "CNRS Section 07" committee members (the scientific council in Computer Science of the CNRS, a French national research institute). In response to these dysfunctions, a subgroup of the CNRS Section 07 committee members, namely Bruno Durand, Chantal Enguehard, Marc-Olivier Killijian and Philippe Schnoebelen, with the help of Stefan Merz and Blaise Genest, have proposed a new voting system that is meant to achieve:

– simplicity: it could be easily adapted to existing devices
– privacy
– full verifiability, even if the electronic devices are corrupted

A few other systems tailored to boardroom election have been proposed such as [11,12]. A feature of the "CNRS Section 07" system is that it does not use cryptography, which makes the system easier to understand and trust, for non experts.

Our contributions. We provide a full review of the voting system proposed by the CNRS Section 07, illustrating the applicability of formal models and in particular, the applicability of the latest definitions and the proof techniques in formal methods. The key idea of the CNRS Section 07 voting system is that each vote appears on the screen, together with a unique identifier (randomly generated by the central device). This unique identifier allows voters to check that their votes have been counted. Due to our attacks on the initial version (that called $F2FV^1$), two variants of it have been proposed: in $F2FV^2$, the random identifier is generated by both the ballot box and the voter while in $F2FV^3$, the random identifier is generated by the voter only. It is interesting to note that this last version is actually close to the protocol devised by Bruce Schneier in [18].

We first describe the three versions and we review in details the possible attacks:

– The initial version $F2FV^1$ is subject to a "clash-attack", using the terminology of [16]. The attack works roughly as follows: if the same identifier is used for two different voters that voted the same way, then a dishonest ballot box may replace one of the ballots by any ballot of its choice. The last version $F2FV^3$ (and thus the Schneier's protocol as well) suffers from the same attack (with relatively small probability) if the random numbers are small, which is likely to be the case in practice.

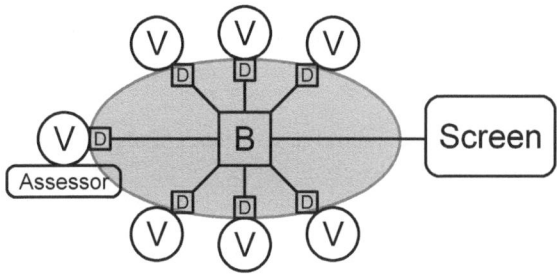

Fig. 1. Schema of the election

- The other attacks are against privacy. Obviously, a dishonest ballot box may know how any voter voted. We discuss other ways for a dishonest ballot box to break privacy. One of the attack works even if the ballot box does not initially know to which a ballot belongs to.

To conduct a more thorough security analysis, we formally model these systems in the applied pi-calculus [1], a process algebra well adapted to security protocols. Computational models where attackers are modeled by polynomial time probabilistic Turing machines are, as a rule, more accurate. However, since the systems here involve no cryptography, we chose the simplicity of the applied pi-calculus, for which several security analyses of voting protocols have already been conducted (e.g. [6,7]).

We focus on two main security properties: vote correctness and privacy. The CNRS Section 07 voting system is primarily designed to ensure that, even if all the electronic devices are corrupted, any approved election outcome reflects the votes of all voters. This property has been introduced by Benaloh and Tuinstra [3] and more precisely defined by Catalano *et al* in [13] and is called *correctness*. We provide a formal definition of this property and prove that the two versions $F2FV^2$ and $F2FV^3$ ensure vote correctness, even if all devices are corrupted (but assuming voters use random numbers). In contrast, privacy cannot be ensured when the central device is corrupted. However, privacy is guaranteed against external users (including voters). Formally, we show privacy for the well established notion of privacy defined in [8], assuming that the electronic devices are honest.

2 Setting

We consider a particular setting, typically for boardroom meetings, where all voters are present in the same room and are given a dedicated voting equipment. In what follows, we assume the individual devices to be linked to a central device. The central device is responsible for collecting the ballots and publishing them. Such systems are standard in many committees (e.g. parliamentary assembly, corporate boards, *etc.*). The particularity of the voting system (and its variants) proposed by the CNRS Section 07 is that it assumes the presence of a screen that each voter can see. This screen ensures that all voters simultaneously see the same data and is the key element for the voting system.

Specifically, the system involves voters and their electronic voting devices, a ballot box (the central device), and a screen. Moreover, a voter is chosen to take on the role of an assessor (for example the president of the committee or her secretary). This is illustrated in Figure 1.

Ballot box. The ballot box is the central device that collects the ballots and tallies the votes. It communicates with the electronic devices of the voters over private individual channels. Once the voting phase is over, the ballot box publishes the outcome of the election on the screen.

Screen. The screen displays the outcome of the election for validation by the voters and the assessor. Since the voters are in the same room, they all see the same screen.

Voter. The voter role has two phases. In the first phase, he casts his vote through her electronic device. In the second phase, he performs some consistency checks looking at the screen and lets the assessor know whether his checks were successful, in which case he approves the procedure.

Personal voting device. Each individual voting device has a pad or some buttons for the voter to express her choice. The device communicates the value of the vote entered by the voter directly to the ballot box.

Assessor. The assessor is a role that can be performed by any voter. He does not hold any secret. He is chosen before the execution of the protocol. The assessor is responsible of some additional verifications. In particular, he checks that each voter has approved the procedure. If one voter has not, he must cancel the vote and start a new one.

3   Face-to-Face Voting System

We describe in details the electronic boardroom voting system designed by the CNRS Section 07 committee. We actually present three versions of it. The three versions have in common the fact that the central device and/or the voters generate a random number that is attached to the vote. Both the vote and the random number are displayed on the screen. This way, each voter can check that his vote (uniquely identified by its random number) is counted in the tally. We could have presented the version that offers the best security guarantees but we think the flaws in the other versions are of interest as well. The three versions differ in who generates the randomness:

- Initial version: The ballot box generates the random identifier for each voter.
- Second version: Both the ballot box and voters generate a random identifier.
- Third version: The voters generate their identifiers.

The three voting systems are summarized in Figure 2 and are described in details in the rest of the section. Since the votes are transmitted in clear to the central device on uniquely identified wires, ballot secrecy is clearly not guaranteed as soon as the central device is corrupted. So for ballot secrecy, we assume that the central device behaves honestly, that is, the secrecy of the ballots will be guaranteed only against external users (including the voters themselves). The major interest of the CNRS Section 07 system is that it ensures vote correctness *even if the central device is corrupted*, that is the voters do not need to trust any part of the infrastructure.

Note that in practice, the "random numbers" used in the remaining of the paper should typically be numbers of 3-4 digits, so that they are easy to copy and compare.

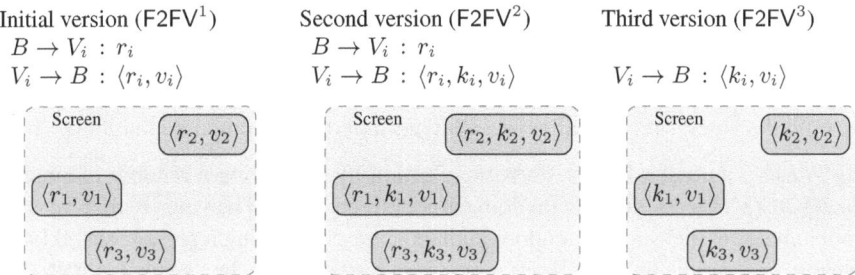

Fig. 2. Voting processes

3.1 Initial System F2FV^1

Voting Phase. The ballot box B starts the election by generating a random number r for each voter V, and sends this random number to the voter. The voter V receives the random number r, uses it to form his ballot $\langle r, v \rangle$ where v is his vote, and sends his ballot to the ballot box. Finally, all the ballots $\langle r, v \rangle$ are displayed on the screen E. This marks the end of the voting process.

Validation Phase. The validation part can then begin. Each voter checks that his ballot is correctly included in the list of ballots displayed on the screen. The assessor waits for each voter to state that his vote appears on the screen. He also checks that the number of ballots matches the number of voters. If all checks succeed, the assessor approves the outcome of the election.

Possible Attacks. The key idea of this system is that each random identifier should be unique, ensuring a one-to-one correspondence between the votes that appear on the screen and the votes cast by the voters. However, a corrupted ballot box may still insert ballots of its choice, mounting a so-called "clash-attack" [16]. The attack works as follows: the (dishonest) ballot box guesses that two voters Alice and Bob are going to vote in the same way. (This could be a pure guess or based on statistical analysis of the previous votes.) The ballot box then sends the *same* nonce r to Alice and Bob. Since Alice and Bob cast the same vote v, they both send back the same ballot $\langle r, v \rangle$. The ballot box is then free to display $\langle r, v \rangle$ only once and then add any ballot of its choice. Both Alice and Bob would recognize $\langle r, v \rangle$ as their own ballot so the result would be validated.

For example, assume there are three voters A, B, and C and the ballot box guesses that A and B vote identically. Suppose A and B cast 0 and C casts 1. The ballot box can replace the two votes for 0 by one vote for 0 and one vote for 1, making the "1" vote win. This can be done by simply sending the same randomness r_a to both A and B.

$$
\begin{array}{lll}
B(I) \rightarrow V_A \ : \ r_a & B(I) \rightarrow V_B \ : \ r_a & B(I) \rightarrow V_C \ : \ r_c \\
V_A \rightarrow B(I) \ : \ \langle r_a, 0 \rangle & V_B \rightarrow B(I) \ : \ \langle r_a, 0 \rangle & V_C \rightarrow B(I) \ : \ \langle r_c, 1 \rangle \\
& B(I) \rightarrow E \ : \ \langle r_a, 0 \rangle & \\
& B(I) \rightarrow E \ : \ \langle r_b, 1 \rangle & \\
& B(I) \rightarrow E \ : \ \langle r_c, 1 \rangle &
\end{array}
$$

3.2   Second System F2FV^2

The attack on the initial system F2FV^1 is due to the fact that the ballot box may cheat when generating random unique identifiers. So a second solution has been proposed, where both the voters and the ballot box generate a part of the random identifier.

Voting Phase. The ballot box B starts the election by generating a random number r for each voter V, then sends this random number to the voter. The voter V receives the random number r, picks a new random number k (possibly using a pre-generated list), and uses it to form his ballot $\langle r, k, v \rangle$ where v is his vote, and then sends his ballot to the ballot box. Finally, all the ballots $\langle r, k, v \rangle$ are displayed on the screen E.

The validation phase works like for the protocol F2FV^1.

Possible Attacks. As we shall see in Section 5.2, this second version ensures vote correctness, even if the ballot box is corrupted. As for the two other variants, privacy is not guaranteed as soon as the central device (the ballot box) is corrupted. Indeed, the central device may leak how each voter has voted or may record it on some memory. However, such attacks against privacy assume a rather strong control of the ballot box, where the attacker can access to the device either during or after the election. We further discuss some more subtle flaws which require a lower level of corruption We describe two different attacks.

Encoding information in the randoms. As already mentioned, a fully corrupted ballot box may transmit how each voter voted since it receives the votes in the clear, from uniquely identified wires. However, F2FV^2 (and F2FV^1) also suffers from offline attacks, where an attacker simply logs the election outcome. Indeed, it makes sense anyway to keep a copy of the screen after each election. The attack works as follows. Instead of generating fully random numbers, the ballot box could be programmed to provide a voter i (where i is the number identifying the voting device used by the voter) with a nonce r_i such that $r_i \equiv i \mod p$, where p is larger than the number of voters. In this way, an intruder could deduce from a ballot $\langle r, k, v \rangle$ the identity of the voter, simply by computing r modulo p. Of course, the identity of the voters could be encoded in the randomness in many other ways, making the detection of such an attack very unlikely. This attack simply assumes the attacker had access to the central device, at least once prior to the election (e.g. during its manufacturing). It does not require the attacker to access the ballot box during nor after the election.

Swallowing ballots. There is a more direct (but easily detectable) way to break privacy, as sketched in Figure 3. Indeed, assume an attacker wants to know to whom a ballot $\langle r_2, k_2, v_2 \rangle$ belongs to. In case the attacker simply controls the display of the screen, he can send a modified set of ballots to the screen. E.g. if he sends $\langle r_2, k_2, v_2' \rangle$ instead of $\langle r_2, k_2, v_2 \rangle$), or if he simply remove this ballot, the voter who submitted the ballot $\langle r_2, k_2, v_2 \rangle$ would then complain, revealing his identity.

Security Guarantees. We show in Section 5 that this second version ensures vote correctness, even if the ballot box is corrupted. It also ensures ballot secrecy, assuming the ballot box is honest.

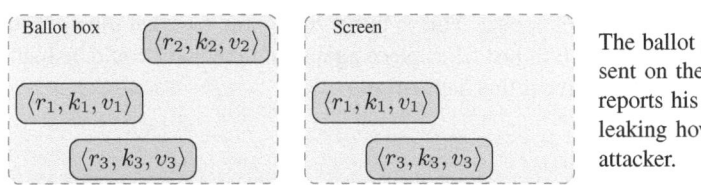

Ballot box $\langle r_2, k_2, v_2 \rangle$ $\langle r_1, k_1, v_1 \rangle$ $\langle r_3, k_3, v_3 \rangle$

Screen $\langle r_1, k_1, v_1 \rangle$ $\langle r_3, k_3, v_3 \rangle$

The ballot $\langle r_2, k_2, v_2 \rangle$ is not sent on the screen. Voter V_2 reports his ballot is missing, leaking how he voted to the attacker.

Fig. 3. Attack against ballot secrecy

3.3   Third System F2FV^3

To circumvent the privacy issue of the second system, when the ballot box is somewhat honest (the attacker cannot access not interfere with it) but has been maliciously programmed, a third version has been proposed, where the random identifier is generated by the voter only.

Voting Phase. Each voter V picks a random number k and uses it to form his ballot $\langle k, v \rangle$ where v is his vote, and then sends his ballot to the ballot box. All the ballots $\langle k, v \rangle$ are displayed on the screen E.
   The validation phase works like for systems F2FV^1 and F2FV^2.

Possible Attack. This third system is vulnerable to the same kind of attacks against vote correctness as the one described for system F2FV^1. Indeed, in case two voters pick the same random number and vote for the same candidate, for instance $(k_A, v_A) = (k_B, v_B)$, the ballot box could remove one of these ballots and replace it by a ballot of its choice without being detected. Note that, due to the birthday theorem, it is not so unlikely that two voters use the same random number. For example, assume voters use 4 digits numbers. Then there is a probability of more than 0.2 to have a collision in a room of 67 members and more than 0.5 in a room of 118 members. In case, only 3 digits numbers are used, there is already a probability of collision of about 0.5 for only 37 members. These figures assume that the voters pick true random numbers. In case they generate numbers "manually", the entropy is usually much lower (e.g. users are sometimes reluctant to generate numbers with repeated digits). In such cases, the probability of collision increases accordingly.
   As mentioned in the introduction, the voting protocol proposed by Bruce Schneier in [18] being very similar, it suffers from the same attack.

Security Guarantees. We show in Section 5 that this third version ensures vote correctness, even if the ballot box is corrupted (providing voters generate true randomness). It also ensures ballot secrecy, assuming the ballot box is honest.

3.4   Common Weaknesses

If a voter claims that her ballot does not appear on the screen, then the election round is canceled and everyone has to vote again. This means that a dishonest voter may choose to cancel an election (e.g. if she's not happy with the result), simply by wrongly claiming that her vote does not appear. This is mitigated by the fact that the advantage of the attack is small (the election just takes place again) and the voter could be blamed as being dishonest or inattentive if this happens too often.

4   Formal Model

The remaining of the paper is devoted to the formal proof of security of ballot privacy and vote correctness for the two systems F2FV^2 and F2FV^3. We use the applied pi-calculus [1] for the formal description of the voting systems. We briefly recall here all the definitions of the applied pi-calculus.

4.1   Syntax

Messages are represented by *terms* built on an infinite set $\mathcal{N}$ of *names* (used to name communication channels or atomic data), a set $\mathcal{X}$ of *variables* and a *signature* Σ, which is a finite set of *function symbols* representing primitives. Since our voting systems do not use any cryptography, we adopt the following simple signature:

$$\Sigma_{pair} = \{\text{ok}, \text{fail}, \text{fst}, \text{snd}, \text{pair}\}$$

where ok and fail are constants ; fst and snd are unary functions and pair is a binary function. The term $\text{pair}(m_1, m_2)$ represents the concatenation of two messages m_1 and m_2, while fst and snd represent the projections on the first and second component respectively. The set of terms $T(\mathcal{X}, \mathcal{N})$ is formally defined by the following grammar:

$$t, t_1, t_2, \cdots ::= x \mid n \mid \text{pair}(t_1, t_2) \mid \text{fst}(t) \mid \text{snd}(t) \qquad x \in \mathcal{X}, n \in \mathcal{N}.$$

We write $\left\{ M_1 /_{x_1}, \ldots, M_n /_{x_n} \right\}$ for the *substitution* that replaces the variables x_i by the terms M_i. The application of a substitution σ to a term N is denoted $N\sigma$. A term is *ground* if it does not contain variables. We also use the following notations: $\langle u_1, \ldots, u_n \rangle$ for $\text{pair}(u_1, \text{pair}(\ldots, \text{pair}(u_{n-1}, u_n)))$ and $\Pi_i^n(u)$ for retrieving the ith element of a sequence of n elements: $\Pi_i^n(u) = \text{fst}(\text{snd}^{i-1}(u))$ for $i < n$ and $\Pi_n^n(u) = \text{snd}^{n-1}(u)$. In particular, $\Pi_i^n(\langle u_1, \ldots, u_n \rangle) = u_i$. We also write $x \in_n y$ for $[x = \Pi_1^n(y)] \vee \cdots \vee [x = \Pi_n^n(y)]$, that is, if x is one of the elements of the sequence y.

The properties of the pair are modeled by an equational theory E_{pair} that states that it is possible to retrieve the two elements of a pair:

$$\text{fst}(\text{pair}(x, y)) = x \qquad\qquad \text{snd}(\text{pair}(x, y)) = y.$$

We consider equality modulo this equational theory, that is, equality of terms is the smallest equivalence relation induced by E_{pair}, closed under application of function symbols, substitution of terms for variables and bijective renaming of names. We write $M == N$ for the syntactic equality.

Protocols themselves are modeled by *processes* and *extended processes*, as defined in Figure 4. Processes contain the basic operators to model a small programming language: 0 represents a process which does nothing, the parallel composition of the two processes

$$\phi, \psi ::= \qquad\qquad\qquad \text{formulae}$$
$$M = N \mid M \neq N \mid \phi \wedge \psi \mid \phi \vee \psi$$

$P, Q, R ::=$	(plain) processes
0	null process
$P \mid Q$	parallel composition
$!P$	replication
$\nu n.P$	name restriction
if ϕ then P else Q	conditional
$u(x).P$	message input
$\overline{u}\langle M \rangle.P$	message output
event$(M).P$	event

$A, B, C ::=$	extended processes
P	plain process
$A \mid B$	parallel composition
$\nu n.A$	name restriction
$\nu x.A$	variable restriction
$\{^M/_x\}$	active substitution

Fig. 4. Syntax for processes

P and Q is denoted by $P \mid Q$, while $!P$ denotes the unbounded replication of P (that is, the unbounded parallel composition of P with itself). The process $\nu n.P$ creates a fresh name n and behaves like P. Tests are modeled by the process if ϕ then P else Q, which behaves like P if ϕ holds and like Q otherwise. Note that like in [6], we extend the applied pi-calculus by letting conditional branches now depend on formulae instead of just equality of terms. Process $u(x).P$ inputs some message (stored in the variable x) on channel u and then behaves like P while $\overline{u}\langle M \rangle.P$ outputs M on channel u and then behaves like P. event$(M).P$ behaves like P, the event is there to record what happens during the execution of the protocol and is typically used to express properties. We write $\nu \tilde{u}$ for the (possibly empty) series of pairwise-distinct binders $\nu u_1. \dots .\nu u_n$. The active substitution $\{^M/_x\}$ can replace the variable x by the term M in every process it comes into contact with and this behavior can be controlled by restriction, in particular, the process $\nu x \left(\{^M/_x\} \mid P\right)$ corresponds exactly to let $x = M$ in P.

Example 1. Let $P(a,b) = c(x).c(y).(\overline{c}\langle\langle x, a\rangle\rangle \mid \overline{c}\langle\langle y, b\rangle\rangle)$. This process waits for two inputs x and y on channel c then performs two outputs, $\langle x, a\rangle$, $\langle y, b\rangle$, in a non-deterministic order, on the same channel.

The *scope* of names and variables are delimited by binders $u(x)$ and νu. The different sets of bound names, bound variables, free names and free variables are respectively written bn(A), bv(A), fn(A) and fv(A). Occasionally, we write fn(M) (respectively fv(M)) for the set of names (respectively variables) which appear in term M. An extended process is *closed* if all its variables are either bound or defined by an active substitution. An *context* $C\,[\_]$ is an extended process with a hole.

A *frame* is an extended process built up from the null process 0 and active substitutions composed by parallel composition and restriction. The *domain* of a frame φ, denoted $\mathrm{dom}(\varphi)$, is the set of variables for which φ contains an active substitution $\{^M/_x\}$ such that x is not under restriction. Every extended process A can be mapped to a frame $\varphi(A)$ by replacing every plain process in A with 0.

4.2 Semantics

The operational semantics of processes in the applied pi-calculus is defined by three relations: *structural equivalence* ($\equiv$), *internal reduction* ($\rightarrow$) and *labelled reduction* ($\xrightarrow{\alpha}$), formally defined in [1]. Structural equivalence is the smallest equivalence relation on extended processes that is closed under application of evaluation contexts, by α-conversion of bounded names and bounded variables. Internal reductions represent evaluation of condition and internal communication between processes while labelled reductions represent communication with the environment. For example, the input and output rules are represented by the following two rules:

$$(\text{IN}) \qquad c(x).P \xrightarrow{c(M)} P\{^M/_x\}$$

$$(\text{OUT-ATOM}) \qquad \bar{c}\langle u \rangle.P \xrightarrow{\bar{c}\langle u \rangle} P$$

Example 2. Let us consider the process $P(a,b)$ defined in Example 1 and the process $Q = \nu r.\bar{c}\langle r \rangle.\bar{c}\langle r \rangle$ that generates a random r and send it twice. A possible sequence of transitions for the process $P(a,b) \mid Q$ is:

$$P(a,b) \mid Q \xrightarrow{\nu r_1.\bar{c}\langle r_1 \rangle} P(a,v) \mid \nu r.\bar{c}\langle r \rangle \mid \{^r/_{r_1}\} \xrightarrow{\nu r_2.\bar{c}\langle r_2 \rangle} P(a,b) \mid \{^r/_{r_1},^r/_{r_2}\}$$

$$\xrightarrow{c(r_1)} c(y).(\bar{c}\langle\langle r,a\rangle\rangle \mid \bar{c}\langle\langle y,b\rangle\rangle) \mid \{^r/_{r_1},^r/_{r_2}\} \xrightarrow{c(r_2)} \bar{c}\langle\langle r,a\rangle\rangle \mid \bar{c}\langle\langle r,b\rangle\rangle \mid \{^r/_{r_1},^r/_{r_2}\}$$

$$\xrightarrow{\nu y_1.\bar{c}\langle y_1 \rangle} \bar{c}\langle\langle y,b\rangle\rangle \mid \{^r/_{r_1},^r/_{r_2},^{\langle r,a\rangle}/_{y_1}\} \xrightarrow{\nu y_2.\bar{c}\langle y_2 \rangle} \{^r/_{r_1},^r/_{r_2},^{\langle r,a\rangle}/_{y_1},^{\langle r,b\rangle}/_{y_2}\}.$$

At the end of the execution, the process is reduced to a frame that contains the terms emitted by the initial process.

Privacy properties are often stated as equivalence relations [8]. Intuitively, if a protocol preserves ballot secrecy, an attacker should not make a distinction between a scenario where a voter votes 0 from a scenario where the voter votes 1. The applied pi-calculus comes with the notion of *observational equivalence*, which formally defines what it means for two processes to be indistinguishable for any attacker. Since observational equivalence has been shown to coincide [1,17] with labelled bisimilarity, which is easier to reason with, we adopt the latter in this paper. Labelled bisimilarity intuitively states that processes should be bisimilar and send indistinguishable messages. In our context, given that the only primitive we consider is pairing, two sequences of messages are indistinguishable to an attacker (formally defined as static equivalence [1]) if and only if they are equal. We therefore present here a simplified version of labelled bisimilarity, which is labelled bisimilarity for the special case of pairing.

Definition 1 (Labelled bisimilarity). *Labelled bisimilarity ($\approx_l$) is the largest symmetric relation $\mathcal{R}$ on closed extended processes such that $A\mathcal{R}B$ implies:*

1. $\varphi(A) = \varphi(B)$;
2. if $A \rightarrow A'$, then $B \rightarrow^* B'$ and $A'\mathcal{R}B'$ for some B';
3. if $A \xrightarrow{\alpha} A'$ such that $\mathsf{fv}(\alpha) \subseteq \mathsf{dom}(A)$ and $\mathsf{bn}(\alpha) \cap \mathsf{fn}(B) = \emptyset$, then $B \rightarrow^* \xrightarrow{\alpha} \rightarrow^*$ B' and $A'\mathcal{R}B'$ for some B'.

Example 3. Let us consider $A = P(a, b) \mid Q$ and $B = P(b, a) \mid Q$. Is $A \approx_l B$? Let us consider the same evolution as in Example 2 except that $c(r_1)$ and $c(r_2)$ are replaced by $c(M)$ and $c(N)$ which represents an action of the intruder, replacing what is sent by Q by something of her choice. In that case, we will have :

$$\varphi(A) = \{^r/_{r_1}, ^r/_{r_2}, ^{\langle M, a \rangle}/_{y_1}, ^{\langle N, b \rangle}/_{y_2}\} \text{ and } \varphi(B) = \{^r/_{r_1}, ^r/_{r_2}, ^{\langle M, b \rangle}/_{y_1}, ^{\langle N, a \rangle}/_{y_2}\}.$$

Since $\varphi(A) \neq \varphi(B)$ we have that $A \napprox_l B$.

4.3 Modeling Protocols in Applied pi-Calculus

We provide a formal specification of the two last variants of the CNRS voting system, in the applied pi-calculus. We do not describe the formal model of the initial voting system since it does not ensure ballot secrecy nor vote correctness.

We model the communications of the ballot box with the voters and the screen by secure channels (resp. c_i and c_B). These channels may be controlled by the adversary when the ballot box is corrupted. The voters and the assessor look at the screen. This communication cannot be altered and is modeled by an authenticated channel c_{eyes}. The assessor also communicates with each voter to check that the voter found his/her ballot on the screen. This is again modeled by an authenticated channel c_{A_i} since we assume that voters cannot be physically impersonated. The channel connections are summarized in Figure 5.

Remark 1. The applied-pi calculus provides an easy way to model both public and secure channel. Public channels are simply modeled by unrestricted names: the attacker can both read and send messages. Secure channels are modeled by restricted names: the attacker cannot read nor send any message on these channels. In contrast, an attacker may read authenticated channels but only authorized users may send messages on them. Since the applied pi-calculus does not provide us with a primitive for authenticated channels, we model authenticated channel by a secure channel, except that a copy of each emission is sent first on a public channel. In particular, we use the notation $\overline{\overline{c}}\langle M \rangle$ for $\overline{c_p}\langle M \rangle.\overline{c}\langle M \rangle$ with c_p a public channel.

Remark 2. The role of the individual voting device is limited: it simply receives the vote from the voter and transmit it to the Ballot Box. W.l.o.g and for simplicity, we identify the voter and her individual device in the model of the voting systems.

Model of F2FV^2. The process for the voter is parametrized by the number n of voters, its secure channel with the ballot box c, its authenticated channel with the screen (c_e) and the auditor (c_a), the public channel c_p and its vote v.

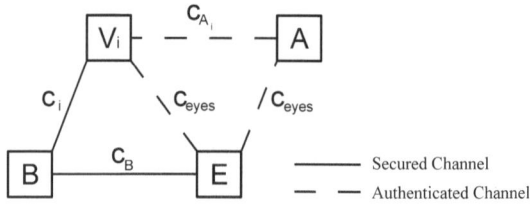

Fig. 5. Players of the Protocol

$$V_n(c, c_e, c_a, c_p, v) =$$
$$\nu k \, . \, c(x) \, . \qquad \text{\% Creates fresh nonce and waits for input on } c.$$
$$\bar{c}\langle\langle x, k, v\rangle\rangle \, . \qquad \text{\% Sends ballot on } c \text{ to the ballot box.}$$
$$c_e(y) \, . \qquad \text{\% Waits for input on } c_e \text{ (results on the screen).}$$
$$\text{if } \langle x, k, v\rangle \in_n y \qquad \text{\% Checks his vote.}$$
$$\text{then } \overline{c_a}\langle\text{ok}\rangle \text{ else } \overline{c_a}\langle\text{fail}\rangle \qquad \text{\% Sends result on } c_a \text{ to the assessor.}$$

The process for the ballot box is parametrized by the number n of voters, the secure channels $c_v^1, \ldots, c_v^n$ with each voter and its secure channel with the screen c_{be}.

$$B_n(c_v^1, \ldots, c_v^n, c_b) =$$
$$\nu r_1, \ldots, r_n \, . \qquad \text{\% Creates fresh randomness.}$$
$$\overline{c_v^1}\langle r_1\rangle \, . \, \ldots \, . \, \overline{c_v^n}\langle r_n\rangle \, . \qquad \text{\% Sends randomness to voters.}$$
$$c_v^1(y_1) \, . \, \ldots \, . \, c_v^n(y_n) \, . \qquad \text{\% Waits for inputs of ballots.}$$
$$(\overline{c_b}\langle y_1\rangle \mid \cdots \mid \overline{c_b}\langle y_n\rangle) \qquad \text{\% Sends ballots in random order to } E.$$

The screen is modeled by a process E_n that simply broadcasts the result given by B_n. It is parametrized by the number n of voters, the authenticated channels c_e with each voter, the secure channel with the bulletin box c_b, and the public channel c_p.

$$E_n(c_b, c_e, c_p) =$$
$$c_b(t_1) \, . \, \ldots \, . \, c_b(t_n) \, . \qquad \text{\% Waits for votes from ballot box.}$$
$$\text{let } r = \langle t_1, \ldots, t_n\rangle \text{ in}$$
$$\overline{c_p}\langle r\rangle \, . \, (! \, \overline{c_e}\langle r\rangle) \qquad \text{\% Displays info for all the boardroom.}$$

The last role is the role of the assessor. It is modeled by a process A_n that waits for the result displayed by the screen and the confirmation of the voters. Then it verifies the outcome and validates the election if everything is correct. The process A_n is parametrized by the number n of voters, the authenticated channels $c_a^1, \ldots, c_a^n$ with each voter, the secure channel with the screen c_e, and the public channel c_p.

$$A_n(c_e, c_a^1, \ldots, c_a^n, c_p) =$$
$$c_e(z') \, . \qquad \text{\% Waits to see result on the screen.}$$
$$c_a^1(z_1) \, . \, \ldots \, . \, c_a^n(z_n) \, . \qquad \text{\% Waits for decision of voters.}$$
$$\text{if } \Psi_n(z', z_1, \ldots, z_n) \qquad \text{\% Checks if everything is fine.}$$
$$\text{then } \overline{c_p}\langle\text{ok}\rangle \text{ else } \overline{c_p}\langle\text{fail}\rangle \qquad \text{\% Sends confirmation or rejection.}$$

where $\Psi_n(p', p_1, \ldots, p_n) = (\bigwedge_{i=1}^{n} p_i = \mathsf{ok}) \wedge (p' = \langle \Pi_1^n(p'), \Pi_2^n(p'), \ldots, \Pi_n^n(p') \rangle)$.

The test Ψ_n ensures that each voter approved the vote ($p_i = \mathsf{ok}$) and that the result contains as many ballots than the number of voters.

Finally the system $\mathsf{F2FV}^2$ is represented by the voter's role V_n and the voting context:

$$P_n^2[\_] = \nu \tilde{\omega}. [\_ \mid B_n(\mathsf{c}_1, \ldots, \mathsf{c}_n, \mathsf{c}_B) \mid E_n(\mathsf{c}_B, \mathsf{c}_{\mathsf{eyes}}, \mathsf{c}_{\mathsf{out}}) \mid A_n(\mathsf{c}_{\mathsf{eyes}}, \mathsf{c}_{A_1}, \ldots, \mathsf{c}_{A_n}, \mathsf{c}_{\mathsf{out}})]$$

where $\tilde{\omega} = (\mathsf{c}_1, \ldots, \mathsf{c}_n, \mathsf{c}_{A_1}, \ldots, \mathsf{c}_{A_n}, \mathsf{c}_B, \mathsf{c}_{\mathsf{eyes}})$ are restricted channels ($\mathsf{c}_{\mathsf{out}}$ is public).

Model of the Protocol $\mathsf{F2FV}^3$. The third protocol only differs from the second one by the fact that the ballot box does not generate any randomness. Therefore, the models of the screen and of the assessor are unchanged. The voter and ballot box models are modified as follows.

$$
\begin{aligned}
&V_n'(c, c_e, c_a, c_p, v) = \\
&\quad \nu k . \overline{c}\langle\langle k, v \rangle\rangle . c_e(x) . \\
&\quad \text{if } \langle k, v \rangle \in_n x \text{ then } \overline{\overline{c_a}}\langle\mathsf{ok}\rangle \text{ else } \overline{\overline{c_a}}\langle\mathsf{fail}\rangle
\end{aligned}
\qquad
\begin{aligned}
&B_n'(c_v^1, \ldots, c_v^n, c_b) = \\
&\quad c_v^1(y_1) . \ldots . c_v^n(y_n) . \\
&\quad (\overline{c_b}\langle y_1 \rangle \mid \cdots \mid \overline{c_b}\langle y_n \rangle)
\end{aligned}
$$

The system $\mathsf{F2FV}^3$ without the voters is represented by the voter's role V_n' and the voting context:

$$P_n^3[\_] = \nu \tilde{\omega}. [\_ \mid B_n'(\mathsf{c}_1, \ldots, \mathsf{c}_n, \mathsf{c}_B) \mid E_n(\mathsf{c}_B, \mathsf{c}_{\mathsf{eyes}}, \mathsf{c}_{\mathsf{out}}) \mid A_n(\mathsf{c}_{\mathsf{eyes}}, \mathsf{c}_{A_1}, \ldots, \mathsf{c}_{A_n}, \mathsf{c}_{\mathsf{out}})]$$

where $\tilde{\omega} = (\mathsf{c}_1, \ldots, \mathsf{c}_n, \mathsf{c}_{A_1}, \ldots, \mathsf{c}_{A_n}, \mathsf{c}_B, \mathsf{c}_{\mathsf{eyes}})$ are restricted channels.

5 Security Properties

We study two crucial properties for voting systems: ballot secrecy and vote correctness. We consider two cases depending on whether the ballot box is corrupted or not. We always assume the screen to be honest. This is however not a limitation. Indeed, requiring the screen to be honest reflects the fact that everyone sees the same screen, which is always the case for people in the same room.

5.1 Ballot Secrecy

Formalizing ballot secrecy may be tricky. For example, even a good voting system reveals how anyone voted in case of unanimity. Early definitions of privacy appear for example in [3]. In what follows, we use a well established definition of ballot secrecy that has been formalized in terms of equivalence by Delaune, Kremer and Ryan in [8]. Several other definitions of privacy have been proposed (see e.g. [15,4]), which measure the fact that the attacker may learn some information, even if he does not know how a certain voter voted.

A protocol with voting process $V(v, id)$ and authority process A preserves *ballot secrecy* if an attacker cannot distinguish when votes are swapped, i.e. it cannot distinguish when a voter a_1 votes v_1 and a_2 votes v_2 from the case where a_1 votes v_2 and a_2 votes v_1. This is formally specified by :

$$\nu \tilde{n}. (A \mid V\{^{v_2}/_x, ^{a_1}/_y\} \mid V\{^{v_1}/_x, ^{a_2}/_y\}) \approx_l \nu \tilde{n}. (A \mid V\{^{v_1}/_x, ^{a_1}/_y\} \mid V\{^{v_2}/_x, ^{a_2}/_y\})$$

where $\tilde{n}$ represents the data (keys, nonces, channels, ...) initially shared between the authority and the voters.

Ballot Secrecy for Voting Protocol F2FV². The voting protocol F2FV² preserves ballot secrecy, even when all but two voters are dishonest, provided that the ballot box, the screen and the assessor are honest. For the sake of clarity, we use the following notation for the ith voter: $V^i(v) = V_n(\mathsf{c_i}, \mathsf{c_{eyes}}, \mathsf{c_{A_i}}, \mathsf{c_{out}}, v)$.

Theorem 1. *Let $n \in \mathbb{N}$, let (P_n^2, V_n) be the process specification for n voters of the voting protocol* F2FV² *as defined in Section 3.2, and let a, b be two names. Then*

$$P_n^2 \left[V^1(a) \mid V^2(b) \right] \approx_l P_n^2 \left[V^1(b) \mid V^2(a) \right]$$

Proof sketch: The proof of Theorem 1 consists in two main steps. First we build a relation $\mathcal{R}$ such that

$$P_n^2 \left[V^1(a) \mid V^2(b) \right] \mathcal{R} \, P_n^2 \left[V^1(b) \mid V^2(a) \right]$$

and such that for any two processes $P \, \mathcal{R} \, Q$, any move of P can be matched by a move of Q such that the resulting processes remain in relation. This amounts to characterizing all possible successors of $P_n^2 \left[V^1(a) \mid V^2(b) \right]$ and $P_n^2 \left[V^1(b) \mid V^2(a) \right]$. The second step of the proof consists in showing that the sequences of messages observed by the attacker are equal (due to the shuffle performed by the ballot box).

Ballot Secrecy for Voting Protocol F2FV³. Similarly, the voting protocol F2FV³ preserves ballot secrecy, even when all but two voters are dishonest, provided that the ballot box, the screen and the assessor are honest.

Theorem 2. *Let $n \in \mathbb{N}$, let (P_n^3, V_n') be the process specification for n voters of the voting protocol* F2FV³ *as defined in Section 3.3, and let a, b be two names. Then*

$$P_n^3 \left[V'^1(a) \mid V'^2(b) \right] \approx_l P_n^3 \left[V'^1(b) \mid V'^2(a) \right]$$

The proof of Theorem 2 is adapted from the proof of Theorem 1.

5.2 Vote Correctness

We define vote correctness as the fact that the election result should contain the votes of the honest voters. Formally, we assume that the voting protocol records the published outcome of the election t in an event $\mathsf{event}(t)$.

Definition 2 (Correctness property). *Let n be the number of registered voters, and m be the number of honest voters. Let $v_1, \ldots, v_m \in \mathcal{N}$ be the votes of the honest voters. Let $V^1, \ldots, V^m$ be the processes representing the honest voters. Each V^i is parametrized by its vote v_i. Let P_n be a context representing the voting system, besides the honest voters. We say that a voting specification $(P_n, \vec{V})$ satisfies* vote correctness *if for every $v_1, \ldots, v_m$, for every execution of the protocol leading to the validation of a result t_r, i.e. of the form*

$$P_n[V^1(v_1)| \ldots |V^m(v_m)] \to^* \nu\tilde{n} \cdot (\text{event}(t_r) \cdot Q \mid Q')$$

for some names $\tilde{n}$ and processes Q, Q', then there exist votes $v_{m+1}, \ldots, v_n$ and a permutation τ of $[\![1, n]\!]$ such that $t_r = \langle v_{\tau(1)}, \ldots, v_{\tau(n)} \rangle$, that is, the outcome of the election contains all the honest votes plus some dishonest ones.

To express vote correctness in the context of the CNRS Section 07 voting system, we simply add an event that records the tally, at the end of the process specification of the assessor (see Appendix for the corresponding modified process A'_n). We show vote correctness for a strong corruption scenario, where even the ballot box is corrupted. Formally, we consider the following context that represents the three voting systems, the only difference between the systems now lying in the definition of voters.

$$P_n'[\_] = \nu\,\tilde{\omega}.\,[\_ \mid E_n(\mathsf{c_B}, \mathsf{c_{eyes}}, \mathsf{c_{out}}) \mid A'_n(\mathsf{c_{eyes}}, \mathsf{c_{A_1}}, \ldots, \mathsf{c_{A_n}}, \mathsf{c_{out}})]$$

where $\tilde{\omega} = (\mathsf{c_{A_1}}, \ldots, \mathsf{c_{A_n}}, \mathsf{c_{eyes}})$, which means that the intruder has access in this scenario to channels $\mathsf{c_1}, \ldots, \mathsf{c_n}$ and $\mathsf{c_B}$ in addition to $\mathsf{c_{out}}$.

To illustrate the correctness property, let first show that F2FV^1 does not satisfy vote correctness when the ballot box is corrupted. First, we introduce $\hat{V}$ the process of an honest voter in F2FV^1:

$$\hat{V}(c, c_e, c_a, c_p, v) = c(x) \cdot \bar{c}\langle\langle x, v\rangle\rangle \cdot c_e(y) \cdot \text{if } \langle x, v\rangle \in_n y \text{ then } \overline{\overline{c_a}}\langle\text{ok}\rangle \text{ else } \overline{c_a}\langle\text{fail}\rangle$$

Let $\hat{V}^i = \hat{V}\{^{\mathsf{c_i}}/_c, ^{\mathsf{c_{eyes}}}/_{c_e}, ^{\mathsf{c_{A_i}}}/_{c_a}, ^{\mathsf{c_{out}}}/_{c_p}\}$. It represents the i-th honest voter. Suppose now, that the first m honest voters cast the some vote: $\forall i \in [\![1, m]\!]$, $v_i = v$. We show how the attack described in Section 3.1 is reflected. Each honest voter receives the same random number r:

$$P_n'[\hat{V}^1(v_1) \mid \cdots \mid \hat{V}^m(v_m)] \xrightarrow{\forall i\in[\![1,m]\!],\ \overline{c_i}\langle r\rangle} P_n'[\hat{V}_r^1(v_1) \mid \cdots \mid \hat{V}_r^m(v_m)]$$

where $\hat{V}_r^i(v_i) = \overline{c_i}\langle\langle r, v_i\rangle\rangle \cdot \mathsf{c_{eyes}}(y) \cdot \text{if } \langle r, v_i\rangle \in_n y_i \text{ then } \overline{\mathsf{c_{A_i}}}\langle\text{ok}\rangle \text{ else } \overline{\mathsf{c_{A_i}}}\langle\text{fail}\rangle$. Then, the honest voters output their vote on channels $\mathsf{c_1}, \ldots, \mathsf{c_m}$ which will always be $\langle r, v\rangle$.

$$P_n'[\hat{V}_r^1(v_1) \mid \cdots \mid \hat{V}_r^m(v_m)] \xrightarrow{\forall i\in[\![1,m]\!],\ \overline{c_i}\langle\langle r,v_i\rangle\rangle} P_n'[\hat{V}_e^1(v_1) \mid \cdots \mid \hat{V}_e^m(v_m)]$$

where $\hat{V}_e^i(v_i) = \mathsf{c_{eyes}}(y) \cdot \text{if } \langle r, v_i\rangle \in_n y_i \text{ then } \overline{\mathsf{c_{A_i}}}\langle\text{ok}\rangle \text{ else } \overline{\mathsf{c_{A_i}}}\langle\text{fail}\rangle$. Corrupted voters also submit their votes (which is transparent in transitions) and we move to the next phase: the corrupted ballot box just has to output one of the honest votes to the screen and $n-1$ other votes. Thus, the final tally t_r showed by the screen will contain only one $\langle r, v\rangle$ but each honest voters will send ok to the assessor since their test will succeed anyway. In that case, we would have $P_n'[\hat{V}^1(v_1)| \ldots |\hat{V}^m(v_m)] \to^* \nu\tilde{n} \cdot \text{event}(t_r)$ for some $\tilde{n}$, but, clearly, t_r is not satisfying the property of the Definition 2 since it only contains one vote v instead of m votes v.

In contrast, the two voting systems F2FV^2 and F2FV^3 satisfy vote correctness, even when the ballot box is corrupted, assuming that the voters check that their ballots appear on the screen.

Table 1. Results for the F2FV[1],F2FV[2], and F2FV[3] protocols. A ✓ indicates provable security while × indicates an attack. We assume an arbitrary number of dishonest voters.

RESULTS		Privacy			Correctness		
System ⟍ Corr. Players	None	Ballot Box	Assessor	None	Ballot Box	Assessor
F2FV[1]	✓	×	✓	✓	×	×
F2FV[2]	✓	×	✓	✓	✓	×
F2FV[3]	✓	×	✓	✓	✓	×

Theorem 3. *The voting specifications* (P'_n, V) *and* (P'_n, V') *satisfy vote correctness.*

Proof sketch. The assessor records the result of the election in an event only if $\Psi_n(p', p_1, \ldots, p_n)$ holds. This formula intuitively represents the fact that every voter has told to the assessor that his ballot was included in the tally, and that the number of ballots in the tally matches the number of voters, i.e. n. Using this information and the fact that each honest voter has generated a random nonce uniquely identifying his ballot, we can show that the voting specifications satisfy vote correctness.

Correctness requires that at least one person in the room checks that no one has complained and that the number of displayed ballots correspond to the number of voters. If no one performs these checks then there is no honest assessor and correctness is no longer guaranteed.

A summary of our findings is displayed on Table 1. The proofs of correctness of F2FV[2] and F2FV[3] in the honest case follow from the proofs in the dishonest case. Privacy is not affected by a corrupted assessor as it actually only performs public verification. So its corruption does not provide any extra power to the attacker. Privacy and correctness for F2FV[1] (in the honest case) follow from the proofs for F2FV[2].

6   Discussion

We believe that the voting system proposed by the CNRS Section 07 committee for boardroom meetings is an interesting protocol that improves over existing electronic devices. We have analyzed the security of three possible versions, discovering some interesting flaws. We think that the two last versions are adequate since they both preserve ballot secrecy and vote correctness. The choice between the two versions depends on the desired compromise between ballot secrecy and vote correctness: the second version ensures better correctness but less privacy since the randomness generated by the ballot box may leak the identity of the voters. Conversely, the third system offers better privacy but slightly less assurance about vote correctness, in case the voters do not use proper random identifiers.

In both cases, vote correctness is guaranteed as soon as:

– Voters really use (unpredictable) random numbers. In practice, voters could print (privately and before the meeting) a list of random numbers that they would use at their will (erasing a number once used). This list of random numbers could typically be generated using a computer. Alternatively, voters may also bring dice to the meeting.
– Each voter casts a vote (possibly blank or null) and checks that his vote (and associated randomness) appears on the screen.

Correctness does not require any trust on the devices while privacy does. This is unavoidable unless the communication between the voters on the ballot box would be anonymized, which would require a much heavier infrastructure. Note that the system is not fair if the ballot box is compromised since dishonest voters may then wait for honest voters to cast their votes, before making their own decision.

In this paper, we have focused on ballot secrecy and vote correctness. As future work, we plan to study stronger notions of privacy. Clearly, the voting system is not coercion resistant. Indeed, an attacker may provide a voter with a list of random numbers, that he should use in a precise order, allowing the attacker to control the votes. However, we believe these systems ensure some form of receipt-freeness, assuming the attacker is given access to the screen only after the election is over but cannot interact with voters before nor during the election.

A weakness of the system relies in the fact that a voter may force to re-run an election by (wrongly) claiming that her vote does not appear on the screen. As already mentioned in Section 3.4, this is mitigated by the fact that the voter could then be blamed if this happens to often. This also means that an honest voter could be blamed if a dishonest Ballot Box intentionally removes her ballot at each turn. It would be interesting to devise a mechanism to mitigate this issue.

Acknowledgment. We would like to thank the anonymous reviewers for their numerous remarks and propositions that helped us to improve the paper.

References

1. Abadi, M., Fournet, C.: Mobile values, new names, and secure communication. In: 28th ACM Symp. on Principles of Programming Languages (POPL 2001), pp. 104–115 (2001)
2. Adida, B.: Helios: web-based open-audit voting. In: 17th Conference on Security Symposium, SS 2008, pp. 335–348. USENIX Association (2008)
3. Benaloh, J., Tuinstra, D.: Receipt-free secret-ballot elections. In: Proceedings of the 26th Annual ACM Symposium on Theory of Computing (STOC 1994), pp. 544–553. ACM (1994)
4. Bernhard, D., Cortier, V., Pereira, O., Warinschi, B.: Measuring vote privacy, revisited. In: 19th ACM Conference on Computer and Communications Security (CCS 2012), Raleigh, USA. ACM (October 2012)
5. Clarkson, M.R., Chong, S., Myers, A.C.: Civitas: Toward a secure voting system. In: 2008 IEEE Symposium on Security and Privacy, pp. 354–368 (2008)
6. Cortier, V., Smyth, B.: Attacking and fixing Helios: An analysis of ballot secrecy. In: 24th IEEE Computer Security Foundations Symposium (CSF 2011), pp. 297–311 (2011)

7. Cortier, V., Wiedling, C.: A formal analysis of the norwegian E-voting protocol. In: Degano, P., Guttman, J.D. (eds.) POST 2012. LNCS, vol. 7215, pp. 109–128. Springer, Heidelberg (2012)
8. Delaune, S., Kremer, S., Ryan, M.: Verifying privacy-type properties of electronic voting protocols. Journal of Computer Security 17(4), 435–487 (2009)
9. Feldman, A., Halderman, A., Felten, E.: Security Analysis of the Diebold AccuVote-TS Voting Machine. In: 2007 USENIX/ACCURATE Electronic Voting Technology Workshop, EVT 2007 (2007)
10. Fujioka, A., Okamoto, T., Ohta, K.: A practical secret voting scheme for large scale elections. In: Zheng, Y., Seberry, J. (eds.) AUSCRYPT 1992. LNCS, vol. 718, pp. 244–251. Springer, Heidelberg (1993)
11. Groth, J.: Efficient maximal privacy in boardroom voting and anonymous broadcast. In: Juels, A. (ed.) FC 2004. LNCS, vol. 3110, pp. 90–104. Springer, Heidelberg (2004)
12. Hao, F., Ryan, P.Y.A., Zielinski, P.: Anonymous voting by two-round public discussion. IET Information Security 4(2), 62–67 (2010)
13. Juels, A., Catalano, D., Jakobsson, M.: Coercion-resistant electronic elections. In: Chaum, D., Jakobsson, M., Rivest, R.L., Ryan, P.Y.A., Benaloh, J., Kutylowski, M., Adida, B. (eds.) Towards Trustworthy Elections. LNCS, vol. 6000, pp. 37–63. Springer, Heidelberg (2010)
14. Kremer, S., Ryan, M.D., Smyth, B.: Election verifiability in electronic voting protocols. In: Gritzalis, D., Preneel, B., Theoharidou, M. (eds.) ESORICS 2010. LNCS, vol. 6345, pp. 389–404. Springer, Heidelberg (2010)
15. Küsters, R., Truderung, T., Vogt, A.: Verifiability, Privacy, and Coercion-Resistance: New Insights from a Case Study. In: IEEE Symposium on Security and Privacy (S&P 2011), pp. 538–553. IEEE Computer Society (2011)
16. Küsters, R., Truderung, T., Vogt, A.: Clash Attacks on the Verifiability of E-Voting Systems. In: IEEE Symposium on Security and Privacy (S&P 2012), pp. 395–409. IEEE Computer Society (2012)
17. Liu, J.: A proof of coincidence of labeled bisimilerity and observational equivalence in applied pi calculus. Technical report (2011)
18. Schneier, B.: Applied Cryptography, ch. 6. John Wiley & Sons (1996)
19. Wolchok, S., Wustrow, E., Halderman, J.A., Prasad, H.K., Kankipati, A., Sakhamuri, S.K., Yagati, V., Gonggrijp, R.: Security analysis of India's electronic voting machines. In: 17th ACM Conference on Computer and Communications Security, CCS 2010 (2010)

Dispute Resolution in Accessible Voting Systems: The Design and Use of Audiotegrity

Tyler Kaczmarek[1], John Wittrock[1], Richard Carback[2], Alex Florescu[1], Jan Rubio[1], Noel Runyan[3], Poorvi L. Vora[1], and Filip Zagórski[4]

[1] Department of Computer Science, The George Washington University[*]
[2] Network and Information Concepts Group, Charles Stark Draper Laboratories
[3] Personal Data Systems
[4] Institute of Mathematics and Computer Science,
Wroclaw University of Technology[**]

Abstract. We describe in detail dispute resolution problems with cryptographic voting systems that do not produce a paper record of the unencrypted vote. With these in mind, we describe the design and use of Audiotegrity—a cryptographic voting protocol and corresponding voting system with some of the accessibility benefits of fully-electronic voting systems and some of the dispute resolution properties of paper-ballot-based systems. We also describe subtle issues with coercion-resistance if accessible systems are not well-designed.

Audiotegrity was designed in response to a request by Takoma Park election officials, tested in a public test organized by the city in June 2011, and used in its municipal election in November 2011. We are not aware of any other precinct-based end-to-end independently-verifiable election for public office where the protocol enabled participation by voters with visual disabilities.

Keywords: end-to-end voting systems, accessible, dispute resolution.

1 Introduction

Several cryptographic voting protocols have been proposed for polling place elections, where voters use voting systems that they do not trust. Many of the corresponding voting systems use paper ballots (Prêt à Voter [20,10], Scantegrity II [8]) scanned after the voter marks her choice(s). Paper ballots are severely limiting from a usability and accessibility perspective. On the other hand, the straightforward replacement of interactions on paper with similar interactions

[*] This work was supported in part by NSF Award Nos. 0831149, 0937267 and 1137973 and by Research Experience for Undergraduates (REU) enhancements to these awards. It was determined to be Exempt, Category 2—GW IRB application 061109.

[**] This research was partially supported by NCN scientific project 2010-2013 - grant number N N206 369839.

J. Heather, S. Schneider, and V. Teague (Eds.): VoteID 2013, LNCS 7985, pp. 127–141, 2013.
© Springer-Verlag Berlin Heidelberg 2013

over an electronic medium does not always preserve a protocol's security properties. This paper makes the following contributions. First, it describes in detail the dispute resolution weaknesses of voting systems where voters do not manually mark ballots. Second, it presents the design and deployment of Audiotegrity, a protocol and corresponding voting system, that seeks a balance between the strong accessibility and usability properties of fully-electronic voting systems and the strong dispute resolution properties of paper-ballot-based ones. Audiotegrity was used by the city of Takoma Park for its municipal election in November 2011.

Audiotegrity provides an electronic interface for the voter to enter a vote, and produces a marked Scantegrity II ballot which is then scanned and processed in the same manner as a hand-marked paper Scantegrity II ballot. From the available descriptions, the version of Prêt à Voter proposed for use in Victoria [6] and STAR-Vote [4] use similar interfaces. The focus of this paper is twofold. First, it presents the security implications of the use of paper vs. electronic interactions in various protocol steps. Second, it describes the design of a protocol that takes these into consideration, and the use of the corresponding system in tests in June 2011 and a real election in November 2011. In particular, we observe that paper ballots or ballot summaries play a role not only in manual recounts, but in the protocol itself, even when the voting system is a good cryptographic system. Paper and physical procedures enable some aspects of dispute resolution and coercion-resistance for human voters, who are not able to make and check digital commitments and signatures in the polling booth.

We note at the outset that we focused on the vote-casting experience. We did not implement interfaces for voters to interact with the website that displays confirmation numbers and audit information. However, voters can use accessible devices, in general, for electronic information displayed on appropriately-designed websites. Voters cannot use personal accessible devices while voting, as such a device would learn the vote.

In section 2 we provide background, and in section 3 we describe related work. In 4 we describe the dispute resolution and coercion-resistance problems with voting systems that do not show the voter a paper record of her unencrypted vote. In section 5 we describe the Audiotegrity protocol and its security properties. In section 6 we describe the dispute resolution and coercion-resistance properties of paper-ballot protocols Prêt à Voter and Scantegrity II and compare them with those of Audiotegrity. In section 7 we describe the use of Audiotegrity in Takoma Park in 2011. We conclude in section 8.

2   Background

In the typical cryptographic voting protocol, each vote is encrypted and all encrypted votes are broadcast on an election website. Voters may treat encrypted votes as receipts and take them home to check that they are correctly broadcast. Encrypted votes are processed in a verifiable manner to obtain the tally.

Vote Encryption: We will focus on precinct-based protocols—where the voter votes from a polling booth, and the cast/audit paradigm proposed by Benaloh [3].

Some protocols use specially-designed paper ballots with the property that a voter can encrypt her vote simply by filling the ballot, see Figure 1.

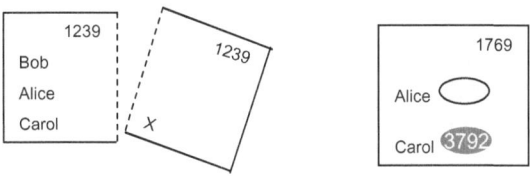

Fig. 1. Marked ballots: Left: *Prêt à Voter* Right: *Scantegrity II*

For example, Prêt à Voter ballots list the candidates in a pseudo-random permutation on the left side of the ballot. The voter marks her choice on the right side and then separates the two ballot halves along a central perforation. The half with the candidate order is shredded and the marked half cast. The serial number provides the information necessary for the voting system to interpret the mark, and the position of the mark is the encryption of the vote.

For another example, the Scantegrity II voter marks ballots that are very similar to optical scan ballots, with a single important difference. Each oval has printed on it, in invisible ink, a confirmation number—the encryption corresponding to this vote choice. When voters filled the oval with a special pen, the confirmation number becomes visible. The same functionality can be achieved through the use of scratch-off surfaces.

Other protocols like Votebox and simple-verifiable voting rely on encryption machines in the polling place to perform the encryption.

Once the vote is encrypted, it is cast or audited, see Figure 2. If the encryption (i.e. the receipt) is audited, the voting system provides a proof that it encrypted the vote correctly, and the proof is public. The corresponding vote cannot be cast as the correspondence between the encryption and the vote is now public, and the vote no longer secret. The voter goes through a fresh encryption process which will again end in a cast or audit.

Voters take home copies of the final cast encryption as well as voting system responses to audits. They may check the presence of these on the election website, and the correctness proofs of the audited encryptions using software obtained from any—and, in fact, several—sources. Thus the voter need not have access to trusted software in the polling booth. The tally is computed in a verifiable manner from the encrypted votes posted on the website. After the election outcome is announced, the tally computation is publicly audited. Anyone can write software to check the audits.

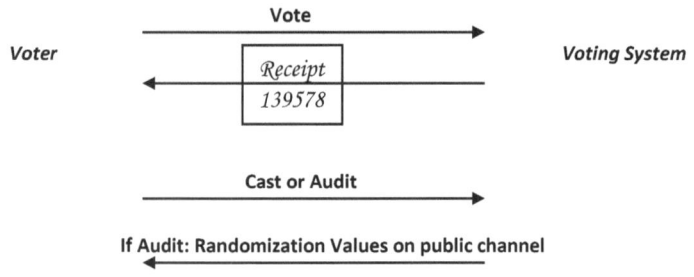

Fig. 2. The Benaloh Cast/Audit Paradigm

3   Related Work

Accessible Interfaces for Voters: The Voting-on-Paper Assistive Device (Vote-PAD) [1] enables voters with visual or dexterity impairments to complete paper ballots. The device consists of a plastic ballot-sleeve, tactile indicators and an audio tape recording, customized for each election and ballot design. Similar devices, called Tactile Ballots, have been used in elections in Rhode Island [13]. Prime III [12] provides a multimodal interface to a voting machine with a voter-verifiable video audit trail (VVVAT) that is a video record of all interactions with the voting machine. A preliminary proposal for accessible audio-based electronic protocols appears in [11]. These protocols, however, are not practical enough for use in real elections.

Dispute Resolution: Saltman [21] and Mercuri [19] were among the first to describe problems with voting systems not following instructions. They demonstrated these problems in non-cryptographic voting systems. We show, in section 4, that similar (though not identical) problems can persist in cryptographic voting systems. Kiayias and Yung provide a dispute-free protocol [16] in the classical cryptographic protocol model (all participants are interactive probabilistic polynomial time Turing machines) which was followed by proposals for several dispute-free protocols in the same model. We examine the problems that arise because voters are not probabilistic polynomial-time Turing machines, as proposed by Adida [2]. Küsters, Truderung and Vogt provide a rigorous definition of accountability for voting and other cryptographic protocols [18]. The definitions used is closely related to our notion of dispute resolution. The problems they identify are not, however, related to the cast/audit paradigm, nor to the use of paper. We have referred briefly to dispute resolution problems with the cast/audit paradigm in [9].

Use of Accessible Voting Systems in Real Elections: The protocol we describe in section 5 is very similar to the STAR-Vote proposal and the version of Prêt à Voter proposed for use in Victoria. Neither proposal describes how voters commit to casting or auditing ballots. The STAR-Vote proposal does not distinguish among spoiled and audited ballots and does not describe how to resolve disputes regarding whether a ballot was audited or cast. The STAR-Vote proposal also does not describe if blank paper ballots are available for voters in case the voting machine does not print the vote as directed.

4   Problems with Dispute Resolution in the Absence of Paper

We first consider a protocol that does not use paper at all: VoteBox. In this instance of the cast/audit paradigm (see figure 3), the voter enters a vote into a voting machine, which provides an encryption of the vote; this encryption is immediately published on the bulletin board. The voter then chooses whether to cast the ballot or audit it. If she chooses to audit it, the machine publishes (or provides) the randomization used in the encryption. If she chooses to cast it, the encrypted value is published among cast ballots. All communication is electronic.

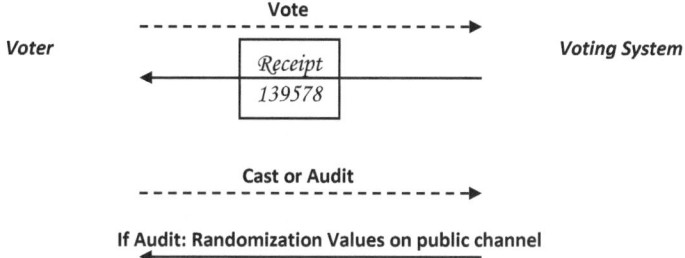

Fig. 3. The channel from voter to voting system is electronic. A dashed line shows interactions that are not verifiable by a third party and hence result in dispute resolution weaknesses.

We consider two problems with VoteBox because the machine may deviate from protocol and not follow the voter's instructions.

The voter provides two sets of instructions: the vote and whether to cast or audit. We consider each separately below.

1. **Machine encrypts a vote other than that cast:** The voter is able to detect the deviation on audit. Hence, if the machine changes a large enough number of votes in this manner, the probability of at least one voter detecting this on audit is large. However, the protocol does not enable the voter to prove such deviation. The channel from voter to voting machine is electronic and there is no record—other than that held by the voting machine—of the voter's command. Hence a third party would not be able to determine whether the voter or the voting machine was lying.
2. **Machine does not follow cast/audit instruction:** The voter is always able to detect the deviation. However, as above, the voter is not able to prove the deviation to a third party.

The reason the above deviations cannot be proven to a third party is that—in both instances—there is no record of the voter's instruction, see figure 3. The fact that the dispute cannot be resolved is an important problem. In particular, the general public cannot distinguish between (a) an incorrect election outcome and (b) a group of dishonest voters calling an honest election into question.

It has been proposed that other approaches—such as auditing a machine in public during the election—may be used to determine whether a machine is truly behaving honestly. However, as with parallel testing, such approaches are vulnerable to "cryptic knocks". An insider present at the polling location might easily warn the voting machine through a side channel that it is being audited. The channel may be implemented in various ways, including a modified election console which can send to the booth a packet that satisfies a predefined property. The channel can also be implemented using different machines working in the same sub-network (i.e. ARP packets) or by equipping the booth with an additional network (3G/WiFi/...) connection. In fact, such an attack is far simpler than the many fairly complex attacks against non-cryptographic systems described in the secure voting systems literature. Source code analysis does not help since the malicious code can be injected at the hardware level (eg. Rakshasa [5]).

We now consider the original version of the simple verifiable voting approach. It proposes that the vote encryption may be provided to the voter on paper (the receipt in figure 3 is provided on paper). The voter may then take the paper to another device to cast or audit it. Here too the two instructions from the voter—the vote and the cast/audit command—are communicated to an electronic device using an electronic interface, where the electronic device holds all records of the commands. Again, disputes between the machine and the voter such as those described above are not resolvable by a third party.

As mentioned earlier, Saltman and Mercuri both pointed out similar problems with fully-electronic non-cryptographic voting systems: the machine need not follow voter instructions. There is a major difference between the (fully-electronic) cryptographic and non-cryptographic voting systems, however: using the cryptographic voting system, a voter can catch a cheating system, even if he or she cannot prove this to others. In the non-cryptographic voting system, the voter does not know whether the system followed instructions.

The ability of the machine to ignore instructions (without the voter being able to prove this) can be used in multiple ways to change the election outcome. First, the machine can encrypt votes for a particular candidate. Second, it can choose to always encrypt the correct vote, audit it on occasion (ignoring whether the voter wanted to cast or audit) and then immediately cast one of its own choice (claiming the voter audited and then entered a vote and chose to cast it). Third, it may claim a vote was audited after a voter thought he or she had cast it. There would be many other combinations.

Note that the weaknesses we demonstrate are *not* weaknesses of the cast/audit approach which greatly simplifies the user experience. These are weaknesses resulting from the type of channel used for communication.

5   Audiotegrity

We describe only the front end of Audiotegrity, designed around the cast/audit paradigm. The back-end corresponds to the voting system used—in our case, Scantegrity II. The voter enters her votes on an electronic interface that produces a printed marked ballot and cryptographic receipt, face down. Before the voter can look at the ballot (which, in the Scantegrity II case contains the receipt value in the form of confirmation numbers), she must declare publicly, at the polling site, whether she wishes to cast or audit the ballot. This is to prevent coercion attacks, such as described in [15]. She may then check that the ballot is marked correctly and make a copy to take home if it is an audited ballot, or else cast it at the scanner.

We first describe the aspects of Scantegrity II relevant to Audiotegrity, and then describe Audiotegrity in more detail.

5.1   Scantegrity

The Scantegrity confirmation numbers are chosen—pseudo-randomly per ballot and per candidate—by the voting system before the election. Also before the election, the voting system publishes commitments to (a) the correspondence between candidates and confirmation numbers for each ballot and (b) the sorted list of confirmation numbers by ballot number. Voters do not need to know this information to cast a valid vote.

Voters who manually fill out paper Scantegrity ballots also fill out the confirmation card manually if they wish to check the numbers later, writing down confirmation numbers they see. There is nothing special about the confirmation card, which is simply provided as an aid to the voter; the voter may note these numbers on any paper or memorize if they can and wish to do so. Those who do not wish to check later may ignore the confirmation numbers.

Immediately after the election, the system publishes the following on the election website:

1. all voted ballot IDs and corresponding voted confirmation numbers (without corresponding candidates);
2. all audited ballot IDs with the correspondence between candidates and confirmation numbers;
3. the tally and that part of the digital audit trail required for tally-correctness audits.

The voter may check the confirmation numbers on her receipt and any copies of audited ballots with those on the election website. Note that a voter who does not care to verify may simply ignore this step. If a voter finds that her confirmation number is not correctly displayed on the website, she may file a dispute, declaring the number she claims should be on the website instead.

The Scantegrity scanner may be programmed to reject overvoted ballots, so that a voted ballot may not be later over-voted by an insider with access to the ballots. (This was not implemented for the election and can result in a dispute resolution problem, but is not a problem with the protocol).

After the period for filing disputes is over (generally a few days after the election), the voting system publishes all voted ballot IDs and the corresponding sorted list of all confirmation numbers. It also provides the information necessary to check the commitments to these values. All disputes by voters may be checked against this information. If, while filing the dispute, the voter provided a confirmation number that is on the list of confirmation numbers committed to for the ballot, but was not listed as a voted confirmation number, it is very likely that the voter was correct. This is because the probability that the voter would correctly guess a voted confirmation number is low. On the other hand, if the number provided by the voter is not on the list of numbers committed to by the voting system, it is unlikely that the voter is correct if ballot audits do not detect problems. Thus dispute resolution in Scantegrity, unlike that in Prêt à Voter), does not depend on digital signatures or an authenticated receipt. The receipt is not what the voter has, but what the voter knows. The purpose of a digital signature is served by the fact that the confirmation numbers on a single contest consist of a very small set of all possible confirmation numbers.

While dispute resolution in Scantegrity is probabilistic and depends on a large-enough number of ballot audits, the dispute resolution problems we identify in section 4 are not resolved by a large-enough number of audits unless we make different assumptions, such as a large enough number of honest voters (an assumption not required by paper ballot systems Scantegrity and Prêt à Voter).

5.2   Audiotegrity

The station has a privacy screen and is not visible from the voting floor. The printer attached to the station is preferably visible to the public and to poll workers, just as the scanner is (it can be outside the privacy-screened area, for example, or the privacy-screened area may be designed so that the voter may vote privately while the printer is visible).

The ballot and confirmation card are of distinct sizes so that it is easy to know the difference by touch and/or sight.

An audio record of the confirmation numbers would be useful (we currently do not provide this). We attempted to match the colors of the marked ovals and the confirmation codes on both types of ballots—the Scantegrity ballots marked manually by voters and the Audiotegrity machine-marked ballots—so that they would be difficult to distinguish on casual, distant examination.

Figure 4 provides a summary of Audiotegrity as a cast/audit protocol, and figure 5 an illustration of the voting process. We follow this with a more detailed description of the protocol.

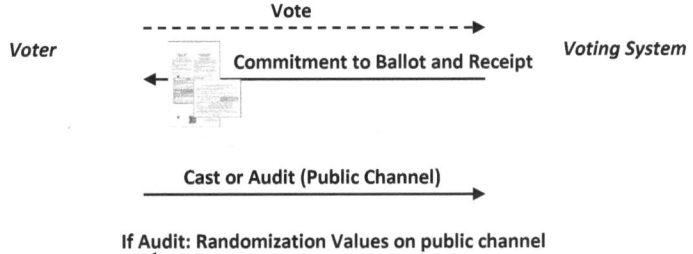

Fig. 4. A summary of the Audiotegrity voting protocol. A dashed line shows interactions that are not verifiable by a third party and hence result in dispute resolution weaknesses.

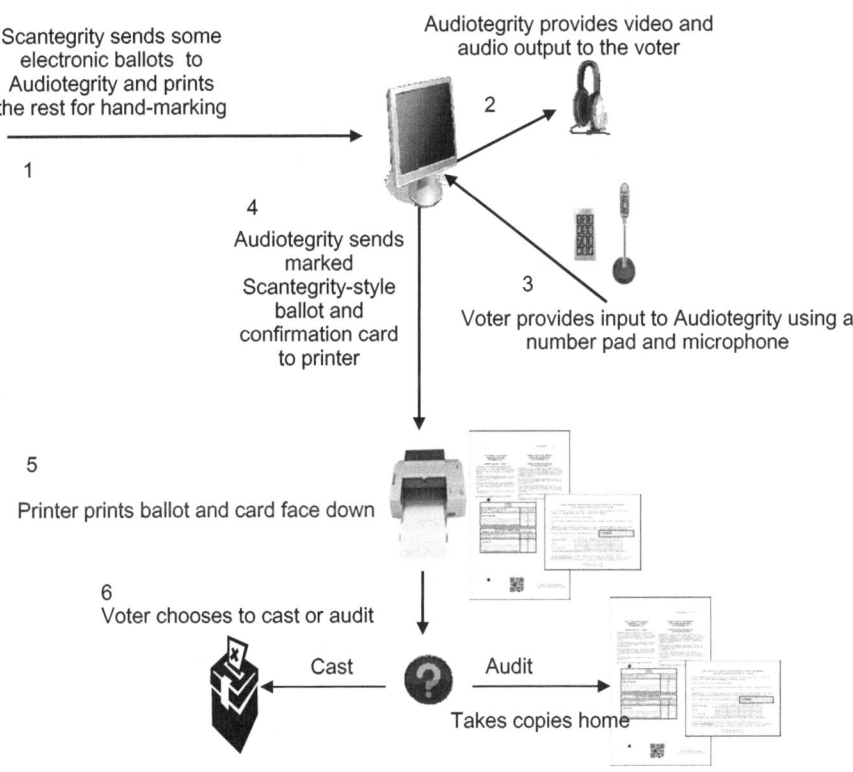

Fig. 5. The Audiotegrity Voting Protocol

Audiotegrity Ballot Casting Protocol

1. *Voter is Authenticated:* The voter is authenticated for voting by the physical process used by the jurisdiction.
2. *Voter Arrives at Station:* The voter is escorted to the station. The voter is assisted in putting on a headset. The location of the keypad designated for input and the printer that will output the ballot is described to the voter, and the voter's Ward number is input to the voting machine.
3. *Set Preferences:* The voter sets her preferences for audio speed and volume (and optionally for text size).
4. *Make Selections:* The voter makes selections. She can record a speak-in choice, which is later interpreted by election officials (write-in votes on Scantegrity ballots are also interpreted by election officials).
5. *Confirm Selections:* The voter confirms her selections.
6. *Ballot Printed:* The voting station prints out face-down:
   - **ballot** an appropriately-marked Scantegrity ballot with Scantegrity confirmation numbers printed in the ovals next to the chosen candidate(s).
   - **confirmation card** a Scantegrity confirmation card which lists the ballot ID and the confirmation numbers for each choice. The voter takes the card home with her; the confirmation numbers reveal nothing about the vote.
7. *Cast or Audit:* Before the voter leaves the station, touches the ballot or identifies any information on it, the voter decides whether to cast or audit the ballot and publicly informs a poll worker of her decision. (Note that if the voter decides to cast or audit her ballot after seeing the confirmation numbers, the protocol is vulnerable to the coercion attack of [15].)
   If the ballot is:
   cast it is treated the same as any other ballot:
   (a) the voter looks at it and checks that it is correctly marked,
   (b) the voter checks that the confirmation card lists the correct confirmation numbers or makes a separate note if she desires,
   (c) the voter is then directed to the scanner where the ballot is cast and scanned in.
   The voter with visual disability is protected by other voters using the same station and detecting printing errors.
   The sighted voter may notice that the ballot is not marked correctly. In the event that this happens, the voter may choose to spoil the ballot and restart the voting process from the head of the line. Spoiled ballots are not treated the same as audited ballots. As with the Scantegrity voting system, spoiled ballots are not revisited.
   audited an election official helps the voter make a copy of the ballot (with confirmation numbers) to take home with her and sets up the machine so she may vote again.
   Both the original audited ballot and the copy bear signatures of both: the voter and the election official. The voter cannot cast an audited ballot because the correspondence between confirmation numbers and candidates is made public in an audited ballot.
8. *Voter Leaves:* The voter leaves, with a ballot receipt corresponding to her single cast ballot and any ballot copies of audited ballots.

5.3 Properties

Note that if the system provides wrong confirmation numbers for the voter's choice of candidate, it is caught during an audit. The voter can prove that the system provided the wrong confirmation number, because her vote is marked on the ballot. If the voting system posts a number online that the voter claims is incorrect, this can be resolved as with Scantegrity, described in section 5.1.

The voting system can mark the wrong candidate on the ballot. This will be detected every time a ballot is marked incorrectly and not only during an audit; however, the voter will not be able to prove that the machine marked the wrong candidate. This is because the channel between the voter and the voting machine is electronic, and all records are held by the voting machine. The voter may spoil the incorrectly-marked ballot and vote again. Because information on spoiled ballots is not made public, this does not introduce a coercion threat.

The proof of incorrect printing is not transferable, and each voter must convince his or herself that the printer is printing correctly. This aspect can, however, be checked without special effort by sighted voters. Voters with visual disability can avail of independent verification provided at the polling place (as defined by the Voluntary Voting Systems Guidelines 1.1 [22, section 7.8]). (We were not able to provide this for the 2011 election). However, because the independent verification is not guaranteed to be independent, voters with visual disability also rely on others using the same stations, and on the system itself not being able to tell the difference between voters. Because personal electronic ballot readers would know the correspondence between vote and confirmation number, voters cannot use these to read unaudited ballots. It would be difficult to monitor and enforce the use of personal readers only on audited ballots. When there is no complaint of incorrect printing, voters with visual disability can rely on the printers printing correctly.

The Audiotegrity audit checks only a single correspondence between candidate and confirmation number for each choice, unlike the Scantegrity II audit which checks all confirmation numbers on the ballot. This does not appear to result in any coercion or integrity related problems.

The machine knows the codes for all Audiotegrity ballots, and no others. Its knowledge of codes is no different from that of the printer for Prêt à Voter or Scantegrity II.

Finally, unlike fully-electronic protocols, this protocol is not "fully-accessible". A voter might need assistance to take the filled-in ballot to the scanner.

6 Comparison of Protocol Properties

We now provide a comparison of the properties of Scantegrity II, Audiotegrity, simple verifiable voting and voting by DRE.

Suppose a cheating Scantegrity II voting system provides incorrect confirmation numbers. This is caught through a ballot audit, and there is never an unresolved dispute that it is cheating in this manner. That is, the proof of cheating is transferable to another voter, and one voter checking helps other voters too.

A cheating Audiotegrity voting system can:
(a) mark the wrong oval (with the confirmation number corresponding to this oval; that is, cast a valid vote for a candidate other than the voter's choice). This is caught without an audit — i.e. it is almost always caught. However, a dispute cannot be resolved and proof of it cheating in this manner is not transferable. Because a voter catches the cheating, she can vote again, including with a paper ballot. This is an unresolved issue for voters with visual disability (in any voting system, to our knowledge).
(b) mark the correct oval with the wrong confirmation number. This is caught in the manner of Scantegrity II, and the dispute is resolvable. The proof of cheating is transferable.

A cheating system based on simple verifiable voting can
(a) print a valid encryption of an incorrect vote, in the manner of the first Audiotegrity attack (a). The system is detected to be cheating by the voter only on audit. A dispute between voter and system—each claiming to be correct—is not resolvable and the proof is not transferable. Repeated instances can prevent a voter from voting. While many complaining voters can draw attention to this problem, the absence of paper ballots means there is no other way to vote. Additionally, a small group of voters can call an honest election into unresolvable dispute. Finally, this is detected by the voter only on audit, so many valid incorrect votes may be cast.
(b) print an invalid encryption, similar to the second Audiotegrity attack (b). This is caught on audit and the dispute is resolvable.

A cheating DRE need not reveal it is cheating, and hence will not be caught cheating as it provides no information about the election.

Voting systems that maintain paper trails such as Scantegrity II and STAR-Vote are vulnerable to coercion from insiders with access to the paper trail, as a voter's ballot ID reveals her entire vote. A level of indirection can be provided through distinct serial numbers and online verification numbers (with a correspondence protected by a shared secret), with the latter being torn off before the ballot is cast (this, again provides a usability challenge) such as described for Scantegrity II [8]. Prêt à Voter, where one half of the ballot is destroyed after the ballot is marked, does not maintain a paper trail. However, the printer that prints Prêt à Voter ballots before the election, or the machine that prints a marked ballot in the proposed solution for elections in Victoria, does know the vote too. Perhaps Prêt à Voter ballots can be printed using the independent-ballot-sheet approach of Punchscan [14]. Clearly, voting systems that do not maintain paper trails cannot carry out statistical manual audits through hand counting of paper ballots.

7   Audiotegrity in Takoma Park

The City of Takoma Park neighbors the city of Washington DC and has a population of about 17,000 with about 10,000 registered voters. The turnout in municipal elections is about 15-25%. In municipal elections, the city elects a mayor and six council members and ballots can also list referendums. Each contest has a write-in option. Takoma Park uses instant-runoff voting, and voters may rank candidates. Ballots are in English and Spanish. There was a single precinct for the 2011 election.

Both city officials and the voting population had experience with cryptographic voting systems as the city had used Scantegrity II in their 2009 municipal election [7]. Election officials wished to use Scantegrity II in 2011 too, but also wished to provide a more accessible alternative. In previous municipal elections that used optical scan technology (including the 2009 election) voters with difficulties handling paper ballots had voted with assistance. We began the design of the system in early 2011, when approached by the Board, and provided demonstrations of prototypes in a couple of election board meetings in the first half of 2011. We received no compensation from Takoma Park for its use of Audiotegrity.

The city of Takoma Park held an open test of Audiotegrity on June 8, 2011 in the Takoma Park Community Center. The test was publicized in the local news media and election officials sent announcements to various special-interest listservs. The test was not restricted to Takoma Park residents, and all who were interested were allowed to test the system. About 25-30 individuals tested the system and about 24 individuals filled out a survey. The purpose of the survey was not usability research, but to obtain feedback on the system in an informal manner, and to make potential users of the interface aware that Takoma Park might choose to use it in the election. A remote voting system was tested at the same time and place. Because we collected the data informally and interacted considerably with participants while they were testing the system, and the number of participants was very small, we do not present the data from our surveys. To obtain a qualitative, independent, albeit brief, assessment of the test, the reader may refer to a blog article [17, last paragraph].

We made some changes based on the criticisms and concerns of some participants: we provided variable speed and volume for the audio and obtained a professional recording for the real election. We also changed the instructions to make them more understandable.

The Audiotegrity system was deployed on November 8, 2011, as an accessible interface to be used alongside Scantegrity II. The protocol used in Takoma Park was different from that described in section 5.2 in a few aspects. No public declaration was required to cast or audit, and the ability to audit the ballot was not publicized widely. This was to simplify the process for the first use of the system. We chose to give audio confirmation codes to the voter before the printing began. Again, this was a consequence of the fact that we were not planning on many voter audits in this election and we wanted to provide voters with visual disability some of the information that sighted voters got. A better way to do this would be to provide digital media with confirmation codes on it.

Audiotegrity was used to cast a few votes including by poll workers and auditors. Audits were made on the system by the election auditor, Neal McBurnett. This election marks one of the first times (if not the first) where the voting system design did not prevent a voter with visual disability from independently casting an E2E ballot in a secret ballot precinct-based public election.

We are not able to provide information on how Audiotegrity votes were audited. We consciously do not keep information on Audiotegrity ballot IDs after the election, in order to reduce the ability to distinguish between Audiotegrity and Scantegrity ballots.

At the election certification meeting, Audiotegrity was called out as a valuable contribution by the chair of the board of elections and a council member.

8   Conclusions

In conclusion, what appear to be small details play an important role in protocol security. Cryptographic protocols assume secure authenticated channels between probabilistic-polynomial-time Turing machine participants. Real elections involve human voters who cannot compute signatures or commitments. Paper plays a role in providing authenticated communication between the voter and the untrusted voting machine. Additional, small changes in procedures can make a difference to security properties. We designed Audiotegrity with these issues in mind. It was used by the City of Takoma Park in its 2011 city election.

Acknowledgements. The Board of Elections and the City Clerk of Takoma Park were very generous with their time and knowledge of electoral practices and voter behavior. Assistant City Clerk, Irma Andia, translated English script into Spanish and read most of the audio. The Communications Department of the city provided the audio recording. Veronica Elsea of Laurel Creek Music shared with us her considerable expertise in audio recording. Neal McBurnett audited ballots.

References

1. Accessible voting without computers, http://www.vote-pad.us/
2. Adida, B.: Advances in Cryptographic Voting Systems. PhD thesis. MIT (2006)
3. Benaloh, J.: Simple verifiable elections. In: EVT (2006)
4. Benaloh, J., Byrne, M., Kortum, P.T., McBurnett, N., Pereira, O., Stark, P.B., Wallach, D.S.: STAR-Vote: A secure, transparent, auditable, and reliable voting system. CoRR, abs/1211.1904 (2012)
5. Brossard, J.: Hardware backdooring is practical. In: DEFCON (2012)
6. Burton, C., Culnane, C., Heather, J., Peacock, T., Ryan, P.Y.A., Schneider, S., Teague, V., Wen, R., Xia, Z.(J.), Srinivasan, S.: Using Pret a Voter in Victoria State Elections. In: EVT/WOTE (2012)
7. Carback, R., Chaum, D., Clark, J., Essex, A., Mayberry, T., Popoveniuc, S., Rivest, R.L., Shen, E., Sherman, A.T., Vora, P.L.: Scantegrity II Municipal Election at Takoma Park: The First E2E Binding Governmental Election with Ballot Privacy. In: USENIX Security Symposium (2010)

8. Chaum, D., Carback, R., Clark, J., Essex, A., Popoveniuc, S., Rivest, R.L., Ryan, P.Y.A., Shen, E., Sherman, A.T., Vora, P.L.: Scantegrity II: end-to-end verifiability by voters of optical scan elections through confirmation codes. IEEE Transactions on Information Forensics and Security 4(4), 611–627 (2009)
9. Chaum, D., Florescu, A., Nandi, M., Popoveniuc, S., Rubio, J., Vora, P.L., Zagórski, F.: Paperless independently-verifiable voting. In: Kiayias, A., Lipmaa, H. (eds.) VoteID 2011. LNCS, vol. 7187, pp. 140–157. Springer, Heidelberg (2012)
10. Chaum, D., Ryan, P.Y.A., Schneider, S.: A practical voter-verifiable election scheme. In: De Capitani di Vimercati, S., Syverson, P.F., Gollmann, D. (eds.) ESORICS 2005. LNCS, vol. 3679, pp. 118–139. Springer, Heidelberg (2005)
11. Popoveniuc, S., Chaum, D., Hosp, B., Vora, P.L.: Accessible voter verifiability. Cryptologia 33(3), 283–291 (2009)
12. Vincent Cross II, E., McMillian, Y., Gupta, P., Williams, P., Nobles, K., Gilbert, J.E.: Prime III: a user centered voting system. In: CHI 2007 Extended Abstracts on Human Factors in Computing Systems (2007)
13. Fresolone, M.: Tactile ballots alternative voting method for the blind, http://www.votersunite.org/info/tactileballots.asp
14. Carback III, R.T., Popoveniuc, S., Sherman, A.T., Chaum, D.: Punchscan with independent ballot sheets: Simplifying ballot printing and distribution with independently selected ballot halves. In: WOTE (2007)
15. Kelsey, J., Regenscheid, A., Moran, T., Chaum, D.: Attacking paper-based E2E voting systems. In: Chaum, D., Jakobsson, M., Rivest, R.L., Ryan, P.Y.A., Benaloh, J., Kutylowski, M., Adida, B. (eds.) Towards Trustworthy Elections. LNCS, vol. 6000, pp. 370–387. Springer, Heidelberg (2010)
16. Kiayias, A., Yung, M.: Self-tallying elections and perfect ballot secrecy. In: Naccache, D., Paillier, P. (eds.) PKC 2002. LNCS, vol. 2274, pp. 141–158. Springer, Heidelberg (2002)
17. Kiser, M.: Internet voting 2.0 and other advances in election technology in takoma park. FairVote Blog (June 9, 2011)
18. Küsters, R., Truderung, T., Vogt, A.: Accountability: Definition and Relationship to Verifiability. In: ACM CCS (2010)
19. Mercuri, R.: Electronic Vote Tabulation Checks and Balances. PhD thesis, University of Pennsylvania, Philadelphia, PA (October 2000)
20. Ryan, P.Y.A.: A variant of the Chaum voter-verifiable scheme. Technical Report 864, School of Computing Science, University of Newcastle upon Tyne (2004)
21. Saltman, R.G.: Effective use of computer technology in vote-tallying. Technical report, NIST (1975)
22. Technical Guidelines Development Committee, Election Assistance Commission. Voluntary voting system guidelines 1.1 (2007), http://www.eac.gov/assets/1/AssetManager/VVSG_Version_1-1_Volume_1_-_20090527.pdf

Mental Models of Verifiability in Voting

Maina M. Olembo, Steffen Bartsch, and Melanie Volkamer

Technische Universität Darmstadt / Center for Advanced Security Research
Darmstadt, Germany
Name.Surname@cased.de

Abstract. In order for voters to verify their votes, they have to carry out additional steps besides selecting a candidate and submitting their vote. In previous work, voters have been found to be confused about the concept of and motivation for verifiability in electronic voting when confronted with it. In order to better communicate verifiability to voters, we identify mental models of verifiability in voting using a questionnaire distributed online in Germany. The identified mental models are, *Trusting*, *No Knowledge*, *Observer*, *Personal Involvement* and *Matching* models. Within the same survey, we identify terms that can be used in place of 'verify' as well as security-relevant metaphors known to the voters that can be used to communicate verifiability.

Keywords: Mental Models, Verifiability, Internet Voting, Voting.

1 Introduction

Internet voting continues to generate great interest, with a recent survey in Germany [1] finding that more than 50% of eligible voters would cast their vote over the Internet for federal elections. Despite this interest, security experts have expressed concern over the integrity of Internet voting, for example Simons and Jones [2]. Verifiability offers some assurance of the integrity of votes cast in an election - both in traditional as well as in Internet-based elections. Voters however, have to carry out additional steps to verify the integrity of their individual votes (and if they are interested, all votes) cast in an election. While in traditional paper-based elections voters are not confronted with verifying (e.g. assuming that poll workers do not ask voters to remain behind to verify that votes are properly tallied), they are in Internet based elections: In the vote casting interface, there might be a button to click on to verify, a link to the bulletin board, or voters get a receipt to verify later on.

Sherman et al. [3] and Volk et al. [4] found that voters are confused about the concept of and motivation for verifiability. Similarly, Schneider et al. [5] report that voters expressed confusion over use of the term 'receipt'. This confusion and lack of understanding and motivation in voters shows the need to investigate mental models of verifiability in voting to base future communication of verifiability on these models. It also shows the need to use a different term or phrase for 'verifying'. In this work we seek to identify mental models of and

J. Heather, S. Schneider, and V. Teague (Eds.): VoteID 2013, LNCS 7985, pp. 142–155, 2013.
© Springer-Verlag Berlin Heidelberg 2013

terms for verifiability. We define mental models as 'voters' knowledge, beliefs and attitudes of verifiability as they cast votes in postal voting and paper-based voting at the polling station'. We use a questionnaire distributed online.

The mental models are identified as *Trusting, No Knowledge*[1], *Observer, Personal Involvement* and *Matching* models. The most appropriate term identified is *check*. While we concentrate in this work on Internet-based verifiable voting systems, our findings are relevant to verifiable e-voting systems in general, as the mental models identified are based on traditional voting systems.

The remainder of this paper is structured as follows: we give background information in Section 2 on verifiability and voting procedures in Germany, followed by a discussion of related work in usable verifiable electronic voting in Section 3. We present the methodology of our study in Section 4, the results in Section 5, and discuss the implications of our findings and future work in Section 6.

2   Background

Background information is provided on the verifiability definitions, and the voting processes in Germany are introduced briefly as the questionnaire was distributed to German citizens.

Verifiability definitions. Verifiability addresses the following three aspects: Cast as intended - the voter can verify that his vote has been cast as he intended; Stored as cast - the voter can verify that his vote is stored for tabulation as he cast it; and Tallied as stored - anybody can verify that all votes have been tallied as they were stored[2].

Voting processes in Germany. In Germany, voters can cast paper votes at the polling station, or register for absentee voting and use postal voting. Postal voting has been provided in Germany since 1956 to cater for voters who for one reason or another cannot cast their vote in person at a polling station [7]. Furthermore, postal voting has continued to experience increasing use, with 21.4% of voters using postal voting for the 2009 federal elections [7]. Another special provision for German elections is that ordinary voters and interested parties are allowed to remain at the polling station, including the location where postal votes are stored and tallied, to observe election processes during set up, voting and the tallying of votes, as long as they do not disrupt the proceedings [8].

3   Related Work

Different techniques have been applied to identify mental models in voting. Schneider et al. [5] carried out a series of focus group sessions to evaluate, among

---

[1] By no knowledge, we refer to participants who were uncertain how to verify votes in postal voting, and paper voting, despite the fact that voters are allowed to observe voting processes in Germany.

[2] While these are the definitions selected for this work, other definitions of verifiability exist in the literature, for example [6].

other issues, voters' understanding of security mechanisms in an early version of Prêt à Voter. Storer et al. [9] also interacted with participants in focus groups and additionally used videotaped scenarios to study voters' attitudes towards a pollsterless remote voting system. Campbell and Byrne [10] investigated voters' mental model of straight party voting using an online survey, while Yao and Murphy [11], used a paper-based survey to evaluate voters' perceptions of, and their intention to use, telephone and web-based interfaces of remote electronic voting systems.

Since few studies have been carried out to specifically investigate voters' mental models in voting, we also considered literature in the field of computer security. Raja et al. [12] carried out a lab study of Vista Basic firewall, and a firewall prototype that included contextual information of the current and future network states. Almuhimedi et al. [13] used a survey and a lab study in web certificate management.

Using semi-structured interviews, Raja et al. [14] explored participants' knowledge, requirements, perceptions and misconceptions about personal firewalls. Friedman et al. [15] tested users' conceptions of web security using semi-structured interviews that included a drawing task. Ho et al. [16] interviewed caretakers of wireless home computer networks to understand how they deployed and secured the networks. Wash [17] conducted interviews to understand users' folk models of attackers and security technologies. Dourish et al. [18] carried out semi-structured interviews to identify people's perceptions of security.

Mental models of computer security [19] and privacy and security [20] were identified from literature and tested in a two-card sorting experiment [21], [22], [23] involving experts and non-experts. Bravo-Lillo et al. [24] used scenarios in open-ended interviews to evaluate mental models of computer security warnings.

We see a variety of approaches used to identify mental models in voting and in computer security. In this study, we distributed a questionnaire online to participants, integrating scenario diagrams to elicit terms for verifiability.

4   Methodology

The research questions and study instruments, participant recruitment, data analysis, and ethical considerations for the study, are described in this section. All study materials were written in English and translated into German. The data collected was translated into English for analysis and reporting. The translations were verified for accuracy by the authors. Additionally, the data collected on terms for verifiability was analyzed in German since future work will investigate their use in Germany.

4.1   Research Questions and Study Instruments

The research question is: *What mental models do participants have of verifiability in postal voting and paper voting at the polling station?* This was explored by asking participants the following questions addressing different aspects of verifiability:

- how they could tell that their individual postal vote was not modified or removed on its way to the town hall and into the ballot box $(Q1_{postal})$.
- how they could tell that their postal or paper vote was not modified or removed from the ballot box, $(Q2_{postal})$ and $(Q2_{paper})$.
- how they could tell that their postal or paper vote was included in the final tally, $(Q3_{postal})$ and $(Q3_{paper})$.
- how they could tell that all postal or paper votes were included in the final tally, $(Q4_{postal})$ and $(Q4_{paper})$.

These questions were derived from the stored as cast and tallied as stored verifiability definitions. Note the problem with the first verifiability step: cast as intended, i.e. making sure that the vote is not modified before being sent is not a concern in paper-based elections and thus is not addressed here. The questionnaire is shown in Table 5 in the Appendix. Participants first answered demographic questions which acted as screening questions to allow exclusion of data from participants who did not meet the requirements (see Subsection 4.2). Scenario diagrams, shown in Figures 1 to 6, were developed by a professional graphic designer and used to obtain terms for verifiability.

4.2 Participant Recruitment

Participants were recruited to form a convenience sample [25]. We did not seek participants representative of the German population, rather we aimed to carry out an exploratory study to identify research questions for further investigation on mental models of verifiability. We therefore do not generalize our findings to the entire population. Invitation emails were first sent to an initial pool of participants known to the authors, then a second email, containing a URL and password to access the questionnaire, was sent to those participants who expressed interest in the study. This approach has been shown to improve response rates [26]. These participants were requested to forward the email to other persons whom they thought would be interested in participating, in a snowballing technique [27]. Participants represented different age groups and professional backgrounds including retired workers. Eligible participants were German citizens, used the Internet, and were over the age of 18 (in order to be eligible to vote in elections). Participants were not offered compensation, instead we asked those interested to provide their email addresses[3] to receive information on the results of the survey [28].

Out of 55 participants who filled out the questionnaire online, 11 did not complete it. We therefore consider data from 44 participants. There were 31 male and 13 female respondents. Ten participants had been educated up to high school level, and 34 had university education. Forty participants reported using the Internet everyday, while four used it every two to three days. Data on participants' age ranges and level of computer proficiency (measured by asking participants whether they install computer programs on their computers) are shown in Table 1 and Table 2, respectively.

---

[3] Participants' email addresses were not linked to their responses.

Table 1. Participants' Age Ranges

Age	Number
19 - 34	16
35 - 44	9
45 - 54	8
55 - 64	8
65+	3

Table 2. Participants' Computer Proficiency

Computer Proficiency	Number
Install on their own	20
Need help to install	10
Others ask them for help	13
Do not install	1

4.3   Data Analysis

Responses were analyzed using content analysis and open coding [29]. In content analysis, participants' responses are analyzed and categorized using explicit rules. Open coding was used in order to obtain emerging themes from participants' responses, rather than beginning the data analysis with pre-selected themes. If one participant mentioned several concepts, each was coded under an appropriate theme. We used spreadsheets to assign the different concepts and themes to each question. For example, a response such as *No knowledge, only trust in regulated procedures and sanctions and mutual control during the count by the people present, as well as to this day minor known cases of abuse* was identified to have the following relevant concepts: No Knowledge, Trust in processes, and Observers present. These concepts were grouped into themes, which form the mental models. One participant could have expressed several concepts that would be classified under different mental models. The concepts identified in this example were then categorized under *No Knowledge, Trusting* and *Observer* models.

Two researchers independently reviewed a subset of the data and identified concepts and emerging themes from participants' responses. A Cohen's Kappa of 0.65 was obtained. Any value above 0.60 indicates acceptable inter-rater reliability [29]. The remaining responses were then analyzed. In coding the data, one question was analyzed in its entirety before researchers moved on to analyze the next question. This process was repeated until all participants' responses to all questions had been analyzed, and emerging themes identified.

We analyzed participants' responses based on the meaning of phrases and the response as a whole, first identifying concepts and themes and then the mental models. We observed that two themes, specifically, trusting and no knowledge, were identified in participants' responses to ($Q1_{postal}$). The remaining themes were identified while analyzing responses from ($Q2_{postal}$) to ($Q4_{postal}$) and from ($Q2_{paper}$) to ($Q4_{paper}$). Concepts within the themes primarily remained the same for the different questions, though there was a slight change, reflecting the differing situations presented in the questions, that is, moving from vote storage to tallying of votes. As such, it is likely that theoretical saturation [30] was attained at this point and unlikely that introducing more participants would reveal any new themes.

Fig. 1. The Ballot Box is Empty   **Fig. 2.** The Voter is Eligible

Fig. 3. The Voter goes alone into **Fig. 4.** Eligible Voters' Votes are in the Voting Booth   the Ballot Box

Fig. 5. The Seal is Broken and the **Fig. 6.** All Votes are Properly Tallied. Ballot Box is Empty   lied

4.4 Ethical Considerations

Ethical requirements for research involving human participants are provided by an ethics commission at the university[4]. The relevant ethical requirements regarding participant consent and data privacy were met. Participants were first informed about the purpose of the study, after which they could decide whether or not to proceed to the questionnaire. They were informed that the purpose of the study was to better understand preferences for Internet voting based on use of traditional voting systems, to avoid causing bias by referring to integrity in voting or verifiability. In order to meet the data privacy requirement, a privacy statement was provided on the questionnaire, assuring participants that their data would only be collected for research purposes, their identity would not be linked to their responses, and their data would not be passed on to third parties. Furthermore, participants' data was only handled by researchers involved in the project.

5   Results

We present the results of this work, first discussing the different mental models of verifiability in voting that have been identified, and metaphors and terms that can be used in reference to verifiability processes.

5.1   Mental Models

A number of mental models were identified from participants' responses. Specifically, *Trusting, No Knowledge, Observer, Personal Involvement*, and *Matching* models were identified. Examples of the concepts identified and accompanying mental models are shown in Table 4 in the Appendix. As mentioned above, themes overlapped with respect to the concepts, for instance, for the *Trusting* and *Observer* models, in the case where participants trust that observers will notice manipulations.

We first discuss each of the mental models and then propose metaphors and terms participants used while answering the questions and which might be used to improve the communication of verifiability. The mental models are reported in this section based on the number of concepts identified; those with a high number of concepts are listed first.

Trusting Model: Participants' responses indicated that they had *blind trust, trust in persons*, or *trust in processes* for integrity of their individual votes and all votes cast in an election. Another new concept was *trust (no option)*, with the participant stating '*I have to trust in it*'. As participants moved from question $Q1_{postal}$ to question $Q4_{postal}$, new concepts emerged such as: *trust in observers* in $Q2_{postal}$, *trust the count* in $Q3_{postal}$, and *trust in the public count of votes* in $Q4_{postal}$, as an example, one participant stated '*... one also has to trust*

---

[4] http://www.intern.tu-darmstadt.de/gremien/ethikkommisson/index.en.jsp

in the count'. The concept of the envelope used in postal voting being sealed was observed, with a participant stating *'...I trust that the sealed envelope is only opened to count my vote'*. Similarly, new concepts were observed across the responses in $Q2_{paper}$ through to $Q4_{paper}$, for example, *trust in the public count of votes.*

No Knowledge Model: Participants' responses indicated they were either not sure how to ascertain the integrity of their individual vote and other voters' votes, or they considered that there was no way for this to be done. Participants stated, for example, *'I don't know', 'You can never know',* and *'Not at all'*. We also noted that many concepts in this model were linked to other concepts from different mental models, for example, one participant responded *'I don't know; I trust',* and another, *'I don't know; I trust that the procedure of the election is properly monitored'.*

Observer Model: Participants referred mostly to observers being present during the vote casting process and the tallying of votes. One participant referred to the presence of observers which assured him of the integrity of his individual vote in $Q1_{postal}$ and a few referred to the presence of observers in $Q2_{postal}$ to $Q4_{postal}$. As an example, one participant said *'Therefore election observers are permitted...',* in response to $Q3_{postal}$. In paper voting, participants expressed assurance of how their vote was handled because *observers were present.* Since *different election workers were present* and likely to have *different party affiliations,* participants also considered them as playing a role in ensuring the integrity of the voting process. Additionally, participants referred to *election workers observing each other,* and the *results being verified by several people.* The election workers were referred to more times in response to $Q2_{paper}$ to $Q4_{paper}$, which could be because participants interact with them more during the voting process, in comparison to postal voting, where voters might never interact with the election workers in person.

Additionally, participants were assured of the integrity of their votes and all votes since they were counted in public. Relevant concepts were observed in $Q3_{postal}$ and $Q4_{postal}$ with one participant indicating *'Due to the fact that the count is done in public...'.* Relevant concepts were identified from $Q2_{paper}$ to $Q4_{paper}$. In the responses given, participants did not specify how the public count could ensure the integrity of individual votes and all votes.

Personal Involvement Model: Participants made reference to being personally involved in the tallying process by *observing the tallying of votes in person* ($Q4_{postal}$) with this participant stating *'I can watch the count of the absentee votes...'.* Other concepts were *submitting the vote personally* ($Q2_{paper}$), *observing in person* ($Q3_{paper}$) and *participating in the public count* ($Q4_{paper}$).

Matching Model: Participants responses made reference to *checking that the final results matched the observed results* ($Q4_{postal}$) and that *the number of votes matched the number of participating voters* ($Q2_{paper}$).

5.2   Further Results

We identified a number of metaphors from participants' responses, which can be tailored to communicate verifiability. Furthermore, terms that participants use to describe verifiability are reported.

Metaphors: A number of metaphors were identified from participants' responses. The *ballot box* was referred to as *being sealed* (in both postal voting and paper voting), and *physically protected* (in postal voting). The *envelope being sealed* gave assurance to one participant that any tampering with his postal vote would be detected *'...because the envelope would have to be opened and the vote then becomes invalid'* ($Q2_{postal}$).

Terms For Verifiability: Terms were obtained from participants' responses to describe the action of the man in black (Figures 1 to 6). These and accompanying English translations are shown in Table 3. Some participants used multiple terms to describe the action. Responses that only appeared once are grouped together under 'Other'.

Table 3. Terms for Verifiability

English translation	German term	Count
To observe	beobachten	18
To check	kontrollieren	10
To verify	überprüfen	6
To monitor	überwachen	5
Other		11

6   Discussion

User studies of voters' interaction with verifiable voting systems, for example in [3] and [31], show that voters are confused about the concept of verifiability. In this work, we have identified the mental models of verifiability of German voters to gain insights on how to improve voters' understanding of verifiability. Specifically, we have identified *Trusting, No Knowledge, Observer, Personal involvement*, and *Matching* mental models.

Our results indicate that there are gaps in voters' knowledge, beliefs and attitudes towards verifiability in voting as more concepts were identified for the *Trusting* and *No Knowledge* mental models. These gaps need to be closed by communicating verifiability. One approach could be to inform voters that the trust-inducing elements present in traditional (paper-based) voting systems, for example, observers, are not the same in Internet voting. The argument could then follow that voters need to personally act as observers, or that they need to carry out extra steps.

Our findings on the mental models can be employed to improve user interfaces for verifiable voting. While one option would be to first identify voters' mental models and then communicate verifiability according to the model(s) that voters have, legal requirements are that all voters receive the same information. Correspondingly, in future work, we will investigate designing an interface that is adequate for several – ideally all – identified mental models. Future work will also consider the effect that this improved communication has on voters checking their votes.

Moreover, the metaphors and terms for verifiability identified in this work will be applied in the improved communication. The identified metaphors, sealed and protected ballot box and sealed envelope, can be exploited to communicate individual verifiability. One option could be in providing a contrast, for example, informing voters that while these aspects are present in postal voting and paper-based voting at the polling station, they are not available in Internet voting, thus prompting the voter to participate in verifiability processes.

Similarly, further research will utilize the German terms that participants used to refer to verifying. While 'observe' is the highest ranking term, we consider that the term 'check' offers more options for use in communicating verifiability to voters. Some sample phrases are 'check the vote preparation process', and 'check the correctness of the counting process'. The appropriateness of these and other phrases will be evaluated in future work.

Since this study targeted German voters, it would be of interest to identify and compare additional mental models in other cultures, as well as to conduct additional quantitative work to determine each mental model's prevalence.

Acknowledgment. Support for this work was provided by CASED (www.cased.de) and Micromata (www.micromata.de). The authors would like to thank the anonymous reviewers for their helpful insights that helped improve the presentation of this work.

References

1. Microsoft: Forsa-Umfrage: Jeder zweite würde online wählen. Digitale Technologien stärken die Demokratie. Bürgerbeteiligung über das Internet fördert Vertrauen in die Politik (2013), http://www.microsoft.com/germany/newsroom/pressemitteilung.mspx?id=533684 (accessed March 22, 2013)
2. Simons, B., Jones, D.W.: Internet voting in the U.S. Communications of the ACM 55(10), 68–77 (2012)
3. Sherman, A.T., Carback, R., Chaum, D., Clark, J., Essex, A., Herrnson, P.S., Mayberry, T., Stefan, P., Rivest, R.L., Shen, E., Sinha, B., Vora, P.: Scantegrity Mock Election at Takoma Park. In: Electronic Voting 2010 (EVOTE 2010), pp. 45–61 (2010)
4. Karayumak, F., Kauer, M., Olembo, M.M., Volk, T., Volkamer, M.: User Study of the Improved Helios Voting System Interface. In: Socio-Technical Aspects in Security and Trust (STAST), pp. 37–44. IEEE (2011)

5. Schneider, S., Llewellyn, M., Culnane, C., Heather, J., Srinivasan, S., Xia, Z.: Focus Group Views on Prêt à Voter 1.0. In: International Workshop on Requirements Engineering for Electronic Voting Systems (2011)
6. Langer, L., Schmidt, A., Buchmann, J., Volkamer, M.: A Taxonomy Refining the Security Requirements for Electronic Voting: Analyzing Helios as a Proof of Concept. In: International Conference on Availability, Reliability, and Security, ARES 2010, pp. 475–480. IEEE (2010)
7. Krimmer, R., Volkamer, M.: Bits or Paper? Comparing Remote Electronic Voting to Postal Voting. In: Andersen, K., Grönlund, A., Traunmüller, R., Wimmer, M. (eds.) Workshop and Poster Proceedings of the Fourth International EGOV Conference, pp. 225–232 (2005)
8. Demirel, D., Henning, M., Ryan, P.Y.A., Schneider, S., Volkamer, M.: Feasibility Analysis of Prêt à Voter for German Federal Elections. In: Kiayias, A., Lipmaa, H. (eds.) VoteID 2011. LNCS, vol. 7187, pp. 158–173. Springer, Heidelberg (2012)
9. Storer, T., Little, L., Duncan, I.: An Exploratory Study of Voter Attitudes Towards a Pollsterless Remote Voting System. In: Chaum, D., Rivest, R., Ryan, P.Y.A. (eds.) IaVoSS Workshop on Trustworthy Elections (WOTE 2006) Pre-Proceedings, pp. 77–86 (2006)
10. Campbell, B.A., Byrne, M.D.: Straight-Party Voting: What Do Voters Think? IEEE Transactions on Information Forensics and Security 4(4), 718–728 (2009)
11. Yao, Y., Murphy, L.: Remote Electronic Voting Systems: An Exploration of Voters' Perceptions and Intention to Use. European Journal of Information Systems 16(2), 106–120 (2007)
12. Raja, F., Hawkey, K., Beznosov, K.: Revealing Hidden Context: Improving Mental Models of Personal Firewall Users. In: Proceedings of the 5th Symposium on Usable Privacy and Security, SOUPS 2009 (2009)
13. Almuhimedi, H., Bhan, A., Mohindra, D., Sunshine, J.S.: Toward Web Browsers that Make or Break Trust. In: Proceedings of the Sixth Symposium on Usable Privacy and Security, SOUPS 2008 (2008)
14. Raja, F., Hawkey, K., Jaferian, P., Beznosov, K., Booth, K.S.: It's Too Complicated, So I turned It Off!: Expectations, Perceptions, and Misconceptions of Personal Firewalls. In: Proceedings of the 3rd ACM Workshop on Assurable and Usable Security Configuration, SafeConfig 2010, pp. 53–62 (2010)
15. Friedman, B., Hurley, D., Howe, D.C., Felten, E., Nissenbaum, H.: Users' Conceptions of Web Security: A Comparative Study. In: Extended Abstracts on Human Factors in Computing Systems, CHI EA 2002, pp. 746–747. ACM (2002)
16. Ho, J.T., Dearman, D., Truong, K.N.: Improving Users' Security Choices on Home Wireless Networks. In: Symposium of Usable Privacy and Security, SOUPS 2010 (2010)
17. Wash, R.: Folk Models of Home Computer Security. In: Proceedings of the Sixth Symposium on Usable Privacy and Security, SOUPS 2010 (2010)
18. Dourish, P., Grinter, B., Delgado de la Flor, J., Joseph, M.: Security in the wild: User Strategies for Managing Security as an Everyday, Practical Problem. Personal and Ubiquitous Computing 8(6), 391–401 (2004)
19. Camp, L.J.: Mental models of computer security. In: Juels, A. (ed.) FC 2004. LNCS, vol. 3110, pp. 106–111. Springer, Heidelberg (2004)
20. Camp, L.: Mental Models of Privacy and Security. IEEE Technology and Society Magazine 28(3), 37–46 (2009)
21. Asgharpour, F., Liu, D., Camp, L.J.: Mental Models of Computer Security Risks. In: Workshop on the Economics of Information Security (2007)

22. Liu, D., Asgharpour, F., Camp, L.J.: Risk Communication in Security Using Mental Models. In: Usable Security (2008)
23. Camp, J., Asgharpour, F., Liu, D.: Risk Communication in Computer Security Using Mental Models. In: Workshop on the Economics of Information Security, WEIS 2007 (2007)
24. Bravo-Lillo, C., Cranor, L.F., Downs, J.S., Komanduri, S.: Bridging the Gap in Computer Security Warnings: A Mental Model Approach. IEEE Security and Privacy 9(2), 18–26 (2011)
25. Charmaz, K.: Constructing Grounded Theory: A Practical Guide through Qualitative Analysis, 1st edn. Sage Publications Limited (2006)
26. Andrews, D., Nonnecke, B., Preece, J.: Conducting Research on the Internet: Online Survey Design, Development and Implementation Guidelines. International Journal of Human-Computer Interaction 16(2), 185–210 (2003)
27. Oppenheim, A.N.: Questionnaire Design, Interviewing and Attitude Measurement. Continuum (2000)
28. Wright, K.B.: Researching Internet-based Populations: Advantages and Disadvantages of Online Survey Research, Online Questionnaire Authoring Software Packages, and Web Survey Services. Journal of Computer-Mediated Communication 10 (2005)
29. Lazar, J., Feng, J.H., Hochheiser, H.: Research Methods in Human-Computer Interaction. John Wiley and Sons (2010)
30. Guest, G., Bunce, A., Johnson, L.: How many interviews are enough? An experiment with data saturation and variability. Field Methods 18(1), 59–82 (2006)
31. Karayumak, F., Michaela, K., Maina, O., Melanie, V.: Usability Analysis of Helios - An Open Source Verifiable Remote Electronic Voting System. In: Proceedings of the 2011 USENIX Electronic Voting Technology Workshop/Workshop on Trustworthy Elections. USENIX (2011)

A   Relevant Study Data

Table 4. Some Identified Concepts Grouped Under Mental Models

Mental Model	Sample of Concepts in Model
Trusting	Trust(Blind) Trust(Processes) Trust(Employees) Trust(Postal service) Trust(Sealed envelope) Trust(Public count of votes) Trust(Observers)
No Knowledge	Don't know No way
Matching	Published results match observed ones Number of voters match number of votes
Observer	Observers Different election workers Public count of votes
Personal Involvement	Can observe personally

Table 5. Questions from the Study Questionnaire

SECTION	QUESTIONS
Demographics	Please select your age range. [18 and under, 19 - 34, 35 - 44, 45 - 54, 55 - 64, over 65] What is your gender? [Male, Female] What is your highest level of education? [High school or less, Some college, Bachelor's degree, Master's degree, PhD] How often do you use the Internet? [Every day, Every two or three days, Once a week, Once every two weeks, Once a month] Which of the following statements is true in most cases? [I need help to install programs on my computer, I install computer programs on my computer, Other people ask me to help them install programs on their computers, I do not install programs on my computer]
Mental Model (Paper Voting)	How can you tell that the paper vote you cast at the polling station was not modified or removed from the ballot box? How can you tell that the paper vote you cast at the polling station was included in the final tally, that is, as it was stored in the ballot box? How can you tell that the paper votes cast at the polling stations are included in the final tally, as they were stored in the ballot box?
Mental Model (Postal Voting)	How can you tell that your postal vote was not modified or removed on its way to the town hall and into the ballot box? How can you tell that your postal vote was not modified or removed from the ballot box? How can you tell that your postal vote was included in the final tally, that is, as it was stored in the ballot box? How can you tell that all postal votes are included in the final tally, as they were stored in the ballot box?
Verifiability Terms	Kindly give one word or phrase to describe what the man in black (in reference to the scenario diagrams) is doing

Prêt à Voter Providing Everlasting Privacy

Denise Demirel[1], Maria Henning[2], Jeroen van de Graaf[3], Peter Y.A. Ryan[4],
and Johannes Buchmann[1]

[1] Technische Universität Darmstadt / CASED, Germany
[2] Project Group Constitutionally Compatible Technology Design (provet),
Universität Kassel, Germany
[3] Departamento de Ciência da Computação, Universidade Federal de Minas,
Gerais,CEP 31270-901, Brazil
[4] University of Luxembourg/ Interdisciplinary Centre for Security and Trust,
Luxembourg

Abstract. This paper shows how Prêt à Voter can be adjusted in order
to provide everlasting privacy. This is achieved by adapting the ballot generation and anonymisation process, such that only unconditional
hiding commitments and zero knowledge proofs are published for verification, thus ensuring privacy towards the public. This paper presents
a security analysis carried out in a collaboration between computer sci-
entists and legal researchers. On the technical side it is shown that the
modified Prêt à Voter provides verifiability, robustness, and everlasting
privacy towards the public. Everlasting privacy towards the authorities
can be achieved by implementing several organisational measures. A legal evaluation of these measures demonstrates that the level of privacy
achieved would be acceptable under German law.

Keywords: Prêt à Voter, everlasting privacy, legal issues, design and
evaluation of e-Voting systems, cryptographic voting schemes.

1 Introduction

1.1 Motivation

The principle of secret suffrage is essential for every democratic election. In order
to fulfil this requirement, the privacy of the ballot cast must not only be assured
at the moment of voting but also after the election. It follows that an election
system must provide everlasting privacy, meaning that even a computationally
unbounded attacker cannot violate voter privacy. This is not only of high importance for secret suffrage but also for free suffrage. The casting of votes would
not be free if voters have to fear the disclosure of their vote on the day of the
election or afterwards. Therefore the validity of vote privacy cannot be bounded
to a specific period of time [13].

Computer based voting brings up huge challenges for technology as how to
guarantee the integrity of the result on the one hand, and ballot privacy on the
other. These challenges can be overcome by issuing cryptographically secured

J. Heather, S. Schneider, and V. Teague (Eds.): VoteID 2013, LNCS 7985, pp. 156–175, 2013.
© Springer-Verlag Berlin Heidelberg 2013

voting receipts, as given in the voting system of Prêt à Voter. Then voters are able to verify that their vote is recorded as cast and that all votes included in the input batch of the count are tallied as recorded. However, in order to provide a private and free election the voters should not be able to generate a proof for their voting decision using the receipt. Especially with respect to everlasting privacy this is not ensured by most verifiable voting systems. If the receipt, for instance, contains the voting decision in encrypted form, an attacker can determine the voting decision as soon as the underlying cryptosystem has been broken.

This paper analyses the use of unconditionally hiding commitments, instead of an encryption scheme in order to guarantee everlasting privacy with the voting system of Prêt à Voter. We chose Prêt à Voter because this is one of the best explored electronic voting systems which provides verifiability on one hand but a familiar way of paper voting one the other hand. Furthermore, Prêt à Voter is planned to be used in the Victoria State Election in Australia [6,7]. However, since electronic voting systems need to fulfil the election principles, not only technical but also legal considerations are important. For this reason, interdisciplinary work is indispensable while looking for electronic voting which is constitutionally compatible. Therefore, in this paper a technical solution for Prêt à Voter is described and evaluated regarding the properties verifiability, everlasting privacy, and robustness, followed by a legal evaluation of the provided level of privacy.

1.2   Related Work

Since its introduction in 2004 [32], Prêt à Voter has been continuously developed and improved. In [31], for instance, Ryan et al. describe the key elements and compare two approaches that use different cryptographic primitives. In [34] a threat analysis is carried out and enhancements are proposed and in [42] Xia et al. show how various election methods can be handled. Furthermore, the authors of [14] analyse the feasibility of Prêt à Voter for German Federal Elections from a technical and legal point of view. However, despite the numerous publications, this is the first paper addressing the aspect of everlasting privacy.

In [19], a voting system is proposed merging the Prêt à Voter ballot layout and the PunchScan tallying and auditing process. The votes are encoded using unconditionally hiding bit commitments providing a simple and everlasting private voting scheme. However, due to the PunchScan back end, an audit table is used instead of a mix-net.

There are other poll-site voting systems where privacy is independent of computational assumptions, for instance, the voting scheme introduced by Moran and Noar [26] and Bingo Voting [4]. But the first solution is based on direct-recording electronic voting machines that keep the cast vote secret while the second one assumes a trusted number generator. Prêt à Voter, where the voters generate an encoded vote by filling out a ballot paper, does not rely on the security of hardware used in the polling station.

Paper based poll-site voting systems that do not depend on computational assumptions regarding privacy are, for instance, ThreeBallot [30], Farnel [3,2], and Split-Ballot [27,28]. The privacy of the ThreeBallot voting system can be violated by a statistical attack [40] and the Farnel voting system enforces a more complex vote casting procedure. Each time a voter casts a vote in the Farnel box a receipt is generated by spinning the box and scanning a subset of its content. Furthermore, the order in which votes are cast determines the probability of each vote to be handed out as a receipt and be verified by other voters. Using Prêt à Voter each voter verifies his or her own vote and the receipts can be generated fast by simply printing the scanned information.

Split-Ballot requires that each ballot paper consists of several layers which are filled out by the voter simultaneously. Two layers are cast and both are needed to reconstruct the vote. Thus, this scheme also provides everlasting privacy but requires a more complex ballot layout and vote casting procedure.

Scantegrity [10,39] uses a commitment scheme and can thus be modified to provide unconditional privacy. However, verifiability is implemented by confirmation codes shown to the voters during the vote casting process. Thus, by making a photo of the filled ballot while the codes are still visible allows the voters to generate a proof of their cast vote. Prêt à Voter ballots are not unique because several ballots show the same candidate order and all information that allows to identify one single ballot paper, like the ID, are hidden under scratch fields (introduced in [33]). Thus, a photo would prove how the voter filled out a ballot but not that this ballot has been cast.

How everlasting privacy can be introduced to a voting system by using a universally verifiable and everlasting private mix-net [5] has been shown for the online voting system Helios [15]. When using a paper based poll-site voting system the mix-net cannot be simply replaced. In this case it needs to be elaborated how the ballots are generated and printed, and how the votes cast can be decoded and counted. Furthermore, the presented Helios voting system provides only everlasting privacy towards the public while in this paper we also discuss under which assumptions the privacy can be ensured towards the authorities.

The structure is as follows: In Section 2, a high-level overview of the classic Prêt à Voter voting scheme is given. In order to provide everlasting privacy the design does not have to be changed but the used cryptographic primitives are different. Thus, in Section 3 the technical details of our solution are described. In Section 4, a security analysis and in Section 5 a legal evaluation of the approach are carried out, followed by conclusion in Section 6.

2   System Overview of the Classic Scheme

2.1   Roles

The following parties participate in the election process.

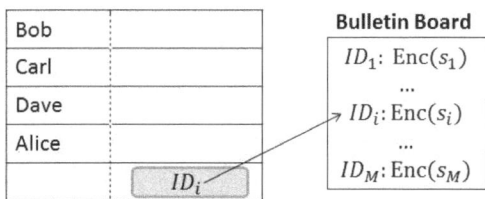

Fig. 1. Ballot Paper Layout used in Prêt à Voter

Election committee. The election committee is responsible for the correct execution of the election procedures. The head of the election committee, for instance, opens and closes the vote casting process, overviews the counting of votes, and announces the election result of the constituency.

Poll workers. The poll workers assist the election committee during the election procedures, for instance, by checking the eligibility of the voters, handing out ballot papers in the polling station, and supervising the vote casting and auditing process.

Voters. Voters are people who cast a vote.

Help Organisation. Help organisations support voters in performing the verification processes.

Auditors. Auditors are experts who run the verification process and check the published proofs. Further, they are in charge of guaranteeing and verifying the randomness of the challenge.

Authorities. The set of authorities consists of all private authorities, e.g. the election committee, poll workers, auditors, printers, and mixes.

Key holders. The set of key holders is a subset of authorities who hold shares of private or access keys, needed to decrypt data or access hardware.

Clerks. The set of clerks is a subset of authorities that generate the ballot data in distributed fashion.

Observers. Observers are interested parties like voters, authorities, and third parties, who verify the correctness of the election process and result.

2.2   System Overview

This section provides a high-level overview of the system and the voter's view. For more information please consult [7,34].

Ballot Form Layout. The Prêt à Voter ballot form consists of two halves which can be separated by a perforation down the middle. The lefthand side shows the candidates in random order. The righthand side contains a box against each name where the voters can mark their choice and includes a link to the used encrypted candidate order (See Fig. 1). This can, for instance, be a hash or a serial number which refers to corresponding data published. The information on the righthand side, which allows reconstruction of the candidate order, is hidden by a scratch field.

Auditing of Ballot Forms. Before the vote casting process, the poll workers publicly audit the well-formedness of a set of randomly selected ballots. This is performed by revealing the scratch fields and verifying that the printed candidate list matches with the encrypted candidate order. In addition voters should be able to perform their own checks. Thus, each voter receives two or more ballots from which he or she chooses one for vote casting while the remaining ballots are audited.

Vote Casting and Vote Capture. The voter authenticates him- or herself, receives a set of ballot papers, audits all ballots except one, and enters the secret polling booth. Then he or she votes for a subset of candidates, e.g. by marking the corresponding boxes with an "x". In order to cast the vote, only the righthand side containing the selected positions and the link to the encrypted candidate order have to be scanned. Thus, the voter detaches and destroys the left hand side, showing the candidate list, and leaves the polling booth. The poll worker checks whether the scratch field is still intact, reveals the information at the bottom of the righthand side, and scans the ballot paper. Then the scanner displays the digitalisation of the receipt (i.e. righthand side of the ballot) and asks the voter to confirm whether it has been recorded correctly. Thus, the voter can cast a fresh ballot, if the information shown does not reflect his or her vote. If the scanned information is correct, the voter confirms. Then his or her encrypted vote is added to the list of votes cast and the voter receives a receipt containing a record of the scanned information signed by the electronic ballot box. In addition, the filled out righthand side is cast to a conventional ballot box allowing to re-scan in case of a malfunction or breakdown.[1]

Anonymisation and Tallying. After the vote casting process, all cast encrypted votes, consisting of the marked positions and the encrypted candidate order, are made anonymous followed by decrypting and tallying.[2] The anonymisation process is usually performed with the help of a mix-net. This technique was introduced by David Chaum in 1981 [9] and allows to make a set of input messages anonymous while the content of the input batch remains unchanged. Prêt à Voter uses an enhancement, the so called reencryption mix-net [29], which permits that the whole anonymisation process can be verified by any interested party. The input set consists of all published encrypted votes. Then each mix of the mix-net successively reencrypts the probabilistic encryption, i.e. by changing the random values of the ciphertexts, and shuffles its input batch. The output of the mix-net is a set of anonymised encrypted votes which is then decrypted and tallied.

---

[1] There are also other specifications of Prêt à Voter where the voter keeps the righthand side as a receipt. However, in order to provide robustness we recommend to collect them in a conventional ballot box.

[2] Another approach is to tally the cast votes homomorphically and decrypted the election outcome. However, in this paper we will focus on the mix-net based approach.

Verification. After the voters received their receipt, they should check the validity of the signature[3], for instance, by using a smart phone App or a device which is made available in the polling station. After the vote casting process all cast encrypted votes are published and the voters can check whether their encrypted vote, printed on the receipt, appears. Furthermore, the whole tallying process can be verified by any interested party. More precisely, during mixing, each mix of the mix-net publishes enough information so that the observers are able to check whether the mixing process was performed correctly, i.e. that the input and the output batch encrypts the same set of votes. There are several approaches to prove correct mixing, e.g. by using a non-interactive zero knowledge argument [20,25] or a generic verification method [36]. In addition, the voting system publishes enough information to allow any observer to verify that the output of the mix-net was decrypted and tallied correctly.

3   Technical Details of Prêt à Voter Providing Everlasting Privacy

This section describes the technical details of the proposed voting scheme. The early Prêt à Voter approaches using re-encryption mix-nets only support cyclic shifts of candidate lists [11,35]. However, if the voter selects more than one candidate per ballot, the distance between various marks reveals information about the vote cast. Thus, later developments [21,41,43] provide arbitrary permutations requiring one encrypted information for each candidate. For legibility, we will describe the improved scheme only for ballots containing a shifted candidate order. However, like elaborated for the original approach [42,37] the described process can easily be adapted to support other tallying methods and ballot papers with arbitrary candidate lists.

3.1   Assumptions Regarding the Operational Environment

In order to provide everlasting privacy and robustness we make the following assumptions regarding the operational environment.

Assumption A. The electoral roll is accurately maintained and voters can cast their vote in a secret polling booth.

Assumption B. There exists a private key server, e.g. a hardware security module [1], that provides only limited access to authorities. The access key is distributed between several key holders such that no single authority has access to the device. The key server is used to store some key material and is not needed during the vote casting process. Thus, it can be stored safely, for instance, in the town hall.

---

[3] The voters can verify the signature by themselves. Nevertheless, they should have the opportunity to ask poll workers for help.

Assumption C. As with most end-to-end verifiable voting schemes, we assume the existence of a secure bulletin board, i.e. one to which only authorised entities can append, nothing can be deleted, and everyone has a consistent read access [22].

Assumption D. The authorities choose the parameters (e.g. keys) for the used cryptographic primitives in a way that the underlying computational problem cannot be broken before the election result has been announced.

Assumption E. A non-trivial subset of authorities acts honestly meaning that they follow the process correctly and do not reveal information private to them (e.g. access or private key shares).

Assumption F. All random values used during the ballot generation, tallying and, verification phase are unpredictable and are chosen at random.

Assumption G. The IT environment provides private channels, which are modification proof and secure against side channel attacks, between the private key server and the first printer, the private key server and the first mix of the mix-net, and successive mixes in the mix-net.

Assumption H. At least one mix of the mix-net is honest and keeps the permutation, used to shuffle its input set, secret.

Assumption I. After each printing step the ballot papers are shuffled before they are loaded to the next printer to prevent that neither poll workers nor printers learn the association between IDs and candidate lists.

Assumption J. After processing encrypted data, all hardware components destroy the information private to them.

Assumption K. A threshold subset of key holders attend the tallying process so that the private key server can be accessed and encrypted data can be decrypted.

The internal data stored on the private key server must be sent to the printer in order to generate the ballot papers and to the mix-net to anonymise the votes cast. Thus, both procedures should be carried out in public to allow any interested party to observe that the printing process is performed correctly (Assumption I), that private channels, like direct cable connection, are used for the communication (Assumption G), and that the hardware components delete all information private to them, for instance, by destroying their memory (Assumption J). For a legal evaluation of these assumptions see Section 5.

3.2 Technical Details

Key Generation. In this section we give a high-level overview of the used cryptographic primitives. For more information please consult [5]. In order to provide everlasting privacy and universal verifiability we need a homomorphic and unconditional hiding commitment scheme (GenCom, Com, Unv) to encode the published auditing information. First a commitment key $ck = \mathsf{GenCom}(1^\kappa)$ for security parameter κ is generated and made public. Then for any message $m \in \mathcal{M}$ and randomly chosen decommitment value $r \in \mathcal{R}$ a commitment $c = \mathsf{Com}_{ck}(m, r) \in \mathcal{C}$ can be generated. $\mathsf{Unv}_{ck}(c, m, r)$ returns m if $m \in \mathcal{M}$

and $r \in \mathcal{R}$ are the correct opening values of $c \in \mathcal{C}$ and $\perp$ if not. Note that the used instantiation for the commitment scheme has to be correct, non-interactive, computational binding, unconditional hiding, and must be additive homomorphic, i.e. $\mathsf{Com}(m, r) \cdot_{\mathcal{C}} \mathsf{Com}(m', r') = \mathsf{Com}(m +_{\mathcal{M}} m', r +_{\mathcal{R}} r')$ for all $m, m' \in \mathcal{M}$ and $r, r' \in \mathcal{R}$.

In order to process the opening values in addition to the commitment scheme, a matching homomorphic public key encryption scheme $(\mathsf{GenEnc}, \mathsf{Enc}, \mathsf{Dec})$ is used. $\mathsf{GenEnc}(1^{\kappa})$ generates a key pair for security parameter κ consisting of a private key sk and a public key pk. The algorithm $\mathsf{Enc}(m)$ encrypts message $m \in \mathcal{M}'$ using random value $r \in \mathcal{R}'$. The function $\mathsf{Dec}(c) = m$ denotes the decryption of ciphertext $\mathsf{Enc}(m) = c \in \mathcal{C}'$ to message $m \in \mathcal{M}'$. Possible instantiations are Paillier encryption with slightly adapted Pedersen Commitments like proposed in [28] and the cryptographic primitive proposed in [12].

For our approach we need two instances of the encryption scheme. One which is homomorphic over the message space $\mathcal{M}$, denoted by $(\mathsf{GenEnc}_{\mathcal{M}}, \mathsf{Enc}_{\mathcal{M}}, \mathsf{Dec}_{\mathcal{M}})$ and $(\mathsf{GenEnc}_{\mathcal{R}}, \mathsf{Enc}_{\mathcal{R}}, \mathsf{Dec}_{\mathcal{R}})$ which is homomorphic over the randomisation space $\mathcal{R}$ of the used commitment scheme. More precisely, having two commitments $c_0 = \mathsf{Com}(m_0, r_0)$ and $c_1 = \mathsf{Com}(m_1, r_1)$, where $m_0, m_1 \in \mathcal{M}$ and $r_0, r_1 \in \mathcal{R}$, and the corresponding opening values in encrypted form $\mathsf{Enc}_{\mathcal{M}}(m_0)$, $\mathsf{Enc}_{\mathcal{R}}(r_0)$, $\mathsf{Enc}_{\mathcal{M}}(m_1)$, and $\mathsf{Enc}_{\mathcal{R}}(r_1)$. Then the encrypted opening values to the commitment $c_0 \cdot c_1 = \mathsf{Com}(m_0 + m_1, r_0 + r_1)$ can be computed by multiplying the encryptions: $\mathsf{Enc}_{\mathcal{M}}(m_0) \cdot \mathsf{Enc}_{\mathcal{M}}(m_1) = \mathsf{Enc}_{\mathcal{M}}(m_0 + m_1)$ and $\mathsf{Enc}_{\mathcal{R}}(r_0) \cdot \mathsf{Enc}_{\mathcal{R}}(r_1) = \mathsf{Enc}_{\mathcal{R}}(r_0 + r_1)$.

Prior to an election two key pairs are generated. The public keys $\mathsf{pk}_{\mathcal{M}}$ and $\mathsf{pk}_{\mathcal{R}}$ are published while the corresponding private keys $\mathsf{sk}_{\mathcal{M}}$ and $\mathsf{sk}_{\mathcal{R}}$ are distributed in threshold fashion among several key holders. During the ballot printing process three printers are used. The second printer generates a key pair $(\mathsf{sk}_{\mathcal{R}'}, \mathsf{pk}_{\mathcal{R}'})$ and the third printer a key pair $(\mathsf{sk}_{\mathcal{M}'}, \mathsf{pk}_{\mathcal{M}'})$ using $(\mathsf{GenEnc}_{\mathcal{R}})$ and $(\mathsf{GenEnc}_{\mathcal{M}})$ respectively. The public keys are published together with the other key material.

Ballot Generation. For the Prêt à Voter voting system providing everlasting privacy, the conventional ballot layout is adopted but instead of the encrypted shift value $\mathsf{Enc}(s)$ the ballot refers to a commitment $\mathsf{Com}(s, t)$ of the used candidate order. Furthermore, the ballot is extended by a third "auditing" strip, containing the "decommitment value" t, which can be detached by a perforation (See Figure 2). After vote casting, all scanned ballots are published showing the position marked by the voter and a unique commitment to the shifted candidate list. In order to provide vote secrecy, no single authority or electronic device must be able to reconstruct the association between the published information and the corresponding secret candidate order. Thus, similar to the original approach the ballot data, i.e. shifted candidate order, commitment, and encrypted opening values, is generated in distributed fashion by the clerks. To generate a set of M ballots each clerk $j \in [1, L]$ performs the following steps:

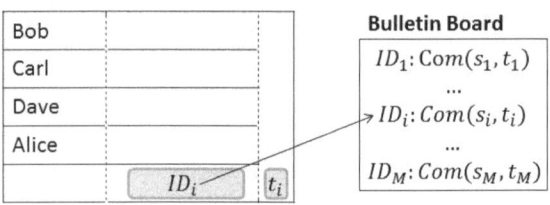

Fig. 2. Ballot Paper Layout of the new version

1. Generate a batch of random seeds $\langle s_i^j \in \mathcal{M} \rangle_{i=1}^M$ denoting a cyclic shift of the candidate names computed (mod n) where n is the number of candidates. The seeds are drawn uniformly at random from the message space.
2. A commitment to each seed $i \in [1, M]$ is generated $\langle \mathsf{Com}_{ck}(s_i^j, t_i^j) \rangle$ using a randomly chosen decommitment value $t_i^j \in \mathcal{R}$. Furthermore, the opening values are encrypted with the public keys $\mathsf{pk}_\mathcal{M}$ and $\mathsf{pk}_\mathcal{R}$ of the key holders, $\langle \mathsf{Enc}_\mathcal{M}(s_i^j), \mathsf{Enc}_\mathcal{R}(t_i^j) \rangle$, and the public keys $\mathsf{pk}_{\mathcal{R}'}$ and $\mathsf{pk}_{\mathcal{M}'}$ of the second and third printer, $\langle \mathsf{Enc}_{\mathcal{M}'}(s_i^j), \mathsf{Enc}_{\mathcal{R}'}(t_i^j) \rangle$. The output of each clerk is securely stored on the private key server.
3. The "full" encrypted information $(\Theta_i^C, \Theta_i^E, \Theta_i^S, \Theta_i^T)$ for ballot i is generated by the private key server by multiplying the output of various clerks:
   $\Theta_i^C = \prod_{j=0}^L \mathsf{Com}_{ck}(s_i^j, t_i^j)$,
   $\Theta_i^E = \langle \prod_{j=0}^L \mathsf{Enc}_\mathcal{M}(s_i^j), \prod_{j=0}^L \mathsf{Enc}_\mathcal{R}(t_i^j) \rangle$,
   $\Theta_i^S = \prod_{j=0}^L \mathsf{Enc}_{\mathcal{M}'}(s_i^j)$ and
   $\Theta_i^T = \prod_{j=0}^L \mathsf{Enc}_{\mathcal{R}'}(t_i^j)$.
4. The private key server generates a link, ID_i, for each ballot $i \in [1, M]$ and publishes the IDs together with the commitments $\{\Theta_i^C\}_{i=1}^M$ on the bulletin board. Then the set of IDs, $\{\mathrm{ID}_i\}_{i=1}^M$, is sent together with $\{\Theta_i^S\}_{i=1}^M$ and $\{\Theta_i^T\}_{i=1}^M$ to the first printer while the corresponding opening values $\{\Theta_i^E\}_{i=1}^M$ are kept secret by the key server.

Ballot Printing. The generated ballot data is printed by a quorum of printers (See Figure 3) similar to the process described in [34][4]. Note that in order to ensure voter privacy assumption E, G, I, and J must hold. Furthermore, the ballots should be printed in public to assure that the described process is performed correctly. For a discussion on this topic from a legal point of view see Section 5.

1. The first printer prints the encrypted seed Θ_S on the lefthand side of the ballot paper, the link ID to the commitment Θ_C at the center, and the encrypted "decommitment value" Θ_T on the righthand side.
2. The printed ID is covered by a scratch field, the ballot papers are shuffled, and loaded into the next printer.

---

[4] Another opportunity is to print the ballots on demand in the polling-station. However, a legal analysis showed that printing in advance should be preferred [14].

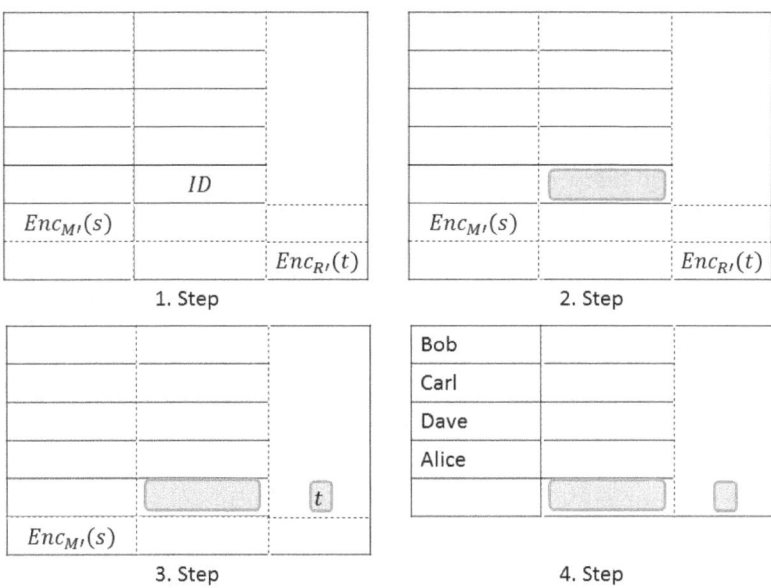

Fig. 3. Ballot printing process

3. The second printer scans and decrypts $\Theta_T = \mathsf{Enc}_{\mathcal{R}'}(t)$ and prints the decommitment value t at the bottom of the righthand side. Then t is covered by a scratch field, Θ_T is removed, the ballot papers are shuffled, and loaded into printer three.
4. The last printer scans and decrypts the seed $\Theta_S = \mathsf{Enc}_{\mathcal{M}'}(s)$ and prints the candidate list shifted by $-s \pmod{n}$ on the lefthand side. Finally the encrypted seed value Θ_S is removed.

Auditing Process. Auditing of ballot forms is very important for the robustness of the voting system. If the ballot papers were not generated properly, the votes cast are not decoded correctly afterwards. In order to check the well-formedness of a ballot paper one simply has to reveal the "decommitment value" t and the link to the commitment $\mathsf{Com}(s, t)$ hidden under the scratch fields. Then he or she can verify whether the value s used to shift the candidate names and t are the opening values of $\mathsf{Com}(s, t)$. This proves integrity of the ballot due to the computational bindingness of the used commitment scheme. In addition, the auditors should check that the revealed shift and "decommitment" values were derived from the defined uniform distribution.

Note that the commitments printed on the ballot forms are published during the tallying process. Thus, if voters get to see the "decommitment" and shift value they can use this information to open the commitment, prove the candidate order of their ballot, and thus the cast vote. Therefore, if a ballot paper is used to cast a vote, the auditing strip, containing the hidden decommitment value t, **must** be detached and destroyed by the poll workers before the voter enters the secret polling booth. Furthermore, ballot papers used for auditing **must not** be used for vote casting.

Anonymisation, Tallying, and Verification Process. Like the conventional Prêt à Voter tallying process, first, the marked position u_i on each cast ballot $i \in [1, K]$ is publicly encoded and homomorphically added to the commitment, that is $\mathsf{Com}(s_i, t_i) \cdot \mathsf{Com}(u_i, 0) = \mathsf{Com}(s_i + u_i, t_i) = \mathsf{Com}(v_i, t_i)$. Note that the marked position and the shift value add up to the position of the chosen candidate with respect to the initial, unshifted candidate list (mod n). Then the commitment to the vote cast, $\mathsf{Com}(v_i, t_i)$, is published next to the scanned ID and marked position on the bulletin board. In addition, the private key server adapts the securely stored encrypted shift values accordingly, $\mathsf{Enc}_{\mathcal{M}}(s_i) \cdot \mathsf{Enc}_{\mathcal{M}}(u_i) = \mathsf{Enc}_{\mathcal{M}}(s_i + u_i) = \mathsf{Enc}_{\mathcal{M}}(v_i)$.

Afterwards, the votes are made anonymous with the help of a mix-net that rerandomises the commitments and encrypted opening values, for instance, by using the mixing procedure presented in [5]. The public commitments, $U = \{\mathsf{Com}(v_i, t_i)\}_{i=1}^{K}$, and the privately stored opening values consisting of the encrypted votes, $V = \{\mathsf{Enc}_{\mathcal{M}}(v_i)\}_{i=1}^{K}$, and the encrypted "decommitment" values, $W = \{\mathsf{Enc}_{\mathcal{R}}(t_i)\}_{i=1}^{K}$, are sent to the first mix using a private channel. The mix-net publicly outputs a set of mixed commitments, $C' = \{\mathsf{Com}(v'_j, t'_j)\}_{j=1}^{K}$, and privately outputs a set of associated anonymised encrypted votes, $V' = \{\mathsf{Enc}_{\mathcal{M}}(v'_j)\}_{j=1}^{K}$, and encrypted "decommitment" values, $W' = \{\mathsf{Enc}_{\mathcal{R}}(t'_j)\}_{j=1}^{K}$. Note that the correctness of the mixing process can be universally verified. After the mixing process, the votes can be decoded and published without violating voter privacy, because the link between single inputs and single outputs has been removed. In order to determine the election outcome, first, the key holders decrypt and publish the votes $\{v'_j\}_{j=1}^{K}$ and "decommitment values" $\{t'_j\}_{j=1}^{K}$. Then any interested party can verify that these are the opening values to the published commitments $C' = \{\mathsf{Com}(v'_j, t'_j)\}_{j=1}^{K}$. Afterwards, the chosen candidates are determined by publicly computing the votes $\{v''_j\}_{j=1}^{K}$, where $v''_j := v'_j \pmod{n}$ for all $j \in [1, K]$, revealing the position marked with respect to the initial, unshifted candidate list. Finally, the number of votes per candidate are counted and the election outcome is announced.

4   Security Analysis from a Technical Point of View

Individual Verifiability. The proposed scheme provides individual verifiability such that the voters can verify that their vote was encoded as intended, cast as encoded, and recorded as cast. If the voter successfully audited some ballots, the correctness of the ballot generation process is ensured with high probability, i.e. the candidate order matches the information the ID refers to. Thus, the auditing process allows the voters to ascertain themselves that using these ballots the vote is encoded as cast. Furthermore, after scanning the encoded vote, the scanner shows its interpretation to the voter and prints a receipt if he or she confirms. Thus, the voter can check that the filled ballot matches the vote printed on the receipt and therefore that the vote is cast as encoded.

Finally, after the vote casting process, the entire input of the tally is published. Thus, each voter can verify that his or her encoded vote printed on the receipt is recorded as cast, such that it is included in the input batch of the tallying process.

Universal Verifiability. The proposed Prêt à Voter voting scheme provides universal verifiability such that any observer can verify that all votes were tallied as recorded. During mixing the mix-net publishes enough information for the observers and the auditors to verify that the commitments to the votes have been processed correctly. After the anonymisation, the commitments are opened what also proves the integrity of the privately processed, encrypted opening values, consisting of the votes and the "decommitment values". Note that if a mix would be able to modify a vote undetected such that the associated commitment can be opened, this is a contradiction to the computational bindingness of the used commitment scheme. For a proof on this statement please consult [5]. In addition, during the subsequent tallying process all intermediate results are published on the bulletin board allowing any interested party to recount the election outcome.

Correctness. It can be shown that by verifying the processing of commitments also the integrity of the associated encrypted opening values is ensured. Assume an authority manipulated one vote, for instance, by adapting the encrypted opening values during ballot generation or by manipulating the key server. Thus, the output of the mix-net contains $\mathsf{Com}(v_i, t_i)$, $\mathsf{Enc}_{\mathcal{M}}(v_i')$, and $\mathsf{Enc}_{\mathcal{R}}(t_i)$ where vote i has been manipulated such that $v_i' \neq v_i$. After carrying out the mixing process and proving its correctness, the opening values, v_i' and t_i are determined. If the commitments could be opened using the modified vote, the authority would have found a second pair of opening values, $\mathsf{Unv}(\mathsf{Com}(v_i, t_i), v_i, t_i) \neq \mathsf{Unv}(\mathsf{Com}(v_i, t_i), v_i', t_i) \neq \perp$, a contradiction to the computational binding property of the commitment scheme.

Everlasting Privacy. The proposed voting system provides everlasting privacy towards observers because only the voter gets to see the secret candidate order. Furthermore, all data printed on the receipts and published on the bulletin board for auditing, like commitments and zero knowledge proofs, provide unconditional privacy. Everlasting privacy towards the authorities can only be provided with the help of organisational measures and is discussed in Section 5 from a legal point of view.

Robustness. Regarding robustness the only difference between the classic Prêt à Voter voting scheme and the solution proposed here is the use of a key server to store the opening values. Without this information the votes cast cannot be determined. Therefore, a backup and recovery concept must be developed that provides a high security standard. However, in some applications even a small probability that the ongoing election might be disturbed is unacceptable.

For such cases a two layer ballot paper, like proposed for Punch Scan [18], can be used. The upper layer shows the secret candidate order and the bottom layer contains the ID that links to the encoded shift value. The voters cast their choices on the top sheet and the marked positions are recorded by the bottom due to holes punched in the upper layer. After filling out the ballot, the top layer containing the vote in plain text is not destroyed but collected in a conventional ballot box for recount while the bottom sheet is scanned. This allows to tally the votes even in case of a malfunction or breakdown of the key server.

5   Security Evaluation from a Legal Point of View

In this section the level of privacy provided by the new version of Prêt à Voter is evaluated from a legal point of view. This evaluation is necessary since the use of electronic voting systems depends on its legal compatibility. Note that German law makes great demands on the legality of parliamentary elections, implying that if a voting system passes the German criteria, it would probably qualify in most countries. For instance, the principle of the public nature of elections requires that all essential steps in the elections are subject to public examinability. However, this issue is beyond the scope of this paper because here we deal with secret suffrage (or, in other words, voter's privacy) only. We refer to [23] for a legal evaluation of the question if verifiability meets the public nature of elections. For a legal analysis of other security properties please consult [14].

As clarified in [13], everlasting privacy is of high importance from a constitutional point of view. Since a free vote is not possible if voters have to fear the disclosure of their voting decision, the privacy of the ballot cast must be assured forever after the election. So the legislator needs to provide a voting procedure that fulfils both everlasting privacy towards the public and towards the authorities. Especially data encrypted with public key cryptography must be protected since this information is secure for several decades only. An exact period of validity cannot be determined but data encrypted with RSA and a key length of 2048 bit, for instance, could be revealed in approximately 20 to 30 years [24,17].

As the technical security analysis of the Section 4 showed, everlasting privacy towards observers can be ensured since only unconditional hiding commitments are published. In order to provide everlasting privacy also towards authorities and technical devices, procedural controls are necessary. It is questionable whether this guarantee can be made dependent on the observance of organisational measures, since the system itself should fulfil the election principles as best as possible. But a comparison with traditional paper based elections and the interpretation of the relevant jurisdiction shows that technical and organisational measures can be implemented in order to achieve such guarantees. For a detailed legal analysis of this aspect please consult Appendix A.

In the following we will evaluate each election step and discuss the needed organisational measures to ensure everlasting privacy towards the authorities.

Key Generation. The parameters for the used cryptographic primitives have to be chosen such that the computational problem cannot be broken before the end of the election. According to § 31 Federal Electoral Act and § 54 Federal Electoral Code, all essential steps in the elections are subject to public observation. Therefore, the public keys for the encryption and commitment scheme have to be published on the bulletin board in order to allow any interested party to verify that the parameters have been chosen properly. Furthermore, the key holders must be chosen in a way that the probability of collaboration can be kept low. According to the current regulations regarding the commonality of the election committee, the key holders could be members of different parties. As regulated in § 9.2 sent 4 Federal Electoral Act, the election committee shall represent the parties of the respective electoral district. Furthermore, when conferring specific competences on the election committee or in specific on the key holders, new penal provisions should be taken into consideration.

Ballot Generation. The ballot data is jointly generated by a set of clerks. As it applies to the key holders, the clerks should be chosen carefully and in correspondence with the existing parties of the respective electoral district. Furthermore, since observers should be able to examine the essential steps of the election, this process must be carried out in public as well.

The data needed to reveal the voting decisions cast on the generated ballots is safely stored in encrypted form on a so-called key server. If an authorised person or a single member of the election committee gets access to the key server and to the data saved in here, particular votes can get linked to particular receipts as soon as the used encryption scheme is broken. Thus, this device must be protected by access control, and the keys are shared between a set of key holders. Furthermore, a certification is indispensable because the key server is an electronic device which is needed for the ballot generation and the ascertainment of the result, and therefore has to be classified as an electronic voting system as defined in § 1 Federal Voting Machine Ordinance. In dependence on the regulations concerning the testing of voting machines, this certification should be allocated to a technique authority, like, for elections in Germany, the *Physikalisch-Technische Bundesanstalt*. This is the supreme technical authority which has long experience with the testing of voting devices and other technical systems [8, p. 2]. According to § 16.2 Federal Voting Machine Ordinance, the key server should be sealed and stored in a way that it is secure against any inspections of unauthorised persons.

Ballot Printing. The ballots are generated and printed in distributed fashion. However, the printers have to process encrypted data, like the seed and random values. It follows that a malicious authority could try to eavesdrop and store this information, wait until the cryptosystem has been broken and reveal the association between receipts and votes cast. Thus, voter privacy can be guaranteed only with the help of certain organisational measures. Private channels like direct cable connections or CDs[5] are used to transfer data from the key server to the printer; the ballots are shuffled by the poll workers after each printing step; and all data private to the printers is deleted afterwards, for instance, by physically destroying the memory. Furthermore, in order to fulfil § 31 Federal Electoral Act and § 54 Federal Electoral Code and the subsequent requirement of public observation, the entire process regarding the application of the key server, including the data transfer, must be carried out in public. All voters and citizen should be able to check that only the authorities access the key servers and that the private channels which are used for data transfer are not subject to manipulation during the ballot printing process.

Without these procedural controls several attacks are possible. If the printing process is not observable, a printer could remove all scratch fields, read and store the encrypted information, and use this data to violate voter privacy. Even worse is if this attack is carried out by the third printer, since this machine sees the seed values in clear and thus does not have to wait until the cryptosystem is broken.

Similar to the key servers the printers need a certification, must be protected by a chain of custody, and have to be checked before use. According to the current regulation of § 7.1 Federal Voting Machine Ordinance, the local authority could be in charge for this. This additional security measures help to prevent that the machines can contain unauthorized soft- or hardware that allows information to be leaked or manipulating data. Furthermore, all electronic systems are prone to eavesdropping of electromagnetic emanations. Therefore, this should be evaluated prior to the election by the technique authority and corresponding security preventive measures should be implemented.

Even though organisational measures would ensure voter privacy if only one printer is used, a distributed printing process should be used. By doing so, the relevant information is not located on one device and a successful attack is harder to carry out. To manipulate a printer successfully, either one needs to have access to the device within the limits of the certification, or one has to manage to get possession of the printer in the polling station. This is more difficult in case more than one printer is used. But to make successful attacks even harder, additional technical measures can be considered. The replacement of printed ballots, for instance, can be made more difficult by watermarks or fingerprints[6] on the ballots which allow verifying their integrity.

Auditing and Vote Casting Process. The auditing procedure must be executed under observation to allow the observers to verify that the process is carried out and that the revealed decommitment values are derived from the defined uniform distribution.

---

[5] Note that if CDs are used they must be publicly destroyed immediately after the printer read out the data.

[6] Note that if fingerprints are used which make the ballot papers unique, the corresponding information must be hidden or destroyed before the ballots are handed out to the voters.

In order to ensure voter privacy during the vote casting process, the electoral roll has to be accurately maintained. A member of the election committee has to remove the auditing strip and immediately destroy it before the ballot is handed out to the voter. If the voter can detach and keep the auditing strip, he or she is able to reveal the used decommitment value and prove a certain candidate order towards an attacker. Furthermore, it has to be ensured that the scratch field is intact after the voter left the polling booth. If the unique code is revealed during the vote casting process, this allows the voter to take a photo of the filled ballot and prove his or her cast voting decision towards a coercer. In traditional paper based elections, a comparable attack is not possible since the picture of a filled ballot paper never proves the insertion of it into the ballot box.

Anonymisation. Before the opening values are decrypted and the election outcome is determined, the cast votes have to be anonymised such that the commitments cannot be linked back to a receipt. Here the same organizational measures as for the printing process are necessary. The hardware must have a certification and be protected by a chain of custody. Furthermore, the whole process must be carried out in public so that any observer can convince him- or herself that the commitments are anonymised before they are opened, that during the process no one tampers with the hardware, and that data is correctly transferred and destroyed afterwards.

6   Conclusion

Despite the large number of poll-site voting systems proposed during the last decades, only a small amount of solutions addresses the aspect of everlasting privacy. A legal evaluation showed that privacy which relies on computational assumptions is just not enough [13]. Thus, in this paper it is shown that everlasting privacy can be introduced to Prêt à Voter by adapting the ballot generation and anonymisation process. Then the proposed voting system is evaluated regarding technical properties and legal regulations. The security analysis shows that the system provides robustness and verifiability. Furthermore, everlasting privacy towards the public is achieved by publishing unconditionally hiding commitments and zero knowledge proofs. The legal evaluation concentrates on the organisational measures needed to ensure everlasting privacy towards the authorities and shows that they are acceptable from a legal point of view. Provided that the use of key servers, private channels, printers, and mix-nets should be observable, any citizen can verify that authorities only get access to the system.

Our results show the importance of interdisciplinary work during the development of electronic voting systems. It allows to combine technical approaches with organisational measures in order to design a solution that is secure and constitutionally compatible.

Acknowledgement. This paper has been developed within the project 'VerKonWa' — Verfassungskonforme Umsetzung von elektronischen Wahlen — which is funded by the Deutsche Forschungsgemeinschaft (DFG, German Science Foundation).

Peter Ryan thanks the FNR Luxembourg for funding the SeRTVS project. Jeroen van de Graaf's research was partially sponsored by PRPq/UFMG, Edital 12/2011.

References

1. Pci hardware security module (hsm),
   https://www.pcisecuritystandards.org/documents
2. Araújo, R., Custódio, R.F., van de Graaf, J.: A verifiable voting protocol based on Farnel. In: Chaum, D., Jakobsson, M., Rivest, R.L., Ryan, P.Y.A., Benaloh, J., Kutylowski, M., Adida, B. (eds.) Towards Trustworthy Elections. LNCS, vol. 6000, pp. 274–288. Springer, Heidelberg (2010)
3. Araujo, R., Ryan, P.Y.A.: Improving the Farnel voting scheme. In: Electronic Voting, pp. 169–184 (2008)
4. Bohli, J.-M., Müller-Quade, J., Röhrich, S.: Bingo Voting: Secure and coercion-free voting using a trusted random number generator. In: Alkassar, A., Volkamer, M. (eds.) VOTE-ID 2007. LNCS, vol. 4896, pp. 111–124. Springer, Heidelberg (2007)
5. Buchmann, J., Demirel, D., van de Graaf, J.: Towards a publicly-verifiable mix-net providing everlasting privacy. In: Financial Cryptography (to appear, 2013)
6. Burton, C., Culnane, C., Heather, J., Peacock, T., Ryan, P.Y.A., Schneider, S., Srinivasan, S., Teague, V., Wen, R., Xia, Z.: A supervised verifiable voting protocol for the victorian electoral commission. In: Electronic Voting, pp. 81–94 (2012)
7. Burton, C., Culnane, C., Heather, J., Peacock, T., Ryan, P.Y.A., Schneider, S., Teague, V., Wen, R., Xia, Z.J., Srinivasan, S.: Using Prêt à Voter in Victoria State Elections. In: Proceedings of the Electronic Voting Technology Workshop/Workshop on Trustworthy Elections (2012)
8. Cabinet of Germany: Bundestags-Drucksache 16/5194 (2007),
   http://dipbt.bundestag.de/dip21/btd/16/051/1605194.pdf
9. Chaum, D.: Untraceable electronic mail, return addresses, and digital pseudonyms. Commun. ACM 24(2), 84–88 (1981)
10. Chaum, D., Essex, A., Carback, R., Clark, J., Popoveniuc, S., Sherman, A.T., Vora, P.L.: Scantegrity: End-to-end voter-verifiable optical-scan voting. IEEE Security & Privacy 6(3), 40–46 (2008)
11. Chaum, D., Ryan, P.Y.A., Schneider, S.: A practical voter-verifiable election scheme. In: De Capitani di Vimercati, S., Syverson, P.F., Gollmann, D. (eds.) ESORICS 2005. LNCS, vol. 3679, pp. 118–139. Springer, Heidelberg (2005)
12. Cuvelier, E., Pereira, O., Peters, T.: Election verifiability or ballot privacy: Do we need to choose? Cryptology ePrint Archive, Report 2013/216 (2013)
13. Demirel, D., Henning, M.: Legal analysis of privacy weaknesses in poll-site evoting systems. Jusletter IT Editions Weblaw (September 2012) ISSN 1664-848X
14. Demirel, D., Henning, M., Ryan, P.Y.A., Schneider, S., Volkamer, M.: Feasibility analysis of Prêt à Voter for German federal elections. In: Kiayias, A., Lipmaa, H. (eds.) VoteID 2011. LNCS, vol. 7187, pp. 158–173. Springer, Heidelberg (2012)

15. Demirel, D., van de Graaf, J., Araújo, R.: Improving Helios with everlasting privacy towards the public. In: Proceedings of EVT/WOTE 2012 (2012)
16. Federal Constitutional Court of Germany: Voting computer judgement. (BVerfGE) - Judicial decisions of the Federal Constitutional Court of Germany 123, 39 (2009), http://www.bverfg.de/entscheidungen/rs20090303_2bvc000307en.html
17. Ferguson, N., Schneier, B.: Practical cryptography. Wiley (2003), http://books.google.nl/books?id=ThVRAAAAMAAJ
18. Fisher, K., Carback, R., Sherman, A.T.: Punchscan: Introduction and system definition of a high-integrity election system. In: Preproceedings of WOTE 2006 (2006)
19. Graaf, J.: Voting with unconditional privacy by merging Prêt à Voter and PunchScan. IEEE Trans. Inf. Forensics Security 4(4), 674–684 (2009)
20. Groth, J.: Short pairing-based non-interactive zero-knowledge arguments. In: Abe, M. (ed.) ASIACRYPT 2010. LNCS, vol. 6477, pp. 321–340. Springer, Heidelberg (2010)
21. Heather, J.: Implementing STV securely in Prêt à Voter. In: CSF, pp. 157–169 (2007)
22. Heather, J., Lundin, D.: The append-only web bulletin board. In: Degano, P., Guttman, J., Martinelli, F. (eds.) FAST 2008. LNCS, vol. 5491, pp. 242–256. Springer, Heidelberg (2009)
23. Henning, M., Demirel, D., Volkamer, M.: Öffentlichkeit vs. verifizierbarkeit - inwieweit erfüllt mathematische verifizierbarkeit den grundsatz der öffentlichkeit der wahl. In: IRIS 2012, pp. 213–220 (2012)
24. Kaliski, B.: Twirl and RSA key size (May 2003), http://citeseerx.ist.psu.edu/viewdoc/download?doi=10.1.1.77.4447&rep=rep1&type=pdf
25. Lipmaa, H., Zhang, B.: A more efficient computationally sound non-interactive zero-knowledge shuffle argument. In: Visconti, I., De Prisco, R. (eds.) SCN 2012. LNCS, vol. 7485, pp. 477–502. Springer, Heidelberg (2012)
26. Moran, T., Naor, M.: Receipt-free universally-verifiable voting with everlasting privacy. In: Dwork, C. (ed.) CRYPTO 2006. LNCS, vol. 4117, pp. 373–392. Springer, Heidelberg (2006)
27. Moran, T., Naor, M.: Split-ballot voting: everlasting privacy with distributed trust. In: ACM Conference on Computer and Communications Security, pp. 246–255 (2007)
28. Moran, T., Naor, M.: Split-ballot voting: Everlasting privacy with distributed trust. ACM Trans. Inf. Syst. Secur. 13(2) (2010)
29. Park, C., Itoh, K., Kurosawa, K.: Efficient anonymous channel and all/Nothing election scheme. In: Helleseth, T. (ed.) EUROCRYPT 1993. LNCS, vol. 765, pp. 248–259. Springer, Heidelberg (1994)
30. Rivest, R.L.: The ThreeBallot voting system (2006)
31. Ryan, P.Y.A., Bismark, D., Heather, J., Schneider, S., Xia, Z.: Prêt à Voter: a voter-verifiable voting system. IEEE Trans. Inf. Forensics Security 4(4), 662–673 (2009)
32. Ryan, P.Y.A., Bryans, J.: A simplified version of the chaum voting scheme. Technical Report CS-TR 843, University of Newcastle upon Tyne (May 2004)
33. Ryan, P.Y.A., Peacock, T.: Prêt à Voter: a systems perspective. Tech. rep. (2005)
34. Ryan, P.Y.A., Peacock, T.: A threat analysis of Prêt à Voter. In: Chaum, D., Jakobsson, M., Rivest, R.L., Ryan, P.Y.A., Benaloh, J., Kutylowski, M., Adida, B. (eds.) Towards Trustworthy Elections. LNCS, vol. 6000, pp. 200–215. Springer, Heidelberg (2010)

35. Ryan, P.Y.A., Schneider, S.A.: Prêt à Voter with re-encryption mixes. In: Gollmann, D., Meier, J., Sabelfeld, A. (eds.) ESORICS 2006. LNCS, vol. 4189, pp. 313–326. Springer, Heidelberg (2006)
36. Sako, K., Kilian, J.: Receipt-free mix-type voting scheme - A practical solution to the implementation of a voting booth. In: Guillou, L.C., Quisquater, J.-J. (eds.) EUROCRYPT 1995. LNCS, vol. 921, pp. 393–403. Springer, Heidelberg (1995)
37. Schneider, S., Srinivasan, S., Culnane, C., Heather, J., Xia, Z.: Prêt á Voter with write-ins. In: Kiayias, A., Lipmaa, H. (eds.) VoteID 2011. LNCS, vol. 7187, pp. 174–189. Springer, Heidelberg (2012)
38. Schreiber, W.: Bundeswahlgesetz Kommentar. Carl Heymanns Verlag (2009)
39. Sherman, A.T., Fink, R.A., Carback, R., Chaum, D.: Scantegrity III: automatic trustworthy receipts, highlighting over/under votes, and full voter verifiability. In: Proceedings of EVT/WOTE 2011, pp. 7–23 (2011)
40. Strauss, C.: A critical review of the triple ballot voting system. Part2: Cracking the triple ballot encryption. Draft Version 1.5, Verified Voting New Mexico (2006), http://www.cs.princeton.edu/~appel/voting/Strauss-ThreeBallotCritique2v1.5.pdf
41. Xia, Z., Schneider, S.A., Heather, J., Ryan, P.Y.A., Lundin, D., Peel, R., Howard, P.: Prêt à Voter: All-in-one. In: Proceedings of WOTE 2007, pp. 47–56 (2007)
42. Xia, Z., Culnane, C., Heather, J., Jonker, H., Ryan, P.Y.A., Schneider, S., Srinivasan, S.: Versatile Prêt à Voter: Handling multiple election methods with a unified interface. In: Gong, G., Gupta, K.C. (eds.) INDOCRYPT 2010. LNCS, vol. 6498, pp. 98–114. Springer, Heidelberg (2010)
43. Xia, Z., Schneider, S.A., Heather, J., Traoré, J.: Analysis, improvement, and simplification of Prêt à Voter with paillier encryption. In: EVT 2008 (2008)

A   Legal Analysis of Organisational Measurements

As the compliance with secret suffrage has to be addressed technically when voting electronically, it is questionable if the guarantee of everlasting privacy can be made dependent on the observance of specific organisational measures.

Since the German constitution does not purport a specific voting procedure the legislator may choose any possible way in order to ensure the election principles as best as possible. The Federal Constitutional Court only reviews whether it has remained within the boundaries of the latitude granted to it by the Basic Law, or whether it has violated a valid constitutional election principle by overstepping these boundaries [16, para 117].

The German legislator imposes a set of security and functionality requirements on electronic voting systems [38, p. 595][8]. Also the Federal Voting Machine Ordinance provides a complex system of security measures that lasts from the certification and the use authorisation up to the voting procedure including the counting and tallying of votes [38, p. 595]. Therefore, organisational measures can be used in order to guarantee the election principles. The same result arises from the judgment of the German Federal Constitutional Court regarding the permissibility of the deployment of electronic voting systems [16]. After this a comprehensive bundle of technical and organisational security measures (e.g. monitoring and safekeeping of the voting machines, comparability of the devices used with an officially checked sample at any time, criminal liability in respect of election falsifications and local organisation of the elections) is not suited *by itself* to compensate for a lack of controllability of the essential steps in the election procedure by the citizen [16, para 126]. This means, as a corollary, that technical and organisational security measures can support the required controllability and the protection of the election principles in general.

These considerations can be transferred to the principle of secret suffrage. Furthermore, even in a traditional paper based election, the guarantee of the secret vote depends on the observance of organisational measures. For example, in Germany the election committee needs to refuse all voters who marked or folded their ballot paper outside of the polling booth. They will get a new ballot paper after they destroyed the old one in the presence of a member of the election committee. Therefore, this will prevent that voters violate the principle of secret suffrage by casting the vote in a detectable way.However, as the legislator purports behaviours which are essential for the guarantee of the secrecy of the vote, it assumes that the election committee acts as intended. For example, in Germany the election committee needs to refuse all voters who marked or folded their ballot paper outside of the polling booth. They will get a new ballot paper after they destroyed the old one in the presence of a member of the election committee. Insofar, it will be prevented that voters violate the principle of secret suffrage by casting their vote in the view of other voters. Therefore, the guarantee of the secrecy of the vote depends on organisational measures even in a traditional paper based election. Consequently, this applies to electronic voting systems as well. Thereby, the conversion of these measures should be controllable by the public since it is part of the election act. In Germany every person is allowed to enter the polling station during the election act and the counting and tallying of votes. Therefore, everyone is able to check whether the election committee follows the provisions correctly. As a result assumptions regarding the operational environment are allowed to a certain extend. But the permissibility of assumptions needs to be questioned in particular cases and for every voting system separately.

Towards a Practical Cryptographic Voting Scheme Based on Malleable Proofs

David Bernhard[1], Stephan Neumann[2], and Melanie Volkamer[2]

[1] University of Bristol, United Kingdom
[2] CASED / TU Darmstadt, Germany

Abstract. Mixnets are one of the main approaches to deploy secret and verifiable electronic elections. General-purpose verifiable mixnets however suffer from the drawback that the amount of data to be verified by observers increases linearly with the number of involved mix nodes, the number of decryptors, and the number of voters. Chase et al. proposed a verifiable mixnet at Eurocrypt 2012 based on so-called *malleable proofs* - proofs that do not increase with the number of mix nodes. In work published at PKC 2013, the same authors adapted malleable proofs to verifiable distributed decryption, resulting in a cryptographic voting scheme. As a result, the amount of data to be verified only increases linearly with the number of voters. However, their scheme leaves several questions open which we address in this paper: As a first contribution, we adapt a multi-party computation protocol to build a distributed key generation protocol for the encryption scheme underlying their voting scheme. As a second contribution, we decompress their abstract scheme description, identify elementary operations, and count the number of such operations required for mixing and verification. Based on timings for elementary operations, we extrapolate the running times of the mixing and verification processes, allowing us to assess the feasibility of their scheme. For the German case, we conclude that the replacement of postal voting by cryptographic voting based on malleable proofs is feasible on an electoral district level.

Keywords: Malleable Proofs, Distributed Key Generation, Performance.

1 Introduction

Since Chaum's seminal work [1], many cryptographic voting schemes have been proposed aiming for secret and verifiable elections. Beside blind signatures and homomorphic tallying, the use of mixnets has gained lots of interest in the research community. The success of the mix-based approach is largely due to recent mathematical achievements with respect to verifiable mixnets for large-scale elections, e.g., Wikström [2–4], Lipmaa and Zhang [5], and Bayer and Groth [6]. In the mix-based approach, the election is usually conducted in the following way: Voters individually encrypt their votes with the public key of the election authority and publish the resulting ciphertexts on a bulletin board. After the declared voting phase, a mixnet is used to anonymize all encrypted votes from

J. Heather, S. Schneider, and V. Teague (Eds.): VoteID 2013, LNCS 7985, pp. 176–192, 2013.
© Springer-Verlag Berlin Heidelberg 2013

eligible voters such that after the anonymization process, individual, encrypted votes can be decrypted by the election authority.

Mixnets are instantiated by independent mix nodes. Each mix node in turn verifies the proofs of all predecessor mix nodes, re-randomises and shuffles the encrypted votes, and adds a non-interactive zero-knowledge proof to its output attesting that it has shuffled correctly. The election authority is instantiated by a set of decryptors (often referred to as trustees). After the anonymization process, each decryptor partially decrypts the list of anonymized ciphertexts and generates a proof that it has partially decrypted this list correctly. Individual plaintexts can be reconstructed by combining a threshold number of partial decryptions. These plaintext votes are used afterwards to calculate the election result. After the tallying, observers (who might be individual voters) verify all proofs generated by all mix nodes and decryptors to convince themselves that the announced election result is correct. The amount of data to be processed by each observer depends linearly on the number of mix nodes, the number of decryptors, and the number of voters.

At Eurocrypt 2012, Chase et al. invented the concept of *malleable proof systems* [7]. Rather than generating individual and independent proofs, malleable proofs allow an individual mix node $i + 1$ to "update" the zero-knowledge proof π_i of mix node i and to add another permutation and randomisation, resulting in proof π_{i+1}. The updated proof is of the same general form as the original one, only the constants having changed. Therefore, the amount of data to be verified only increases linearly with the number of decryptors and voters but is independent of the number of mixers. Chase et al. propose using the DLIN encryption scheme [8] and Groth-Sahai proofs [9] in the DLIN setting to instantiate their construction. The appeal of malleable proofs has motivated work published recently at PKC 2013 [10]. In this work, the authors adapt malleable proofs to distributed decryption and thereby instantiate a cryptographic voting scheme (henceforth referred to as the CKLM13 scheme), which forms the basis of the current work. In CKLM13, the amount of data to be processed by each observer only increases linearly with the number of voters.

Our Contribution. While the underlying ideas and constructions are of great theoretical value, so far the practical use of malleable proofs within cryptographic voting schemes was beyond the scope of the work by Chase et al. [10]. Specifically, two practical questions remain open, which are addressed in our paper. 1) Though proposing a cryptographic voting scheme based on malleable proofs, to date there is no distributed key generation protocol for DLIN known and therefore CKLM13 implicitly relies on a single trusted key distribution party. 2) The concept and the instantiation of malleable proofs for cryptographic voting have been highly theoretical and an evaluation of the real-world feasibility of tallying and verification in terms of computational efficiency is pending.

To address the first problem, we propose a distributed key generation protocol for the DLIN encryption scheme. This allows us to extend the CKLM13 scheme to a fully distributed cryptographic voting scheme. We do so by adapting a multi-party computation (MPC) protocol invented by Smart and Geisler [11] to the

DLIN encryption scheme. The distributed key generation protocol comes at the cost of the assumption that at most $t < n/3$ election administrators (decryptors) are actively cheating. While we concede that cryptographic elections should be verifiable even if all administrators are dishonest, we point out that this problem has not previously been addressed at all for the DLIN encryption scheme: to the best of our knowledge, no DLIN key generation algorithm has been proposed to date that is secure against even *one* dishonest participant.

In the remainder of this work, we refer to this extended version of CKLM13 as our *modified CKLM13* scheme. To answer the second question, we investigate the CKLM13 scheme in detail and expand its abstract description. This allows us to identify and count elementary operations. Using timings from the MIRACL pairing-based cryptography library [12], we draw conclusions about the real-world feasibility of cryptographic voting schemes based on malleable proofs. With reference to the election statistics of Darmstadt, Germany, we conclude that the postal voting process can be replaced by cryptographic voting based on malleable proofs, while on a city level the application of cryptographic voting based on malleable proofs is beyond practical use.

Structure. The remainder of this work is structured as follows: In Section 2, we provide the reader with preliminaries used throughout the paper. Section 3 is dedicated to the construction of a distributed key generation protocol for the DLIN encryption scheme. Thereafter, in Section 4, we analyze the Groth-Sahai proofs used in CKLM13 with respect to elementary operations. Based on implementation timings of the underlying cryptography, we draw conclusions about the feasibility of the modified scheme. Finally, we conclude our paper and give directions for future work in Section 5.

2   Preliminaries

In this section we introduce the notation and cryptographic concepts that we use in our work.

Notation. We denote assignment of value a to variable x by $x \leftarrow a$; assigning to x a value chosen uniformly at random from set S we denote by $x \leftarrow S$. In cryptographic groups we denote group elements by capital letters and integers (modulo the group order) by small ones. Algorithm names are set in SansSerif.

Public-Key Threshold Encryption. A public-key encryption scheme is a triple of algorithms (KeyGen, Encrypt, Decrypt) where KeyGen takes a security parameter as input and produces a public and a secret key; Encrypt takes a message and a public key and produces a ciphertext and Decrypt is deterministic, takes a secret key and a ciphertext as input and returns a message.

A threshold encryption scheme is characterised by two parameters, a number of decryptors n and a security threshold $t < n$. Informally, the properties we want are that any subset of at least $t + 1$ decryptors can jointly decrypt ciphertexts but no set of size at most t can gain any information from ciphertexts. In particular, at no point in a setup–encryption–decryption cycle is any one party or subset of size at most t in possession of a full decryption key. Following Fouque, Pointcheval and Stern [13], a threshold key generation scheme is defined by a 4-tuple of algorithms[1]: KeyGen takes a security parameter as input and outputs a public key pk and n key shares sk_i for the decryptors; Encrypt takes a message m and a public key pk and outputs a ciphertext c; Decrypt takes a ciphertext c and a key share sk_i and outputs a decryption share d_i; Combine takes a ciphertext c and a set of at least $t + 1$ decryption shares d_i and outputs either a message m or the special symbol $\perp$ to denote failure. For any public key pk and set of key shares $(sk_i)_{i=1}^n$ produced by KeyGen, for any message m and any ciphertext c produced by Encrypt on m and pk and for any subset $S \subseteq \{1, \ldots, n\}$ of size $|S| = t + 1$ it must hold that if for all $s \in S$ we compute $d_s \leftarrow$ Decrypt(c, x_s) then Combine$(c, (d_s)_{s \in S})$ returns m. This property is known as *correctness*.

DLIN Encryption. As opposed to many other cryptographic voting schemes, CKLM13 builds upon the DLIN (also known as BBS after its authors [8]) encryption scheme, which relies on the weaker *decisional linear Diffie-Hellman* (DLIN) assumption rather than the *decisional Diffie-Hellman* (DDH) assumption to achieve IND-CPA security. The scheme lives in a cyclic group $\mathbb{G}$ with generator G of some order q, a prime power.

A secret key is a pair $(x, y) \leftarrow \mathbb{Z}_q \times \mathbb{Z}_q$ and the corresponding public key is $(X, Y) = (G^x, G^y)$. To encrypt a $M \in \mathbb{G}$ one picks a pair $(r, s) \leftarrow \mathbb{Z}_q \times \mathbb{Z}_q$ and computes $(A, B, C) \leftarrow (X^r, Y^s, MG^{r+s})$. To decrypt one recomputes M as $C/(A^{1/x}B^{1/y})$ where the inversions are taken over the field $\mathbb{F}_q$. DLIN encryption, like ElGamal, is homomorphic: the componentwise group operation on two ciphertexts is a ciphertext for the group operation on the two underlying messages. This property allows a ciphertext to be re-randomised by adding an encryption of the neutral element in $\mathbb{G}$ which forms the basis for the use of DLIN encryption in mixnets. Creating a threshold version of DLIN encryption is the subject of Section 3.

Pairing-Based Cryptography. A *pairing group* is a triple of groups $(\mathbb{G}_1, \mathbb{G}_2, \mathbb{G}_T)$ of some order q with an efficiently computable bilinear, non-degenerate map e : $\mathbb{G}_1 \times \mathbb{G}_2 \to \mathbb{G}_T$ i.e. for generators G_1, G_2 of $\mathbb{G}_1, \mathbb{G}_2$ respectively and integers a, b we have $e(aG_1, bG_2) = e(G_1, G_2)^{ab}$ and $e(G_1, G_2)$ is again a generator of $\mathbb{G}_T$.

The only known implementations of such groups that are useful for cryptography are based on elliptic curves; such an implementation is called *symmetric* if $\mathbb{G}_1 = \mathbb{G}_2$ and *asymmetric* if the two groups are different and no efficient homomorphisms are known between them.

Shamir's Secret Sharing Scheme. Shamir's secret sharing scheme [14] allows a party to share a secret among any n parties such that any subset of $t \leq n$ parties can reconstruct the secret but any smaller subset gains no information about the secret. Each party obtains as a share the value of a degree-t bounded polynomial at a distinct index over a suitable finite field such that the secret is

---

[1] The original definition also contains verification keys, which we view as part of the public key, and mentions decryption proofs explicitly which we view as part of the decryption shares.

the value at some other index (usually 0). Given any t shares, the secret can be reconstructed by interpolation using Lagrange coefficients.

3   Key Generation with Multi-party Computation

Voting is among the most security-sensitive applications that can be conducted over the Internet. Therefore, complex trust distribution concepts are in place to prevent malicious collaborations among internal/external attackers from violating the desired security properties. As opposed to ElGamal, which is often considered the standard in the cryptographic voting community, the DLIN encryption scheme does not come with a distributed key generation protocol. Hence, the CKLM13 scheme [10] implicitly relies on a trusted key distribution party, which forms a crucial security bottleneck of the overall scheme. This section is organised as follows: First, we explain the distinction between a key generation algorithm and a protocol and show why we want the latter, but for DLIN this does not follow directly from the former. Next, we give the key generation algorithm for DLIN, introduce multi-party computation and deploy it to turn the algorithm into a protocol. We analyse our new protocol with respect to efficiency and security. Finally, we show how our protocol greatly simplifies the threshold decryption operation.

3.1   Security of Threshold Encryption: Algorithm versus Protocol

The definition of threshold encryption (for example, [13]) only postulates a key generation *algorithm* which gives security if it is run by a trusted party who then securely distributes the key shares to the decryptors. In practice, what is required however is a key generation *protocol* that the decryptors can run jointly and that, following our informal specification, never puts any one party in possession of a key with which it could decrypt messages directly [16].

For the ElGamal encryption scheme, constructing a threshold key generation protocol is comparatively easy although not without subtleties [17]. This may be a reason that the distinction between threshold key generation algorithms and protocols is usually not made in the literature. For DLIN however, it is not an easy task to construct a secure key generation protocol from the algorithm, without a trusted party.

DLIN encryption uses two public keys X and Y. Since their use is completely symmetric, we discuss the problem relating only to a single public key $X = G^x$ for some secret x. During decryption, one raises a ciphertext component A to the power $1/x$. The threshold key generation *algorithm* therefore picks an x, creates a public key G^x, computes $\bar{x} \leftarrow 1/x$ and creates shares $\bar{x}_i$ of $\bar{x}$ — the decryptors get shares of the *inverse* of the element used as the exponent of the public key. One could try and build a protocol that starts with all parties generating shares of x and interpolating G^x. However, the shares of the inverse $1/x$ are not the same as the inverses of shares of x and there is no easy method to obtain one from the other. One might think that one could simply start with shares of $\bar{x} = 1/x$ instead but then one cannot easily compute the public key which is now $G^{1/\bar{x}}$.

3.2   A Threshold Algorithm

To construct a threshold scheme for DLIN encryption, we start with Shamir's secret sharing scheme. This gives a key generation algorithm but not yet a protocol: pick a DLIN key pair and Shamir-share the decryption keys. Shamir's scheme has homomorphic properties that allow shares to be used for decryption without ever reconstructing the key. In more detail, if $\mathbb{G}$ is a cyclic group of order q with generator G and $(x_i)_i$ are Shamir-shares of a secret x in $\mathbb{F}_q$ then $(G^{x_i})_i$ are Shamir-shares of G^x since $\mathbb{G}$ can be viewed as a vector space over $\mathbb{F}_q$ and the polynomial p defined by the shares can be lifted from $\mathbb{F}_q$ to G. This leads to the following threshold DLIN scheme.

KeyGen *(algorithm.)* For given t and n, pick secret keys $x, y \leftarrow \mathbb{F}_q$. Compute $\bar{x} \leftarrow 1/x$ and $\bar{y} \leftarrow 1/y$ over $\mathbb{F}_q$. Create a (t, n) Shamir-sharing of $\bar{x}$ and give each decryptor her share $\bar{x}_i$; repeat for $\bar{y}$. Output the public key $(X, Y) \leftarrow (G^x, G^y)$.

Encrypt Like for non-threshold DLIN encryption.

Decrypt(A, B, C) For the decryptor with shares $\bar{x}_i, \bar{y}_i$, create a decryption share as $D_i \leftarrow A^{\bar{x}_i} B^{\bar{y}_i}$.

Combine Given any set of at least $t + 1$ decryption shares $(D_s)_{s \in S, |S| > t}$, interpolate D as the value at 0 of the degree-t-bounded polynomial p such that $p(s) = D_s$ for all $s \in S$. The final decryption is $M \leftarrow C/D$.

This scheme still leaves open two questions. The first is how to check if the values D_s provided by the decryptors are correct - Chase et al. [10] suggest using malleable proofs here. Our solution to the second problem will remove the need for such proofs completely. The second problem to which Chase et al. do not provide a solution is, as mentioned, how to turn the key generation algorithm above into a protocol and eliminate the trusted party that generates keys.

3.3   Multi-party Computation

Multi-Party Computation (MPC) [18] is the theory of cryptographic protocols in which a set of parties $\{P_i\}$, each holding some secret input x_i, jointly compute some function $(y_i)_i = f((x_i)_i)$ of their inputs in a manner as secure as if everyone sent their x_i to a trusted party who computed f and returned the appropriate y_i to each P_i.

Our starting point is the MPC protocol by Smart and Geisler [11] for identity-based schemes that require exponent inversion. The key technique in this protocol is a development of an idea by Bar-Ilan and Beaver [19] for group element inversion. Smart and Geisler's protocol was originally given for distributed decryption in a class of identity-based encryption schemes making use of exponent inversion; another protocol by Kate and Goldberg [20] achieves distributed key generation for this class of schemes but their techniques do not translate into our scenario: in IBE, one party ends up in possession of a decryption key whereas in an election, no-one should ever be able to decrypt individual ballots.

We make two minor modifications to the Smart-Geisler protocol. First, we adapt the protocol to DLIN encryption. Secondly, the original protocol runs a fast key generation followed by comparatively costly MPC for decryption whereas we are considering a scenario in which decryption operations are much more time-critical than key generation so we prefer to use MPC to generate keys and a faster decryption operation. (Technically, Smart and Geisler propose generating shares of x where the public key is $X = G^x$ and using MPC to raise an element to $1/x$ at decryption time; we generate shares of $\bar{x} = 1/x$ for decryption and use MPC to compute the public key as $G^{1/\bar{x}}$.)

Security Threshold. Our protocol, as an artifact of the MPC protocol that we use, requires a security threshold $t < n/3$. We assume that broadcasting a value to all parties and sending a value privately to another party are possible. Our protocol is then secure against up to t parties actively cheating i.e. sending false values during the protocol. Constructing such a protocol for larger t we leave as an open problem. In return for this restriction on the size of t, we obtain not only the first threshold DLIN key generation *protocol* but also a very efficient one that allows us to dispense with the zero-knowledge proofs that threshold schemes usually require at decryption time.

Secure Interpolation. When reconstructing a degree-t Shamir-shared secret, as long as at least $t + 1$ of the shares are correct the presence of any incorrect shares can be detected if the following secure interpolation procedure is used. Pick a set $S \subseteq \{1, \ldots, n\}$ of any $t + 1$ indices and interpolate the secret from these (as the value at 0 of the degree-t bounded polynomial going through (i, x_i) for all $i \in S$, where x_i is the share at index i). Next, again using the set S interpolate the values of the polynomial at the indices of all other shares outside S and check that these points correspond to the actual shares received. If any of these checks fail, abort the setup protocol.

3.4   Our Protocol

Our MPC protocol will let each decryptor obtain a decryption key share $\bar{x}_i$ and all decryptors will obtain a public key $X = G^x$ where $\bar{x} = 1/x$. (To obtain the shares for the other public key component Y too, one runs the protocol twice in parallel.) We give the protocol from the point of view of a party P_i. In our protocol, we denote by $x^{(j)}$ a value received from party j, either as a broadcast or a private message; for $j = i$ this refers to the local variable x of party P_i (this notation allows us to iterate or sum over indices). We denote values that are common to all players with a star, i.e. u^*.

PRSS. We begin by setting up a Pseudo-Random Secret Sharing (PRSS) [15]. Details are in the full version of our paper. This allows all parties to repeatedly draw values x_l for any label l that form a sharing of some fresh random secret x_l^*. This need only be done once for each set of decryptors; they can generate many sets of keys with the same PRSS by picking fresh labels each time.

Decryption Key Shares. Once the PRSS is set up, draw a value $\bar{x}$ that will be your decryption key share. Also draw a further value r. (W.l.o.g. the labels for $\bar{x}$ and r are known to all parties.) Compute[2] $u \leftarrow \bar{x} \cdot r$. Since $\bar{x}$ and r were both degree-t shares of their respective secrets, the shares u are now degree-$2t$ shares of a value u^*.

Round 1: Sharing u. Locally create a degree-t sharing of u and send each P_j her share u_j. This can be achieved by letting $c_0 \leftarrow u$ and picking random coefficients $c_1, \ldots, c_t \leftarrow \mathbb{Z}_q$ to define a polynomial $p(x) = \sum_{k=0}^{t} c_k x^k$ and letting $u_j \leftarrow p(j)$ for all j.

Round 2: Interpolating u'. Collect shares $u^{(j)}$ from all other parties and interpolate u' from the values $(u^{(j)})_{j=1}^{n}$ as the value at zero of a polynomial of degree $2t$. This and all following interpolations must be done securely in the sense defined above, i.e. check that all received shares lie on a polynomial of correct degree and abort the protocol if any checks fail. Broadcast your value of u' to all parties.

Round 3: Reconstructing u^*. Receive values $u'^{(j)}$ from all other players and interpolate u^* from these values. All parties now hold a common value u^* which is the product of the secrets r^* and $\bar{x}^*$ defined by the shares r and $\bar{x}$ respectively. Compute your public key share $X \leftarrow G^{r/u^*}$ and broadcast this to all parties.

Round 4: Public Key. Receive shares $X^{(j)}$ from all parties and interpolate X^* from these values. X^* is the public key. We repeat that interpolation must be done securely, i.e. checking all other shares against the subset used for interpolation.

To generate the two public keys for DLIN encryption (X^* and Y^* in the notation of this section) the respective rounds of the two protocols can be combined, giving the same communication cost (number of messages) as for a single public key.

3.5 Efficiency and Security

Efficiency. It is well-known that MPC can in theory be used to compute any functionality yet in practice, the resulting protocols are too slow to be usable, usually due to a massive communication overhead. Our MPC protocol has a communication cost (in number of rounds or messages sent) equivalent to one single MPC multiplication, even for both public keys X and Y since they can be computed in parallel. This is definitely efficient enough to be run in practice: the cost of using MPC for the setup is dwarfed by the cost of malleable proofs so we expect key generation to account for only a small proportion of the running time of the whole protocol. Moreover, the PRSS setup which is the most expensive part of the setup can be run once for a group of parties and the PRSS obtained can then be re-used for many elections, generating new keys using fresh labels each time. Further, setup is a much less time-critical operation than tallying in a typical deployment of a voting scheme. Therefore, we omit a full analysis of the computational cost of the setup protocol.

---

[2] All operations take place in the ring $\mathbb{Z}_q$ so "mod q" is implicit in any operation.

Security. Textbook MPC theory says that our MPC protocol is secure against passive adversaries, i.e. who do not send false values during the protocol. However, the simple nature of our protocol together with the security threshold $t < n/3$ yields active security for free. The only operations which parties perform on values that they have received from other, potentially malicious parties are interpolations of polynomials of degree at most $2t$. Therefore, since for each such interpolation there are at least $2t + 1$ correct shares, the malicious parties cannot send incorrect values without causing the protocol to abort. It is important that all interpolations are done securely, i.e. after computing the desired value from any set S of $t+1$ (or $2t+1$) shares it must be verified that all further shares lie on the polynomial defined by the shares in S of the correct degree-bound. We do not care about resilience of the setup protocol against malicious parties causing the protocol to abort: in an election scenario, if a decryptor is caught cheating during key generation then one will probably want to choose a new decryptor and re-run the whole setup.

3.6   Threshold Decryption

To decrypt a ciphertext (A, B, C), each decryptor P_i holding shares $\bar{x}_i$ and $\bar{y}_i$ publishes $D_i = A^{\bar{x}_i} B^{\bar{y}_i}$. This is again a degree-t Shamir-share of $D = A^{1/x} B^{1/y}$. To combine decryption shares and complete a decryption, one interpolates D securely from any $t + 1$ shares $(D_i)_i$ (i.e. checks that all further shares lie on the polynomial defined by the ones used to decrypt). This secure interpolation ensures correctness of the decrypted result if $t < n/3$. On the other side, at the current state, correctness of the election result cannot be ensured against thresholds $t \geq n/3$. As a consequence, zero-knowledge proofs do not provide any benefit at decryption time, which allows us to discard them at decryption time.

If any shares appear incorrect then one can isolate the incorrect shares using Reed-Solomon decoding [21] and still recover the correct decryption as long as $t < n/3$, so up to t malicious decryptors can neither cause a false result to be announced nor prevent the correct result from being computed. This is a significant improvement of the efficiency of the decryption process compared to the original CKLM13 scheme (in which it is proposed using another round of malleable proofs) and could be applied to other voting schemes as well.

4   Computational Analysis of the Proofs in CKLM13

In this section we analyze the computational cost of the malleable proofs underlying the mixnet in the CKLM13 scheme [10]. Since Chase et al. only give an abstract description of their proofs we need to make a reasonable choice of a concrete setting in which to instantiate them. The only known implementation that yields somewhat efficient malleable proofs is that of Groth-Sahai (GS) proofs [9] in a pairing group; this is again an abstract concept for which we need to choose specific groups.

4.1   Choice of Setting

Elliptic curves form the basis of all known implementations of pairing groups which are widely believed to have cryptographic security properties. For such groups, the relevant parameters are q, the logarithm of the group size (roughly: the *bit length* of group elements) and k, the *embedding degree* of the group [22]. As a rule of thumb, the cost of operations in such a group is proportional to q^2 whereas security is proportional to $q \cdot k$; a rough estimate is that for given q, k, the security level is equivalent to a $qk/24$ bit symmetric key. It is clear that choosing k as large as possible results in the greatest efficiency at a desired security level. The parameter k is determined by details of the construction of the underlying elliptic curve; the best known choice is a Barreto-Naehrig (BN) curve [23] which achieves $k = 12$. For this reason, BN curves are the standard choice for implementing pairing-based cryptography nowadays. In this case, to get the equivalent of 128-bit security [24] requires group elements of bit-length $q = 256$ bits.

Choosing BN curves gives an *asymmetric* pairing group, i.e. a triple of groups $(\mathbb{G}_1, \mathbb{G}_2, \mathbb{G}_T)$ with a pairing $e : \mathbb{G}_1 \times \mathbb{G}_2 \to \mathbb{G}_T$ such that no efficient homomorphisms between $\mathbb{G}_1$ and $\mathbb{G}_2$ are known in either direction[3]. However, the CKLM13 scheme is given in a *symmetric* setting where $\mathbb{G}_1 = \mathbb{G}_2$ so to deploy it on a BN curve requires some modifications that are well established in the literature. Despite the cost of additional equations incurred in the transformation from symmetric to asymmetric settings, the resulting asymmetric protocols usually greatly outperform their symmetric ancestors. We therefore choose to analyse the cost of the CKLM13 malleable proofs in a $q = 256$ bit BN curve with the necessary modifications to the protocol.

For CKLM13, we require two modifications. First, instead of the DLIN assumption (which only applies to a single group), we require what is technically known as SDLIN (symmetric DLIN) [25], the assumption simply states that DLIN holds in both groups $\mathbb{G}_1$ and $\mathbb{G}_2$ of the setting. This is commonly believed to be the case in groups derived from elliptic curves and the switch from DLIN to SDLIN does not change the protocol. Secondly, since we are using an asymmetric setting, any group element that appears both in groups $\mathbb{G}_1$ and $\mathbb{G}_2$ in the symmetric protocol needs to be replaced by a pair of elements in the asymmetric protocol and "guarded" by an additional equation in the proof. This technique is standard in converting pairing-based schemes from the symmetric to the asymmetric setting.

4.2   Overview of Groth-Sahai Proofs

Groth-Sahai (GS) proofs are based on pairing groups and can be instantiated under several assumptions for several types of equations. We assume an initial set of parameters is given that describe groups $(\mathbb{G}_1, \mathbb{G}_2, \mathbb{G}_T)$ of some order p a

---

[3] All three groups are in fact isomorphic but security stems in part from the fact that no efficient way to compute isomorphisms between $\mathbb{G}_1$ and $\mathbb{G}_2$ is known.

prime or prime power, with generators (G_1, G_2, G_T) respectively and a bilinear map $e : G_1 \times G_2 \to G_T$. This setting is provided by BN curves; we can abstract away any further details of the curves for the moment. Of interest to us are so-called Pairing Product Equations (PPE) under the SDLIN security assumption. A PPE is an equation with vectors of variables $\underline{a}$ over G_1 and $\underline{b}$ over G_2 of the form

$$v \bullet \underline{b} \cdot \underline{a} \bullet w \cdot \underline{a} \bullet \Gamma \bullet \underline{b} = t$$

where $\cdot$ is the group operation in G_T and $\bullet$ is a scalar product over the pairing, i.e. $\underline{a} \bullet \underline{b} := \prod_i e(a_i, b_i)$ and $\underline{a} \bullet \Gamma \bullet \underline{b} := \prod_i \prod_j e(a_i, b_j)^{\Gamma_{ij}}$. v, w and t are constants in G_1, G_2 and G_T respectively.

A GS proof proves that the prover knows an assignment of values to a number of variables which satisfies a set of equations. These values are often known as a *witness*. The prover starts by making a *commitment* to each value and then produces a *proof pair*[4] of elements for each equation. The entire proof consists of a commitment for every variable appearing in the equations and a proof pair for each equation. *Verifying* a GS proof involves evaluating a verification equation for each given equation involving the commitments to the variables, the constants in the original equation and the proof pair.

Mathematical Overview. In this section we give some of the mathematical ideas necessary to understand how our costing of GS proofs works; the reader can skip the mathematical overview if so inclined without missing the essence of our paper.

The SDLIN GS proofs [25] use modules $B_1 := (G_1)^3, B_2 := (G_2)^3, B_T := (G_T)^9$ that can be seen as groups of vectors and matrices over the original groups and inherit a bilinear pairing $e_B : B_1 \times B_2 \to B_T$. Thus, a basic operation (addition or multiplication) in a module costs 3 respectively 9 operations in the underlying group; the pairing e_B costs 9 e-pairings.

All variables must be committed to; for the vector $\underline{a}$ over G_1 this is done by picking a matrix R_1 of random integers modulo p and computing commitments $c \leftarrow \iota(\underline{a}) + R_1 \cdot U_1$ where ι is an inclusion map from G_1 to B_1 and U_1 is a matrix of constants defined in the setup information. The process for $\underline{b}$ over G_2 is analogous.

A GS proof of a PPE in the DLIN setting is a pair $(\theta, \pi) \in (B_1)^3 \times (B_2)^3$ computed according to the following equations.

$$\pi \leftarrow R_1^\top \iota_2(w) + R_1^\top \Gamma \iota_2(\underline{b}) + R_1^\top \Gamma R_2 U_2 - T^\top U_2 \qquad (\Pi)$$

$$\theta \leftarrow R_2^\top \iota_1(v) + R_2^\top \Gamma^\top \iota_1(\underline{a}) + T U_1 \qquad (\Theta)$$

Here R_1, R_2 are the random elements used to commit to elements in $\underline{a}, \underline{b}$ respectively, T is a matrix of random integers modulo p chosen to randomise the proof of this PPE and U_1, U_2 are matrices of constants defined in the setup information.

---

[4] This is our terminology. Such a pair is commonly just called a "proof" but we wish to distinguish between the elements associated with a particular equation and the proof as a whole.

Verification of such a proof involves checking the following equation. Here c, d are the commitments to $\underline{a}, \underline{b}$ respectively and $\otimes$ is the scalar product over the pairing e_B in the B-modules.

$$\iota_1(\boldsymbol{v}) \otimes \boldsymbol{d} \ \cdot \ \boldsymbol{c} \otimes \iota_2(\boldsymbol{w}) \ \cdot \ \boldsymbol{c} \otimes \Gamma\boldsymbol{d} \ \stackrel{?}{=} \ \iota_T(t) \ \cdot \ U_1 \otimes \pi \ \cdot \ \theta \otimes U_2 \qquad (\text{V})$$

To count the number of operations in the CKLM13 scheme, we must deal with several small issues. First, the original paper describes the protocol in terms of a set of equations that are "almost" PPEs — almost, because they use abbreviations in their notation and our first step is to expand these into actual PPE that can be processed by the GS proof system. Secondly, we make the necessary changes to deploy the protocol in an asymmetric setting. Thirdly, starting with the equations to create and verify proofs of PPE we optimise them for the specific equations in CKLM13, i.e. we remove terms that cancel out or have all-zero coefficients.

4.3   Results

We let L be the number of votes shuffled in a run of the mixnet. Of the $4L$ variables and 11 equations given in CKLM13, equations 1–4 are simple PPE, 5 and 6 together require L supporting variables and equations to expand into a full PPE, 7 and 8 are linear PPE, 9–11 are quantified ($\forall i : 1 \leq i \leq L$) so are in fact L PPE each. To map these into an asymmetric setting requires another $2L$ supporting variables and $4L$ supporting equations. All together we end up with $8 + 8L$ equations of which the first 8 have L-fold products each and the remaining $8L$ have only constant-size products; in total we have $4L$ variables in $\mathbb{G}_1$ and $7L$ in $\mathbb{G}_2$.

Analysing the equations and taking into account components that have all-zero coefficients (which therefore contribute nothing to the cost of computation), we find an upper bound on the computation cost as presented in Table 1. Detailed calculations are in the full version of our paper.

Table 1. Number of elementary operations in proof creation and verification in CKLM13

Task	$\mathbb{G}_1$ mult.	$\mathbb{G}_2$ mult.	$\mathbb{G}_1$ op.	$\mathbb{G}_2$ op.	$\mathbb{G}_T$ op.	Pairing
Create proof	$163L + 72$	$183L + 72$	$134L + 48$	$167L + 48$		
Verify proof					$657L + 252$	$657L + 324$

For the remainder of this work, we refrain from considering group operations in $\mathbb{G}_1$, $\mathbb{G}_2$, and $\mathbb{G}_T$, because these are about the factor *bit-length of group elements* faster than multiplications [26] and consequently do not influence the feasibility analysis significantly. The following formula allows us to estimate the running time of an individual mix node and the voter's verification:

Table 2. Operation timings for Barreto-Naehrig curve over 256-bit prime fields with embedding degree 12 with the MIRACL library and the Beuchat et al. implementation

Elementary Operation	MIRACL	Beuchat et al.
$\mathbb{G}_1$ Multiplication	0.22 ms	n.a.
$\mathbb{G}_2$ Multiplication	0.44 ms	n.a.
Pairing	2.32 ms	0.39 ms

$$s(L) = (163 \times L + 72) \times \mathbb{G}_1 \text{ Multiplication Time } +$$
$$(183 \times L + 72) \times \mathbb{G}_2 \text{ Multiplication Time } +$$
$$(657 \times L + 324) \times \text{ Pairing Time}$$

Optimisations. We stress that our results are only an upper bound on the cost of computing a CKLM13 proof as there are several feasible optimisations that we have not yet considered. We mention some possible optimisations in the full version of our paper.

Timings. To the best of our knowledge, the MIRACL cryptography C library [12] is the most established open-source library to support BN curves. Recent timings taken on a 2.4 GHz Intel i5 520M processor [27] lead to the results provided in Table 2 (second column). The fastest claimed results for pairings on 256-bit BN curves which we are aware of are from Beuchat et al. [28, 29] who compute a pairing in 0.39 ms, compared to 2.32 ms currently achievable with MIRACL. However, times for multiplications using their implementation are not available (ref. to Table 2 third column). As pairings are the most expensive operation in the CKLM13 scheme, in the following, we hypothetically assume Beuchat et al.'s pairing time of 0.39 ms, while all other costs are assumed to be equal to MIRACL. The hypothetical timings for Beuchat et al.' implementation are considered in parallel to the MIRACL timings.

To bring these numbers into relation to real-world elections, we consider cryptographic voting as substitution for postal voting in the German case. In the German federal election 2009, 62.2 millions citizens were eligible to vote [30]. On average, electoral districts in Darmstadt, Germany have a size of 1100 voters, while for postal votes on average 3.5 electoral districts are aggregated. In 2009, 21.4% of the eligible voters cast their vote via postal voting. Considering all eligible voters, this results in 13.3 millions postal votes, while for each postal voting district in Darmstadt, Germany, this results in 824 postal votes. Table 3 summarizes the expected running times for one mix node both for the MIRACL library and the hypothetical Beuchat et al. implementation. It should be noted that the running time for the voter's verification is close to the running time of an individual mix node. These timings show that malleable proof based cryptographic voting schemes are feasible for a moderate number of voters, however their efficiency does not compare with Wikström's work or Bayer and Groth's work that achieve mix proofs and their verification for 100.000 ElGamal ciphertexts in around 2 minutes [3, 6].

Table 3. Expected running times for individual mix nodes in the CKLM13 scheme with different numbers of voters

Number of voters	MIRACL	Beuchat et al.
10	17.2 s	3.9 s
824 (Electoral District)	$\approx 22, 5$ min	≈ 5.1 min
1.000	$\approx 27, 3$ min	≈ 6.2 min
100.000	≈ 45 h	≈ 10 h
10.000.000	≈ 190 d	≈ 43 d
13.300.000 (German Federal Election)	≈ 252 d	≈ 57 d

5   Conclusion

In this work, we build upon the CKLM13 cryptographic voting scheme [10], which is based on the concept of malleable proofs invented in [7]. As opposed to existing mix-based approaches, CKLM13 allows to generate verification data which is independent of the number of mix nodes and the number of decryptors involved in the tallying process. However, so far the theoretical innovations are far from practical use. To bridge the gap between innovation and practice, in this paper, we have addressed two crucial questions which remain open in CKLM13. First, we propose a distributed key generation protocol for the DLIN encryption scheme based upon a multi-party computation protocol due to Smart and Geisler [11] and therefore succeed in ensuring security against up to $n/3$ misbehaving participants. By construction of the protocol, we do not achieve security against $n/3$ or more dishonest decryptors whatever happens in the decryption phase; for fewer than $n/3$ dishonest decryptors however the correctness of the election result is verifiable even without any proofs of correct decryption, allowing us to omit them for the time being. Secondly, we investigate CKLM13 in detail and identify elementary operations underlying their constructions. We count the number of such operations used for a single mix node. Based on timings from the MIRACL library, we calculate the running time for single mix nodes, which is almost the same as the running time of a voter verifying the election result.

We base our conclusion upon data obtained from the German Federal election in 2009. It turns out that the replacement of postal voting by cryptographic voting based on malleable proofs would be feasible on an electoral district level. Assuming that three mix nodes are in place with an average number of 824 absentee voters, tallying the election and the voter's verification of the result can be finalized in 90 minutes. This corresponds to the time needed to tally the postal votes in Darmstadt, Germany [31]. However, the results obtained in this work also show that the application of large-scale malleable proof based cryptographic voting is not feasible today. The tallying process on a city level (100.000 eligible voters) would require more mix nodes to be involved. Considering malleable proof based cryptographic voting on city level with five mix nodes and the voter's verification would result in a running time close to two weeks.

We guide future research in several directions: The constructed distributed key generation protocol for the DLIN encryption scheme is based on the assumption that $t < n/3$ participants are actively cheating (for both privacy and verifiability). Privacy against up to $t < n/2$ cheating administrators should be possible with standard MPC techniques. According to Smart [32], implementing our key generation protocol on top of SPDZ [33], for which a practical implementation exists, should even give privacy and verifiability against up to $t = n - 1$ cheaters [32]. For verifiability against even n out of n cheating decryptors, we believe that this is achievable more cheaply than by using another round of malleable proofs by exploiting the pairing operation directly, but leave this idea for future work. Either way, the malleable proofs in the mixnet constitute the dominating cost of the CKLM13 protocol (should one wish to use malleable proofs of correct decryption, these can be based on a much simpler set of GS equations). This justifies our choice to restrict our formal analysis of computational costs in the CKLM13 protocol to the mixing phase. Even though carefully designed, we leave the analysis and the correctness proof of the constructed protocol as a task for future work.

The feasibility estimations of this work are an upper bound on the real cost in a full implemented version of the modified CKLM13 scheme. For instance, expressions of the form $\sum_{i=1}^{l} v_i X_i$ in a group $\mathbb{G}_j, j \in \{1, 2\}$ we counted as l products and $l - 1$ sums, yet algorithms exist [22] to perform such operations more efficiently. One might also consider applying batch techniques [34] because proofs have large numbers of equations of very similar form. Thereby, the number of pairings required to verify a proof might be significantly reduced. Finally, there exist cryptographic libraries providing better performance than MIRACL. The works of Beuchat et al. [28, 29] show that pairing times can be reduced to 1/5 of the MIRACL timings, which would speed up the mixing and verification process by a factor 5. For the future, Beuchat et al.'s implementation should be extended towards a full cryptographic library such that ultimately an cryptographic voting scheme based on malleable proofs can be deployed.

Acknowledgements. The authors would like to thank Dr. Essam Ghadafi for comments on Groth-Sahai proofs and suggesting some optimisations, Prof. Nigel P. Smart and Dr. Ashish Choudhary for comments on multi-party computation, Markulf Kohlweiss for comments on the design of the CKLM12/13 protocols and Dr. Hugo Jonker for organising a PhD workshop on voting in 2012 at which the authors of this paper met and came up with the ideas for this paper. Finally, the authors would like to thank the anonymous reviewers for their helpful comments.

This work has been supported in part by EPSRC via grant EP/H043454/1, in part by the German Science foundation (DFG) via the project "ModIWa2 - Juristisch-informatische Modellierung von Internetwahlen", and in part by the German Federal Ministry of Education and Research (BMBF) via the project "BoRoVo - BoardRoomVoting".

References

1. Chaum, D.L.: Untraceable electronic mail, return addresses, and digital pseudonyms. Communications of the ACM 24(2), 84–90 (1981)
2. Wikström, D.: A commitment-consistent proof of a shuffle. In: Boyd, C., González Nieto, J. (eds.) ACISP 2009. LNCS, vol. 5594, pp. 407–421. Springer, Heidelberg (2009)
3. Terelius, B., Wikström, D.: Proofs of restricted shuffles. In: Bernstein, D.J., Lange, T. (eds.) AFRICACRYPT 2010. LNCS, vol. 6055, pp. 100–113. Springer, Heidelberg (2010)
4. Wikström, D.: A commitment-consistent proof of a shuffle. Cryptology ePrint Archive, Report 2011/168 (2011), http://eprint.iacr.org/
5. Lipmaa, H., Zhang, B.: A More Efficient Computationally Sound Non-Interactive Zero-Knowledge Shuffle Argument. IACR Cryptology ePrint Archive, 394 (2011)
6. Bayer, S., Groth, J.: Efficient Zero-Knowledge Argument for Correctness of a Shuffle. In: Pointcheval, D., Johansson, T. (eds.) EUROCRYPT 2012. LNCS, vol. 7237, pp. 263–280. Springer, Heidelberg (2012)
7. Chase, M., Kohlweiss, M., Lysyanskaya, A., Meiklejohn, S.: Malleable Proof Systems and Applications. In: Pointcheval, D., Johansson, T. (eds.) EUROCRYPT 2012. LNCS, vol. 7237, pp. 281–300. Springer, Heidelberg (2012)
8. Boneh, D., Boyen, X., Shacham, H.: Short Group Signatures. In: Franklin, M. (ed.) CRYPTO 2004. LNCS, vol. 3152, pp. 41–55. Springer, Heidelberg (2004)
9. Groth, J., Sahai, A.: Efficient Non-interactive Proof Systems for Bilinear Groups. In: Smart, N.P. (ed.) EUROCRYPT 2008. LNCS, vol. 4965, pp. 415–432. Springer, Heidelberg (2008)
10. Chase, M., Kohlweiss, M., Lysyanskaya, A., Meiklejohn, S.: Verifiable Elections That Scale for Free. In: Kurosawa, K., Hanaoka, G. (eds.) PKC 2013. LNCS, vol. 7778, pp. 479–496. Springer, Heidelberg (2013)
11. Geisler, M., Smart, N.P.: Distributing the Key Distribution Centre in Sakai–Kasahara Based Systems. In: Parker, M.G. (ed.) Cryptography and Coding 2009. LNCS, vol. 5921, pp. 252–262. Springer, Heidelberg (2009)
12. CertiVox: MIRACL Crypto SDK, https://certivox.com/solutions/miracl-crypto-sdk/ (accessed March 22, 2013)
13. Fouque, P.A., Poupard, G., Stern, J.: Sharing Decryption in the Context of Voting or Lotteries. In: Frankel, Y. (ed.) FC 2000. LNCS, vol. 1962, pp. 90–104. Springer, Heidelberg (2001)
14. Shamir, A.: How to share a secret. Communications of the ACM 22, 612–613 (1979)
15. Cramer, R., Damgård, I., Ishai, Y.: Share Conversion, Pseudorandom Secret-Sharing and Applications to Secure Computation. In: Kilian, J. (ed.) TCC 2005. LNCS, vol. 3378, pp. 342–362. Springer, Heidelberg (2005)
16. Pedersen, T.: A Threshold Cryptosystem without a Trusted Party. In: Davies, D.W. (ed.) EUROCRYPT 1991. LNCS, vol. 547, pp. 522–526. Springer, Heidelberg (1991)
17. Gennaro, R., Jarecki, S., Krawczyk, H., Rabin, T.: Secure Distributed Key Generation for Discrete-Log Based Cryptosystems. In: Stern, J. (ed.) EUROCRYPT 1999. LNCS, vol. 1592, pp. 295–310. Springer, Heidelberg (1999)
18. Cramer, R., Damgård, I., Nielsen, J.B.: Multiparty Computation, an Introduction, http://www.cs.au.dk/~jbn/smc.pdf (accessed March 22, 2013)

19. Bar-Ilan, J., Beaver, D.: Non-cryptographic fault-tolerant computing in constant number of rounds of interaction. In: Proceedings of the Eighth Annual ACM Symposium on Principles of Distributed Computing, Edmonton, Alberta, Canada, August 14-16, pp. 201–209. ACM (1989)

20. Kate, A., Goldberg, I.: Asynchronous distributed private-key generators for identity-based cryptography. IACR Cryptology ePrint Archive, 355 (2009)

21. McEliece, R.J., Sarwate, D.V.: On sharing secrets and Reed-Solomon codes. Communications of the ACM 24, 583–584 (1981)

22. Cohen, H., Frey, G. (eds.): Handbook of elliptic and hyperelliptic curve cryptography. CRC Press (2005)

23. Barreto, P.S.L.M., Naehrig, M.: Pairing-friendly elliptic curves of prime order. In: Preneel, B., Tavares, S. (eds.) SAC 2005. LNCS, vol. 3897, pp. 319–331. Springer, Heidelberg (2006)

24. European Network of Excellence in Cryptology II: Ecrypt II Yearly Report on Algorithms and Key Sizes, http://www.keylength.com/en/3 (accessed March 22, 2013)

25. Ghadafi, E., Smart, N.P., Warinschi, B.: Groth–Sahai Proofs Revisited. In: Nguyen, P.Q., Pointcheval, D. (eds.) PKC 2010. LNCS, vol. 6056, pp. 177–192. Springer, Heidelberg (2010)

26. Smart, N.P.: Personal communication

27. CertiVox: CertiVox Wiki, Benchmarks and Subs, https://wiki.certivox.com/display/EXT/Benchmarks+and+Subs (accessed March 22, 2013)

28. Beuchat, J.L., Diaz, J.E.G., Mitsunari, S., Okamoto, E., Rodriguez-Henriquez, F., Teruya, T.: High-Speed Software Implementation of the Optimal Ate Pairing over Barreto-Naehrig Curves. Cryptology ePrint Archive, Report 2010/354 (2010)

29. Mitsunari, S.: High-Speed Software Implementation of the Optimal Ate Pairing over Barreto-Naehrig Curves, http://homepage1.nifty.com/herumi/crypt/ate-pairing.html (accessed March 22, 2013)

30. Der Bundeswahlleiter: Pressemitteilung (February 16, 2009)

31. Citizens Registration Office, D.E.M.N.: Personal communication

32. Smart, N.P.: Personal communication

33. Damgard, I., Keller, M., Larraia, E., Pastro, V., Scholl, P., Smart, N.P.: Practical Covertly Secure MPC for Dishonest Majority — or: Breaking the SPDZ Limits. Cryptology ePrint Archive, Report 2012/642 (2012)

34. Blazy, O., Fuchsbauer, G., Izabachène, M., Jambert, A., Sibert, H., Vergnaud, D.: Batch Groth–Sahai. In: Zhou, J., Yung, M. (eds.) ACNS 2010. LNCS, vol. 6123, pp. 218–235. Springer, Heidelberg (2010)

35. Knuth, D.: The Art of Computer Programming, vol. 4A. Addison-Wesley Professional (2011)

A Practical Coercion Resistant Voting Scheme Revisited

Roberto Araújo[1] and Jacques Traoré[2]

[1] Universidade Federal do Pará, Faculdade de Computação, Rua Augusto Corrêa 01,
66075-110, Belém/PA, Brazil
rsa@ufpa.br
[2] Orange Labs, 42 rue des Coutures, BP 6243, 14066 Caen Cedex, France
jacques.traore@orange.com

Abstract. The scheme of ABRTY (Araújo et al., CANS 2010) is one of the most promising solutions for internet voting nowadays. It fights realistic coercive attacks and can be applied in large scale voting scenarios as it has linear time complexity. However, this scheme has two intrinsic drawbacks. As it does not allow revocation of credentials of ineligible voters, voters need to obtain fresh credentials before each new election. Also, authorities could generate valid but illegitimate credentials unnoticed. In this work, we present solutions for these drawbacks and show a modified version of ABRTY's scheme. In addition, we describe a weakness of a receipt-free voting scheme proposed by Acquisti in 2004.

1 Introduction

A number of researchers consider internet voting as impracticable. The reason is the risks inherent to its environment. Malwares, for instance, may infect voters' computers to break the secrecy of the vote. Hackers, in turn, could compromise voting systems around the world. In addition, due to its uncontrolled environment, internet voting is susceptible to coercion and vote-selling.

In order to deal with these problems, Juels, Catalano, and Jakobsson (JCJ) [17] introduced the first coercion-resistant scheme that considers a powerful adversary. This adversary cannot succeed in issuing receipts (receipt-freeness), threatening voters to abstain from voting, revealing private data, or even casting random votes.

The idea behind JCJ's proposal is that a voter is able to deceive adversaries about her true vote intention. That is, the voter receives a valid credential (e.g. an alphanumeric string) in a secure manner. When she wants to cast her vote, she uses this credential. A voter under coercion, however, can make a fake credential and give it to the coercer. Later on, she can vote again using her valid credential. The coercer has no way to distinguish between the credentials used. Unfortunately, the earliest implementation of this idea is inefficient for large scale voting scenarios. This idea, though, inspired efficient solutions such as Araújo et al. [3], Spycher et al. [25], and Essex et al. [13].

J. Heather, S. Schneider, and V. Teague (Eds.): VoteID 2013, LNCS 7985, pp. 193–209, 2013.

One of the requisites of coercion-resistant voting schemes as JCJ is that a voter has to receive her credential in a trustworthy way. As this takes into account a untappable channel between the registrars and the voter, this process is supposed to be performed in a registration place. At this place, she obtains her credential after proving to the registrars that she is eligible for voting in an election.

A desirable property of credentials is to employ them in more than one election. In other words, once the voter obtained her credential, she can use it in several upcoming elections. This reduces costs and affords more convenience as voters do not need to revisit the registration place. However, it is necessary to prevent a voter from participating in an election for which she is not eligible for. To this end, authorities must be able to revoke credentials of these voters.

In contrast, if credentials cannot be used in a second election or more, voters need to visit the registration place again before each new election. This would be impractical for large scale voting scenarios.

Based on JCJ's proposal, ABRTY [3] introduced one of the most promising solutions for internet voting nowadays. The scheme is efficient for large scale scenarios as it has linear time complexity and was shown secure. ABRTY's scheme, though, has two intrinsic drawbacks that can discourage its use.

In ABRTY's solution, authorities have no way to revoke credentials. That is, they cannot disallow a voter in a specific election without performing this for all voters. As a consequence, all voters need to revisit the registration place to obtain fresh credentials.

Another drawback of ABRTY's scheme is that a majority of malicious registrars could generate valid (but illegitimate) credentials without being noticed. This means that votes cast using these credentials could appear in the final tally. Schläpfer et al. [21] and Spycher et al. [25] pointed out this problem.

These are important drawbacks of ABRTY's solution, but fortunately they can be fixed. In this work, we introduce techniques to fix these drawbacks and present a modified version of ABRTY's scheme accordingly. We also show that Acquisti's protocol [1] is not coercion-resistant and that its credentials can only be used once.

This text is organized as follows: the next section presents an overview of ABRTY's scheme and its drawbacks. Section 3 shows the improvements to ABRTY's solution and introduces an improved variant scheme. Finally, we present our conclusions in Section 4. In Appendices, we briefly describe the scheme of Acquisti and show its weaknesses.

Related Work on Coercion-Resistance

Juels, Catalano, and Jakobsson (JCJ) presented the first coercion-resistant scheme in 2005 at WPES [17]. Following JCJ's work, several coercion-resistant schemes were proposed. Acquisti [1] introduced a scheme in which the vote and the credential are combined, and which strongly relies on homomorphisms. Meng [18] proposed a solution similar to Acquisti's protocol. Clarkson et al. [11] presented a variant of Prêt-à-Voter [7] scheme suitable for internet voting and based on decryption mix nets.

Schweisgut [23] and more recently Clarkson et al. [10] proposed schemes which mitigate the inefficiency problem of the JCJ's solution. The former scheme relies on decryption mix nets and a tamper-resistant hardware, whereas the latter is a modified version of JCJ's proposal. ABRTY [3] showed that the scheme of Schweisgut is not coercion-resistant.

Smith [24] presented an efficient scheme with linear work factor. Weber et al. [28], however, pointed out problems of Smith's proposal and presented a protocol that combines the ideas of JCJ with a variant of Smith's mechanism. Unfortunately, both solutions are not coercion-resistant as shown by Araújo et al. [2]. The problem of Smith's scheme was also noted independently by Clarkson et al. [10].

Araújo, Foulle, and Traoré [2] presented the first practical and secure coercion-resistant scheme. Their proposal, different from the previous ones, employs credentials with a special structure that allows the scheme to achieve a linear work factor. Based on [2], ABRTY [3] introduced a different scheme that uses new anonymous credentials derived from the group signature scheme of Boneh et al. [4] and formally proved that their scheme is coercion-resistant.

From Araújo et al.'s proposals [2,3], other promising efficient schemes appeared. Spycher et al. [25] introduced a protocol where voters indicate their credentials on an electoral roll. Spycher et al. [26] improved [25] later on. Clark et al. [9] introduced a proposal that uses special passwords as credentials. Schläpfer et al. [21] showed a scheme that links the votes to the voter roll.

However, the complexity of the schemes of Spycher et al. [25], Clark et al. [9], and Schläpfer et al. [21] depends on a security parameter β to balance efficiency against coercion-resistance: the complexity is in $O(\beta N)$ for Clark et al. [9] and Schläpfer et al. [21] and in $O(N + \beta n)$ for Spycher et al. [25], where N is the number of submitted ballots and n is the number of registered voters.

More recently, Essex at al. [13] introduced a promising scheme that authorizes votes during the voting phase. Unfortunately, as pointed out by the authors, this scheme is not efficient for real world elections as it "requires a registration process that is quadratic in the number of eligible voters".

As the schemes of Spycher et al. [25], Clark et al. [9], and Schläpfer et al. [21] depend on a security parameter and the solution of Essex at al. [13] has an inefficient registration phase, only the schemes of Araújo et al. [2,3] are truly linear in N (see Schläpfer et al. [21] for a detailed performance comparison analysis of these schemes). In addition, the security of [2,25,9,21,13] are only conjectured.

2   The ABRTY's Scheme and Its Drawbacks

In this section, we briefly introduce ABRTY's scheme [3]. In addition, we recall a drawback presented by Spycher et al. [25] and introduce another one.

2.1   An Overview of ABRTY's Proposal

The scheme of ABRTY follows the principle introduced by JCJ. The voter receives a credential in a secure manner. She uses it to cast her valid vote and may generate fake credentials to deceive adversaries. However, the credential employed in ABRTY's solution, which is based on Boneh et al.'s group signature scheme (BBS for short) [4], has a mathematical structure that ensures its security.

Cryptographic Building Blocks. ABRTY's scheme requires a set of cryptographic building blocks. It relies on a threshold El Gamal cryptosystem and a universally verifiable mix net. In addition, the scheme requires several zero-knowledge proof protocols. It prevents adversaries from using El Gamal malleability by means of Schnorr signatures [22]. It uses a protocol to prove that a ciphertext contains a vote for a valid candidate such as the proposal of Hirt and Sako [14]. ABRTY's solution also uses a protocol for proving the equality of discrete logarithms relative to different bases owing to Chaum and Pedersen [6], a protocol for proving knowledge of a representation as Okamoto [19] and a plaintext equivalence test [15]. Also, it requires a Web Bulletin Board (WBB). The security of its credentials depends on the q-Strong Diffie-Hellman (q-SDH) [4] and the Strong Decisional Diffie-Hellman Inversion (SDDHI) assumptions [3].

The Scheme. It considers a set of voters, a set of registrars that make valid credentials for the voters and help the talliers in the tallying phase, and a set of talliers that compute the final tally. Let $E_X(Y)$ be the encryption of Y with the public key X. In the setup phase, a set of authorities generate the key material and publish the corresponding public parameters on a WBB. In particular, the authorities define a cyclic group $\mathbb{G}$ with prime order p and four generators $g_1, g_2, g_3, o \in \mathbb{G}$. The Decision Diffie-Hellman problem (DDH) must be hard in $\mathbb{G}$. The talliers cooperate to generate a key pair by means of the threshold El Gamal cryptosystem, i.e. the public key T and its corresponding private key $\widehat{T}$. The registrars also cooperate to generate a key pair, namely the public key $R = g_3^y$ and its corresponding private key $\widehat{R} = y$.

Registration Phase. After proving to the registrars that she is eligible, the voter receives her credential securely, through a untappable channel. In order to compute a credential, the registrars select two random numbers $r, x \in \mathbb{Z}_p$ and compute: $A = (g_1 g_3^x)^{\frac{1}{y+r}}$, where g_1, g_3 are public generators and y is the secret key of the registrars. The credential σ is composed of three parts, namely $\sigma = (A, r, x)$. The voter must keep the value x in secrecy. The parts (A, r) can be stored in a device or be sent by email to the voter without compromising the security of the scheme.

Voting Phase. The voter selects a random number $s \in \mathbb{Z}_p$, uses her credential $\sigma = (A, r, x)$ to compute $B = A^s$ and makes a tuple containing: her encrypted vote, her encrypted credential and a set of non-interactive zero-knowledge proofs (NIZKPs). In other words, she makes the tuple $\langle E_T[v], B,$

$E_T[B^{s^{-1}}], E_T[B^{rs^{-1}}], E_T[g_3^x], o^x, P\rangle$, where v is her vote intention, $B = A^s$, g_3 and o are public generators and P is a set of NIZKPs. This set is composed of a proof that $E_T[v]$ contains a vote for a valid candidate, proofs that the voter knows the plaintext underlying the ciphertexts, a proof that the plaintext of $E_T[B^{rs^{-1}}]$ is different from 1 as well as a proof that the discrete logarithm of o^x in the basis o is equal to the discrete logarithm of the plaintext of $E_T[g_3^x]$ in the basis g_3. The voter then uses an anonymous channel to send her tuple to the WBB and thereby casting her vote.

Tallying Phase. The tallying takes place after the voting phase. It comprises 5 steps. The talliers first read all tuples posted on the WBB and verify all proofs on each tuple. They discard tuples with invalid proofs and then process the tuples that passed the tests. A tuple now has the following format: $\langle E_T[v], E_T[B^{s^{-1}}], E_T[B^{rs^{-1}}], E_T[g_3^x], o^x\rangle$. The talliers then eliminate tuples posted using the same credential (i.e duplicates). For this, they compare all o^x by means of a hash table. If the talliers detect a duplicate, they use the time of posting on the WBB to verify the last posted tuple. The talliers keep the last posted tuple that now is composed of: $\langle E_T[v], E_T[B^{s^{-1}}], E_T[B^{rs^{-1}}], E_T[g_3^x]\rangle$. After that, they send all tuples $\langle E_T[v], E_T[B^{s^{-1}}], E_T[B^{rs^{-1}}], E_T[g_3^x]\rangle$ to a verifiable mix net. The mix net output a set of permuted and re-encrypted tuples of the form: $\langle E_T[v]', E_T[B^{s^{-1}}]', E_T[B^{rs^{-1}}]', E_T[g_3^x]'\rangle$, where $E_T[\cdot]'$ is the reencryption of $E_T[\cdot]$.

The talliers now check the valid credentials. For this, they perform the following steps: (1) they instruct the registrars to cooperatively compute $E_T[B^{s^{-1}}]'^y = E_T[B^{ys^{-1}}]'$ and $E_T[B^{ys^{-1}}]' \cdot E_T[B^{rs^{-1}}]' = E_T[B^{ys^{-1}+rs^{-1}}]'$ by using the secret key y; (2) the talliers compute $C = E_T[B^{ys^{-1}+rs^{-1}} g_1^{-1} g_3^{-x}]'$ from $E_T[B^{ys^{-1}+rs^{-1}}]'$, $E_T[g_3^x]'$, and the public parameter g_1. (3) they now cooperatively select a random number $z \in \mathbb{Z}_p$, compute C^z and decrypt C^z. If they obtain 1 after decrypting C^z, the credential is valid; otherwise, the credential is invalid. In order to finish the tallying phase, the talliers discard all tuples with invalid credentials, cooperatively decrypt $E_T[v]'$ of the tuples with valid credentials, and publish the voting results on the WBB.

2.2   The Drawbacks

The scheme of ABRTY was shown secure in the random oracle model, under the q-Strong Diffie-Hellman and Strong Decisional Diffie-Hellman Inversion assumptions. It can be used in large scale voting scenarios as it has a linear time complexity. Unfortunately, this scheme has two intrinsic drawbacks.

As Spycher et al. [25] presented, "a majority of colluding registrars could compute valid (but illegitimate) credentials unnoticed". In other words, after proving that she is eligible, each voter receives a valid credential from the registrars. Although an adversary cannot forge a credential after the registration because this requires breaking the q-SDH assumption, a majority of registrars could act as adversaries during this phase. These malicious registrars could make valid (but illegitimate) credentials as the scheme does not verify whether they generated a credential to an eligible voter (i.e. a legitimate credential) or not. Thus, a valid (but illegitimate) credential would pass the tests performed in the tallying phase such that the corresponding vote would be counted.

Besides the drawback presented by Spycher et al., the scheme has another one: it does not allow revocation of credentials. In any new election, the number of eligible voters may change. Some voters may have their right to vote revoked after participating in an election, for instance. Also, a voter may be allowed to vote in several elections, but may not vote in others. In order to satisfy these scenarios, authorities must be able to revoke credentials when necessary.

The credentials employed in ABRTY's scheme may be used in several elections as long as the same key y is employed. However, in principle a credential cannot be revoked. Because only the voters know their credentials, the authorities are not able to revoke a credential. In addition, even if the authorities store all credentials and put them in a black list, this would be of no help. There is no way in the tallying phase to decide whether a revoked credential has been used or not. Indeed the credentials are published on the WBB in an encrypted form. Clark et al. [9] and Essex et al. [13] pointed out a similar drawback.

3   Improving ABRTY's Scheme

As presented above, ABRTY's scheme does not allow authorities to revoke credentials. In addition, a majority of colluding registrars could issue valid but illegitimate credentials. Aiming at eliminating these drawbacks, we present here new mechanisms that improve ABRTY's solution. Also, we introduce a version of ABRTY's scheme that employs our mechanisms.

3.1   Revoking Credentials

Although the design of ABRTY's scheme makes revocation difficult, it has some properties that help accomplish this. Recall from ABRTY's scheme that, upon registering, a voter receives a credential $\sigma = (A, r, x)$. The element x must be transmitted via an untappable channel. Conversely, the elements $\langle A, r \rangle$ can be sent by post or even by email. This does not compromise the credential's security as long as the SDDHI assumption holds.

Based on this, it is possible to use a similar method as the technique employed by Boneh et al. [4] to revoke membership certificates in their group signature scheme. That is, in order to revoke credentials and perform new elections, the authorities could execute the following steps:

Besides generating and issuing a credential to a voter, the registrars store the *public part* (A, r) of the credential in a list L_C. Suppose we wish to revoke the credential of a voter V^*. To perform this, the registrars first retrieves from L_C the public part of the credential of V^* (i.e. (A^*, r^*)) and then update their public key. The new public key is $(\widetilde{g}_1, \widetilde{g}_3, \widetilde{R})$ where $\widetilde{g}_1 = g_1^{1/(y+r^*)}, \widetilde{g}_3 = g_3^{1/(y+r^*)}$ and $\widetilde{R} = \widetilde{g}_1^y$. The secret key y remains unchanged. The registrars then publish the values $(\widetilde{g}_1, \widetilde{g}_3, \widetilde{R}, r^*)$ in a revocation list RL.

Let us show now how unrevoked voters update their credentials. Consider an unrevoked voter whose credential is (A, r, x). Given $(\widetilde{g}_1, \widetilde{g}_3, \widetilde{R}, r^*)$ obtained from RL, the voter computes $\widetilde{A} = \widetilde{g}_1^{\frac{1}{r-r^*}} \widetilde{g}_3^{\frac{x}{r-r^*}} A^{\frac{-1}{r-r^*}}$ and sets her new credential to be $(\widetilde{A}, r, x)$. Notice that since the values r and r^* are randomly chosen by the registrars, then with high probability we have $r \neq r^* \bmod p$.

One can verify that $(\widetilde{A}, r, x)$ is a valid credential for the new public key $(\widetilde{g}_1, \widetilde{g}_3, \widetilde{R})$ by computing:

$$
\begin{aligned}
\widetilde{A}^{y+r} &= \widetilde{g}_1^{\frac{y+r}{r-r^*}} \widetilde{g}_3^{\frac{(y+r)x}{r-r^*}} A^{\frac{-(y+r)}{r-r^*}} \\
&= \widetilde{g}_1^{\frac{y+r}{r-r^*}} \widetilde{g}_3^{\frac{(y+r)x}{r-r^*}} g_1^{\frac{-1}{r-r^*}} g_3^{\frac{-x}{r-r^*}} \\
&= \widetilde{g}_1^{\frac{y+r}{r-r^*}} \widetilde{g}_3^{\frac{(y+r)x}{r-r^*}} \widetilde{g}_1^{\frac{-(y+r^*)}{r-r^*}} \widetilde{g}_3^{\frac{-(y+r^*)x}{r-r^*}} \\
&= \widetilde{g}_1 \widetilde{g}_3^{x}
\end{aligned}
$$

This process can be repeated several times if there are more than one credential to revoke. Using similar arguments as the ones given in [4], one can prove that under the q-SDH assumption the revoked voter V^* cannot construct a valid credential for the new public key $(\widetilde{g}_1, \widetilde{g}_3, \widetilde{R})$. However, if the revoked voter V^* was under coercion in a previous election, then the coercer can now check using the new public key $(\widetilde{g}_1, \widetilde{g}_3, \widetilde{R})$ if V^* previously revealed a fake credential or a valid one. Indeed, if V^* gave him (A^*, r^*, x'), he just has to test whether $A^* \overset{?}{=} \widetilde{g}_1 \widetilde{g}_3^{x'} = g_1^{1/(y+r^*)} g_3^{x'(1/(y+r^*))}$.

We therefore propose another method in order to avoid this problem. It allows credentials of eligible voters to be used in more than one election as follows:

- In the *setup phase*, besides generating their key pair (namely $R = g_3^y$ and $\widehat{R} = y$) as usual, the registrars cooperatively make a new key pair: $\langle \mathcal{R}, \widehat{\mathcal{R}} \rangle$. $\mathcal{R}$ is the public key and $\widehat{\mathcal{R}}$ is its corresponding shared private key. This key pair will be used for the purpose of revocation later on.
- During the *registration phase*, the registrars cooperatively generate a credential $\sigma = (A, r, x)$ for each voter. After that, the registrars use the public key $\mathcal{R}$ to cooperatively compute the encryption of $g_1 g_3^x$ (namely $E_{\mathcal{R}}[g_1 g_3^x]$) and store this ciphertext in a list L_1.
- For each new election, instead of using the same shared private key $\widehat{R} = y$, the registrars generate a new shared private key y' (i.e. now $R = g_3^{y'}$ and $\widehat{R} = y'$) and furnish the voters with new values $\langle A' = (g_1 g_3^x)^{\frac{1}{y'+r'}}, r' \rangle$. They compute this from the values $E_{\mathcal{R}}[g_1 g_3^x]$ stored in L_1 and from a randomly chosen value r'. That is, $A' = (g_1 g_3^x)^{\frac{1}{y'+r'}}$ is cooperatively computed by raising $E_{\mathcal{R}}[g_1 g_3^x]$ to the power $\frac{1}{y'+r'}$ using the technique of Wang et al. [27]. After that, $E_{\mathcal{R}}[(g_1 g_3^x)^{\frac{1}{y'+r'}}]$ is cooperatively decrypted to retrieve A'.

- The new credential is the tuple $\langle A', r', x \rangle$ where x is the secret value obtained by the voter during her first registration. The others elements of the credential (i.e. A' and r') could be sent by mail to the voter or even published on a dedicated website.

This novel method makes possible the revocation of credentials in ABRTY's scheme. For each new election, the authorities need a new shared private key y and the eligible voters receive fresh values $\langle A', r' \rangle$. Voters who belong to a revocation list or are not allowed to vote will not receive an updated credential. The voter does not have to revisit the registration place and register again in order to obtain her new credential. She can download the new parts of her credential $\langle A', r' \rangle$ from WBB, for instance. To complete her credential, the voter employs the same x of the credential that she received when she registered for the first time. Thus, the voter does not need to replace the whole credential (i.e. $\sigma = (A, r, x)$) before each new election.

Note that, if a malicious voter has a revoked credential $\langle A_m, r_m, x_m \rangle$ and obtains the new values $\langle A', r' \rangle$ of another voter, she may use the credential $\langle A', r', x_m \rangle$ to vote. However, the vote tuple computed with this credential will not pass the tests in the tallying phase. When the authorities use $E_{\mathcal{R}}[g_1 g_3^x]$ to generate the new parts $\langle A' = (g_1 g_3^x)^{\frac{1}{y'+r'}}, r' \rangle$ of the credential to a voter, they employ the same exponent x that the voter received in the registration phase. As the malicious voter does not have the correct exponent x, her vote tuple will be removed from the tally during the verification process. That is, to verify the valid credentials, the authorities use the values $E_T[g_3^{x_m}], E_T[B^{s^{-1}}], E_T[B^{r's^{-1}}]$ from the malicious voter's tuple and compute $C = E_T[B^{y's^{-1}+r's^{-1}} \ g_1^{-1} g_3^{-x_m}]'$ next, where $B = (A')^s = ((g_1 g_3^x)^{\frac{1}{y'+r'}})^s$ for a random s. By performing this, the authorities obtain the ciphertext C that encrypts $g_3^{x-x_m}$ instead of the value 1. This will make the tuple invalid after the authorities apply the plaintext equivalence test.

3.2   Defeating a Majority of Colluding Registrars

ABRTY's scheme allows the computation of valid (but illegitimate) credentials by a majority of malicious registrars. These fraudulent credentials could be used for ballot stuffing. Although this drawback reduces the security of the scheme, fortunately it can be fixed. We present now a method that identifies any valid (but illegitimate) credential and that allows removing these credentials from the tallying. The method was inspired by the works of Smith [24] and Weber et al. [28].

Comparison and Computation of Fingerprints. Before introducing our solution, we briefly recall the method of comparison and computation of fingerprints owing to Weber et al. This technique is used to blind and compare plaintexts inside ciphertexts without leaking any information about the true plaintexts. The method works as follows: in order to blind a plaintext of an El

Gamal ciphertext, a set of n authorities jointly generate a secret shared value z. These authorities then apply their shares of z to each ciphertext to blind the corresponding plaintext. The authorities now decrypt all ciphertexts to obtain the blinded plaintexts (i.e. fingerprints). For example, from a ciphertext $C = E_T[m]$ of a message m, the fingerprint will be equal in this case to m^z. To compare the fingerprints, the authorities can use a hashtable algorithm.

Taking into account Weber et al. technique as a building block, we introduce our solution as follows:

- In the *registration phase*, after computing a credential $\sigma = (A, r, x)$ to the voter, the registrars cooperatively compute: $E_T[A]$, where T is the public key of the talliers. The registrars may issue a designated verifier proof [16] to prove that $E_T[A]$ encrypts the same A of the voter credential.
- Let ID_{voter} be a voter unique identification number (i.e. a number associated to the voter's name in the electoral roll) and L_2 be a public list of legitimate credentials. For each voter, the registrars store in L_2 the pair $\langle E_T[A], \text{ID}_{\text{voter}}\rangle$.
- In order to check that only legitimate credentials have been used in the *tallying phase*, the talliers proceed as follows:
  - After eliminating duplicates and invalid ballots (i.e. those with invalid proofs or invalid credentials), the talliers obtain the list LV containing the remaining ballots.
  - The talliers send the ciphertexts $E_T[A]$ of L_2 to a verifiable mix net and obtain L_2';
  - By means of Weber et al.'s technique, the talliers raise all the ciphertexts in L_2' and LV (only the values $E_T[A]$) to a random secret exponent and decrypt the resulting ciphertexts. Let L_2'' and LV' denote the new lists;
  - The talliers use a hashtable to verify whether every element in LV' belongs to L_2''. If there is an element in LV' that does not match with an element in L_2'', then this means that either someone has broken the Boneh et al. [4] group signature scheme or that the registrars produced valid but illegitimate credentials. In any case, the talliers remove ballots corresponding to illegitimate credentials from the list L_2''.

3.3   The Improved Variant of ABRTY's Scheme

Based on the mechanisms introduced above, we describe now an improved version of ABRTY's scheme. This version eliminates the drawbacks of the original proposal while keeping the same security properties of it.

The new version employs the same cryptographic primitives as the original one (see Section 2.1). In addition, the new scheme requires the global blind comparison mechanism due to Weber et al. [28] and the method of Wang et al. [27]. It has four phases: setup, registration, voting, and tallying.

However, there are two ways to perform the setup and the registration phases. For a first election, the authorities execute these phases for the first time. All voters need to visit the registration place once to obtain their credentials.

For a second election (or more), as there are previous election parameters and registered voters, the authorities execute different setup and registration phases. Voters that registered before do not need to visit the registration place again. Authorities, in turn, can revoke credentials.

Therefore, there are two states for the scheme. It can be either used in a first election or in several elections (i.e. a second election or more). The scheme is described below.

For a *first election*, the scheme requires the following setup and registration phases:

Setup phase for a first election. If the scheme is used for the first time, the voters do not have any credential and need to obtain them to vote. In this case, the authorities establish first a cyclic group $\mathbb{G}$ (the DDH must be hard in $\mathbb{G}$) with prime order p and five generators $g_1, g_2, g_3, g_4, o \in \mathbb{G}$. The talliers now cooperate to compute the El Gamal key pair for which the public key is denoted by T and the private key is denoted by $\widehat{T}$. The registrars cooperate to compute two pair of keys: a public key $R = g_3^y$ and its secret key $\widehat{R} = y$, and an El Gamal public key $\mathcal{R}$ and its secret key $\widehat{\mathcal{R}}$. The authorities publish all public material on a WBB.

Registration phase for a first election. After authenticating a voter that has an identification number $\mathrm{ID}_{\mathrm{voter}}$, the registrars select two random numbers $r, x \in \mathbb{Z}_p$ and cooperatively computes $A = (g_1 g_3^x)^{\frac{1}{y+r}}$. Then, they issue the credential $\sigma = (A, r, x)$ to the voter via an untappable channel [1]. The registrars now cooperate to encrypt $g_1 g_3^x$ with their public key $\mathcal{R}$ and store the pair $\langle E_{\mathcal{R}}[g_1 g_3^x], \mathrm{ID}_{\mathrm{voter}} \rangle$ in a list L_1 on the WBB. In addition, they encrypt A with the public key T and store the pair $\langle E_T[A], \mathrm{ID}_{\mathrm{voter}} \rangle$ in a list L_2 on the WBB.

After receiving her credential, a voter can participate in several elections. However, as the voter may not be allowed to vote in some elections, the authorities have to update the credentials of the eligible voters before each new election. It is not necessary for voters to revisit the registration place. Thus, if the scheme is used in a second election (or more), it requires slightly different setup and registration phases. These phases are presented next:

Setup phase for several elections. If the scheme is used a second time or more, all voters (or some of them) already have their credentials. In this case, the authorities (talliers and registrars) can either keep all credentials or revoke some of them. If the authorities do not need to revoke credentials, they can keep all but one parameter used in the last election. That is, they replace the generator $o \in \mathbb{G}$ used in the last election by a new one: $o' \in \mathbb{G}$. The authorities publish the new generator $o' \in \mathbb{G}$ as well as the other parameters

---

[1] Although we do not consider the issue of "panic passwords" [8] in this paper, we would like to emphasize that the technique introduced by Clark et al. [9] to generate such passwords also applies to our scheme.

of the last election, namely the cyclic group $\mathbb{G}$ with prime order p, the other three generators $g_1, g_2, g_3 \in \mathbb{G}$, and the key pairs $\langle T, \widehat{T} \rangle$, $\langle R, \widehat{R} \rangle$ and $\langle \mathcal{R}, \widehat{\mathcal{R}} \rangle$. Conversely, if the authorities need to revoke credentials, they replace the generator $o \in \mathbb{G}$ as before and execute an extra step. The registrars replace their key pair $\langle R = g_3^y, \widehat{R} = y \rangle$ used in the last election by a new one. For this, they cooperatively generate the new key pair: $\langle R = g_3^{y'}, \widehat{R} = y' \rangle$, where $\widehat{R} = y'$ is a secret key shared among the registrars. This new key pair is used to update credentials of voters allowed to vote and to generate credentials for new voters in the current election. All public material is published on the WBB.

Updating the credentials of eligible voters. If some voters are not allowed to vote in the new election, the authorities need to update the credentials of the eligible voters. In order to perform this, the registrars read from L_1 all tuples $\langle E_{\mathcal{R}}(g_1 g_3^x), \mathrm{ID}_{\text{voter}} \rangle$. They created this list in the first election (see the setup phase of the first election above). By inspecting the values $\mathrm{ID}_{\text{voter}}$, the registrars identify tuples of voters that can vote in the new election. For each of these tuples, the registrars cooperatively select a random $r' \in \mathbb{Z}_p$, compute $\frac{1}{y'+r'}$ using their new secret key $\widehat{R} = y'$ and power $E_{\mathcal{R}}(g_1 g_3^x)$ to $\frac{1}{y'+r'}$ by means of the method of Wang et al. [27]. Then, they cooperatively decrypt $E_{\mathcal{R}}[(g_1 g_3^x)^{\frac{1}{y'+r'}}]$ to obtain $A' = (g_1 g_3^x)^{\frac{1}{y'+r'}}$. Next, they publish $\langle \mathrm{ID}_{\text{voter}}, A', r' \rangle$ on the WBB. The voters allowed to vote can now visit the WBB to identify their IDs and read their new pair $\langle A', r' \rangle$. Because each eligible voter employs the same secret x generated for the first election, the new credential is: $\langle A', r', x \rangle$. Finally, for each voter $\langle \mathrm{ID}_{\text{voter}} \rangle$ allowed to vote, the registrars replace $E_T[A]$ by $E_T[A']$ in L_2.

Observe that a voter without a credential can register to vote in any election as long as she visits the registration place to obtain one. In order to issue this credential, the registrars employ their secret key $\widehat{R} = y'$ to generate the credential $\sigma = (A, r, x)$. In addition, they update the lists $L1$ and $L2$ with the values $\langle E_{\mathcal{R}}[g_1 g_3^x], \mathrm{ID}_{\text{voter}} \rangle$ and $\langle E_T[A], \mathrm{ID}_{\text{voter}} \rangle$, respectively.

From the setup and registration phases presented above, the voting and tallying phases are described as follows:

Voting Phase. The voter performs the same steps as in the original scheme (see Section 2). That is, she makes the tuple $\langle E_T[v], B, E_T[B^{s^{-1}}], E_T[B^{rs^{-1}}], E_T[g_3^x], o^x, P \rangle$ and sends it through an anonymous channel to the WBB. Note that if the voter can vote in several elections, she uses her updated credential $\langle A', r', x \rangle$ and the new generator o'.

Tallying Phase. The talliers first read all tuples from the WBB, verify all proofs and discard tuples with invalid proofs. The remaining tuples are now composed of $\langle E_T[v], E_T[B^{s^{-1}}], E_T[B^{rs^{-1}}], E_T[g_3^x], o^x \rangle$. After that, they eliminate tuples posted using the same credential (i.e. duplicates). In other words, the talliers use a hash table to compare all values o^x. If a duplicate is detected, they use the time of posting on the WBB to identify the last posted tuple and keep only this last posted tuple. Then, the talliers exclude the values o^x of the remaining tuples and send these new tuples to a mix net. After permuting and reencrypting these tuples, the mix net outputs tuples of the form $\langle E_T[v]', E_T[B^{s^{-1}}]', E_T[B^{rs^{-1}}]', E_T[g_3^x]' \rangle$, where $E_T[\cdot]'$ is the reencryption of $E_T[\cdot]$. Now, the talliers check whether the credentials are valid or not and verify whether they are legitimate. For this, they perform the next steps.

- They use the remaining tuples to *check the validity of the credentials*. This process is similar to the original scheme (see Section 2.1). In case of several elections, however, the registrars have to use their new key $\langle R = g_3^{y'}, \widehat{R} = y' \rangle$ generated for the current election;
- Let LV be a list containing the approved tuples (i.e. tuples with valid credentials), the talliers send LV to a mix net and obtain LV'. They also send the ciphertexts $E_T[A]$ of L_2 to a mix net and obtain L_2';
- By means of Weber et al.'s technique, they cooperate to compute a random value r and raise all values $E_T[A]$ of LV' to r as well as the values of L_2';
- They decrypt the resulting lists and verify whether every plaintext in LV' belongs to an element in L_2'. If a match does not exist, they remove the corresponding tuple from the next step;
- In order to finish this phase, the talliers cooperatively decrypt $E_T[v]'$ of the tuples with legitimate credentials and publish the voting results on the WBB.

4   Conclusion

The voting scheme of ABRTY is coercion-resistant and has linear time complexity. As presented, this solution has drawbacks that can limit its use. In this paper, we presented solutions for these drawbacks. In addition, we introduced a new version of ABRTY's scheme which uses these solutions. The new version allows for the revocation of credentials, and identifies valid (but illegitimate) credentials. This improves the original scheme as a collusion of malicious registrars cannot succeed when issuing illegitimate credentials and eligible voters do not need to register again before each new election.

Acknowledgements. The first author's work was partially supported by the "Fundação Amazônia Paraense (FAPESPA)" under the project: Rede de Pesquisa em TIC. The second author's work has been supported by the French "Agence Nationale de la Recherche" under the LYRICS ANR-11-INSE-013 Project.

References

1. Acquisti, A.: Receipt-free homomorphic elections and write-in ballots. Cryptology ePrint Archive, Report 2004/105 (2004), http://eprint.iacr.org/
2. Araújo, R., Foulle, S., Traoré, J.: A practical and secure coercion-resistant scheme for remote elections. In: Chaum, D., Kutylowski, M., Rivest, R.L., Ryan, P.Y.A. (eds.) Frontiers of Electronic Voting, Dagstuhl, Germany. Dagstuhl Seminar Proceedings, vol. 07311. Internationales Begegnungs- und Forschungszentrum für Informatik (IBFI), Schloss Dagstuhl (2008)
3. Araújo, R., Ben Rajeb, N., Robbana, R., Traoré, J., Youssfi, S.: Towards practical and secure coercion-resistant electronic elections. In: Heng, S.-H., Wright, R.N., Goi, B.-M. (eds.) CANS 2010. LNCS, vol. 6467, pp. 278–297. Springer, Heidelberg (2010)
4. Boneh, D., Boyen, X., Shacham, H.: Short group signatures. In: Franklin, M. (ed.) CRYPTO 2004. LNCS, vol. 3152, pp. 41–55. Springer, Heidelberg (2004)
5. Brickell, E.F. (ed.): CRYPTO 1992. LNCS, vol. 740. Springer, Heidelberg (1993)
6. Chaum, D., Pedersen, T.P.: Wallet databases with observers. In: Brickell (ed.) [5], pp. 89–105
7. Chaum, D., Ryan, P.Y.A., Schneider, S.: A practical voter-verifiable election scheme. In: De Capitani di Vimercati, S., Syverson, P.F., Gollmann, D. (eds.) ESORICS 2005. LNCS, vol. 3679, pp. 118–139. Springer, Heidelberg (2005)
8. Clark, J., Hengartner, U.: Panic passwords: Authenticating under duress. In: Provos, N. (ed.) HotSec. USENIX Association (2008)
9. Clark, J., Hengartner, U.: Selections: Internet voting with over-the-shoulder coercion-resistance. In: Danezis (ed.) [12], pp. 47–61
10. Clarkson, M.R., Chong, S., Myers, A.C.: Civitas: Toward a secure voting system. In: IEEE Symposium on Security and Privacy, pp. 354–368. IEEE Computer Society (2008)
11. Clarkson, M.R., Myers, A.C.: Coercion-resistant remote voting using decryption mixes. Workshop on Frontiers in Electronic Elections (2005)
12. Danezis, G. (ed.): FC 2011. LNCS, vol. 7035. Springer, Heidelberg (2012)
13. Essex, A., Clark, J., Hengartner, U.: Cobra: toward concurrent ballot authorization for internet voting. In: Proceedings of the 2012 International Conference on Electronic Voting Technology/Workshop on Trustworthy Elections, EVT/WOTE 2012, p. 3. USENIX Association, Berkeley (2012)
14. Hirt, M., Sako, K.: Efficient receipt-free voting based on homomorphic encryption. In: Preneel, B. (ed.) EUROCRYPT 2000. LNCS, vol. 1807, pp. 539–556. Springer, Heidelberg (2000)
15. Jakobsson, M., Juels, A.: Mix and match: Secure function evaluation via ciphertexts. In: Okamoto, T. (ed.) ASIACRYPT 2000. LNCS, vol. 1976, pp. 162–177. Springer, Heidelberg (2000)
16. Jakobsson, M., Sako, K., Impagliazzo, R.: Designated verifier proofs and their applications. In: Maurer, U.M. (ed.) EUROCRYPT 1996. LNCS, vol. 1070, pp. 143–154. Springer, Heidelberg (1996)
17. Juels, A., Catalano, D., Jakobsson, M.: Coercion-resistant electronic elections. In: Atluri, V., De Capitani di Vimercati, S., Dingledine, R. (eds.) WPES, pp. 61–70. ACM (2005)
18. Meng, B.: An internet voting protocol with receipt-free and coercion-resistant. In: CIT, pp. 721–726. IEEE Computer Society (2007)

19. Okamoto, T.: Provably secure and practical identification schemes and corresponding signature schemes. In: Brickell (ed.) [15], pp. 31–53
20. Paillier, P.: Public-key cryptosystems based on composite degree residuosity classes. In: Stern, J. (ed.) EUROCRYPT 1999. LNCS, vol. 1592, pp. 223–238. Springer, Heidelberg (1999)
21. Schläpfer, M., Haenni, R., Koenig, R., Spycher, O.: Efficient vote authorization in coercion-resistant internet voting. In: Kiayias, A., Lipmaa, H. (eds.) VoteID 2011. LNCS, vol. 7187, pp. 71–88. Springer, Heidelberg (2012)
22. Schnorr, C.-P.: Efficient signature generation by smart cards. J. Cryptology 4(3), 161–174 (1991)
23. Schweisgut, J.: Coercion-resistant electronic elections with observer. In: Krimmer, R. (ed.) Electronic Voting. LNI, vol. 86, pp. 171–177. GI (2006)
24. Smith, W.: New cryptographic election protocol with best-known theoretical properties. In: Workshop on Frontiers in Electronic Elections (2005)
25. Spycher, O., Koenig, R.E., Haenni, R., Schläpfer, M.: A new approach towards coercion-resistant remote e-voting in linear time. In: Danezis (ed.) [12], pp. 182–189
26. Spycher, O., Koenig, R.E., Haenni, R., Schläpfer, M.: Achieving meaningful efficiency in coercion-resistant, verifiable internet voting. In: Kripp, M.J., Volkamer, M., Grimm, R. (eds.) Electronic Voting. LNI, vol. 205, pp. 113–125. GI (2012)
27. Wang, H., Zhang, Y., Feng, D.: Short threshold signature schemes without random oracles. In: Maitra, S., Veni Madhavan, C.E., Venkatesan, R. (eds.) INDOCRYPT 2005. LNCS, vol. 3797, pp. 297–310. Springer, Heidelberg (2005)
28. Weber, S.G., Araújo, R., Buchmann, J.: On coercion-resistant electronic elections with linear work. In: 2nd Workshop on Dependability and Security in e-Government (DeSeGov 2007) at 2nd Int. Conference on Availability, Reliability and Security (ARES 2007), pp. 908–916. IEEE Computer Society (2007)

A   A Weakness of Acquisti's Coercion-Resistant Scheme

A number of schemes proposed in the literature aim at satisfying the coercion-resistant property. However, many of them do not accomplish this. In this appendix we show that Acquisti's scheme [1] does not fulfills this property either. In addition, we present another drawback of this scheme.

A.1   An Overview of the Scheme

The solution of Acquisti [1] employs an idea similar to the scheme of JCJ. A voter obtains a valid credential from the authorities and use it when she want to cast a valid vote. A voter under coercion may deceive adversaries by giving them fake credentials. However, in Acquisti's scheme, the voter receives from the authorities encrypted shares of her credential and later on combines her credential along with her vote intention. In the next paragraphs we give a short description of Acquisti's scheme.

In a setup phase, the authorities compute two sets of keys of an asymmetric cryptosystem with homomorphic property (e.g. Paillier cryptosystem [20]).

One set encrypts credentials and has a public key T_C. The other set encrypts votes and contains a public key T_V. In addition, the authorities compute another set of asymmetric keys of a non-homomorphic cryptosystem. Each authority also generates a share v_i of a vote such that the sum of the shares of all authorities is equal to a vote v for a valid candidate. This is performed for all valid candidates. After computing the shares, each authority generates two ciphertexts for each candidate. He encrypts his share v_i with T_C and T_V apart. Each authority then publishes his two ciphertexts on a bulletin board. Let $E_{T_C}[v_i]$ and $E_{T_V}[v_i]$ be the resulting ciphertexts of a share v_i.

Registration Phase. For each voter, each authority generates random numbers as shares of credentials. Let σ_i represents a share produced by an authority A_i. A_i encrypts σ_i with the public key for credentials T_C, signs the resulting ciphertext, and publishes the signed ciphertext on the bulletin board. After that, A_i encrypts the share σ_i with the public key for votes T_V and adds a designated verifier proof [16] that the ciphertext published on the bulletin board and the ciphertext computed using T_V contain the same σ_i. A_i then encrypts the ciphertext and the proof with the voter's public key and sends the resulting ciphertext to the voter. The authority does not publish the encryption with the public key T_V.

Voting Phase. After decrypting the ciphertexts received from the authorities and verifying that the proofs are correct, the voter multiplies all encrypted shares of her credential (via the homomorphic property of the cryptosystem) and obtains $E_{T_V}[\sigma]$. The voter then reads from the bulletin board the encrypted shares $E_{T_V}[v_i]$ corresponding to the candidate she wants to vote for and multiplies them to obtain $E_{T_V}[v]$. Now, the voter multiplies the two resulting ciphertexts (i.e. $E_{T_V}[\sigma]$ and $E_{T_V}[v]$) and obtains $E_{T_V}[\sigma + v]$. To finish the process, the voter encrypts $E_{T_V}[\sigma + v]$ with the public key of the non-homomorphic cryptosystem and then publishes the resulting ciphertext on the bulletin board.

Tallying Phase. When the voting phase ends, the authorities multiply the shares of all valid encrypted credentials published in the registration phase. As before, this is performed via the homomorphic property of the cryptosystem. The result is a list of entire encrypted credentials $E_{T_C}[\sigma]$ that is sent to a mix net. The mix net outputs a list of $E_{T_C}[\sigma]'$, where $E_{T_C}[\cdot]'$ is the reencryption of $E_{T_C}[\cdot]$. The authorities then remove the encryption layer of the ciphertexts (this is performed using the private key of the non-homomorphic cryptosystem) posted by the voters and obtain a list of ciphertexts $E_{T_V}[\sigma + v]$. The authorities send this list to a mix net that outputs a new list containing $E_{T_V}[\sigma + v]'$.

For each candidate v_i, the authorities read from the bulletin board the corresponding encrypted shares $E_{T_C}[v_i]$ and multiply them. After processing the encrypted shares of all candidates, the authorities obtain a list of ciphertexts $E_{T_C}[v]'$ that contains an encrypted vote for each candidate. Now, for each encrypted credential $E_{T_C}[\sigma]'$, the authorities choose an encrypted vote $E_{T_C}[v]'$. The authorities then decrypt the resulting multiplication of $E_{T_C}[\sigma]'$ and $E_{T_C}[v]'$

(i.e. $E_{T_C}[\sigma+v]'$), and decrypt all ciphertexts $E_{T_V}[\sigma+v]'$. If the resulting plaintext of $E_{T_C}[\sigma+v]'$ matches one of the plaintexts of $E_{T_V}[\sigma+v]'$, the credential is valid and the vote is counted. Otherwise, the authorities combine $E_{T_C}[\sigma]'$ with another encrypted vote $E_{T_C}[v]'$ and repeat the process. If no match is found, the same process is performed with another encrypted credential.

A.2   The Weakness

We show now that the scheme of Acquisti is not coercion-resistant. In particular, an adversary can force a voter to reveal a credential and use a strategy to check later on whether the credential he received is valid or not.

Suppose the voter gives the coercer an encrypted credential $E_{T_V}[\sigma']$. The coercer then employs this ciphertext to compute a new ciphertext in such a way that their underlying plaintexts satisfy a specific relation R. In order to perform this, he first reads the encrypted shares of a vote $E_{T_V}[v_i]$ corresponding to a particular candidate and multiplies them to obtain $E_{T_V}[v]$. After that, he multiplies $E_{T_V}[v]$ to $E_{T_V}[\sigma']$ and obtains $E_{T_V}[v + \sigma']$. Now, the coercer defines the relation R. For example, he selects a value t as before and computes $E_{T_V}[v + \sigma']^t = E_{T_V}[t \cdot (v+\sigma')]$. The adversary then encrypts $E_{T_V}[t \cdot (v+\sigma')]$ and $E_{T_V}[v+\sigma']$ apart with the public key of the non-homomorphic cryptosystem and publishes the resulting ciphertexts on the bulletin board.

After the voting period, the coercer waits until the authorities compute the voting results. As explained above, in this process, the authorities first mix the ciphertexts $E_{T_V}[\sigma + v]$ posted by the voters after removing the outer encryption layer. They then mix the valid credentials ciphertexts $E_{T_C}[\sigma]$ after multiplying their encrypted shares $E_{T_C}[\sigma_i]$. After that, they multiply the mixed values $E_{T_C}[\sigma]'$ to $E_{T_C}[v]$ after obtaining the entire encrypted votes from the shares $E_{T_C}[v_i]$; let $E_{T_C}[X]'$ be the mix net output of a ciphertext $E_{T_C}[X]$, for a message X.

The authorities then decrypt $E_{T_V}[\sigma + v]'$ and $E_{T_C}[\sigma + v]'$, and match their plaintexts to verify whether a vote is valid or not. While processing all ciphertexts, the authorities publish the ciphertexts related information on the bulletin board. At the end of this phase, anyone can check which votes belong to the valid credentials. Now, in order to verify the relation R, the adversary reads from the bulletin board a plaintext $\sigma + v$ corresponding to a ciphertext $E_{T_V}[\sigma + v]'$ and computes $t \cdot (v + \sigma)$ from it. After that, he searches on the bulletin board for a plaintext $t \cdot (v + \sigma)$ of $E_{T_V}[t \cdot (v + \sigma)]'$ that matches the value $t \cdot (v + \sigma)$ he just has computed. If a match exist (which means that, with overwhelming probability, he has identified the ballot $\sigma' + v$ he submitted in an encrypted form), the adversary verifies whether $\sigma + v$ of $E_{T_V}[\sigma + v]'$ has a corresponding valid credential $\sigma + v$ of $E_{T_C}[\sigma + v]'$ on the bulletin board. A match now indicates that the credential received by the coercer is valid. If the value $t \cdot (v + \sigma)$ generated by the adversary does not match any plaintext on the bulletin board, he chooses another credential and repeats the process.

A.3   Another Drawback of Acquisti's Solution

In many election scenarios, voters do not need to register again before each new election. That is, once registered, a voter can vote in many forthcoming elections. The solution of Acquisti, however, does not provide this convenience to voters. They have to register before each new election.

Recall that in his scheme, in order to verify whether a ciphertext $E_{T_C}[\sigma + v]$ matches to a ciphertext $E_{T_V}[\sigma + v]$, the authorities need to decrypt these ciphertexts and publish their respective plaintexts on the bulletin board. Although the credentials (σ) as well as the votes (v) are unknown to the voters as they only know these values in an encrypted form, an adversary could exploit plaintexts $\sigma + v$ to retrieve several arbitrary credentials.

Indeed, suppose that the adversary wants to retrieve the credential of an arbitrary voter V. Let σ' be the credential of the adversary and v' the candidate he chooses. In order to identify his vote during the tallying phase, the adversary first computes the ballot $E_{T_V}[v' + \sigma']$ and publish it on the bulletin board. Then, he uses the same technique as described in the previous section. That is, he chooses a random value t, computes $E_{T_V}[t \cdot (v' + \sigma')]$, and sends this ciphertext to the bulletin board. After the authorities decrypt all ciphertexts $E_{T_V}[\sigma + v]$, the coercer can identify his ballot $\sigma' + v'$. Now, he just has to choose another valid ballot for the same candidate v'. Let us denote this valid ballot by $\sigma + v'$. Then, by subtracting $\sigma' + v'$ from $\sigma + v'$, he will obtain $\sigma - \sigma'$. He can then use the public key T_V to encrypt $\sigma - \sigma'$ in order to obtain $E_{T_V}[\sigma - \sigma']$. Since he knows $E_{T_V}[\sigma']$ (because this is his credential), he can retrieve $E_{T_V}[\sigma]$ via the homomorphic property of the cryptosystem. To do this, he just has to multiply $E_{T_V}[\sigma - \sigma']$ by $E_{T_V}[\sigma']$. We tacitly assume here that the computation operator on the underlying homomorphic encryption scheme is multiplication.

Author Index